SOLO

SOLO

Backcountry adventuring in Aotearoa New Zealand

Hazel Phillips

MASSEY UNIVERSITY PRESS

For Rob Hosking. For all the tracks
you didn't get to tramp, and the book
you didn't get to write.

CONTENTS

PREFACE

IN PART, THIS BOOK is the story of my quest to find home. It's also about feminism and its intersection with mountaineering.

Perhaps the biggest contrast in mountaineering can be found in the difference between historic climber Freda du Faur, who wrote *The Conquest of Mount Cook and Other Climbs*, and early author and mountaineer Samuel Turner. Both were admirable climbers in their own right, each with notable firsts. Du Faur was the first woman to summit Aoraki/Mount Cook; Turner, first to solo. Du Faur wrote a book on her climbs, while Turner wrote several. Du Faur emerges as a punchy character, pushing boundaries and bending gender norms, whereas Turner simply comes across as an arrogant egotist.[1]

Having read a number of books on mountaineering, adventuring and wilderness experiences — from du Faur and Turner to Peter Graham's biography, Lydia Bradey's *Going Up Is Easy* and international bestsellers such as *Into the Wild* (Jon Krakauer) and *Wild* (Cheryl Strayed) — it's clear to me that men remain unconscious of their gender as it relates to these activities, while for women it is very much a consideration. That's not to say that women dwell on the physical aspects (management of menstruation in the wilderness, for example), but more on confidence and ability (or lack thereof), or on the discrimination they experience. Even though women now make up a greater proportion of, say, attendees on snowcraft courses, we still feel 'othered'. Alpine clubs accept women members, there are plenty of women guides — so why are we still so astounded to see a woman in the wilderness? At what point do we, as women, not only *become* normal, but also *feel* normal?

This book is also about risk and death. Among those backcountry stories I unearthed there are some real tragedies.

A friend commented that while writing this book I'd become quite obsessed with people who have perished in the wilderness. My treatment of them may at times sound glib but I trust that any family member of the deceased mentioned who reads this will know that I've considered this, and the stories of their folk, with the utmost respect and regard.

When you spend a lot of time in the wilderness, and especially when you have a few near-death episodes, you think a lot about how it might end for you. This awareness is nearly always with me and perhaps that's why I take such an interest in these stories. If you, too, are interested, I recommend the two books by Paul Hersey listed in the select bibliography.

Most of all, I think about it in conjunction with the value of these experiences: is it worth it, the risk? It's a question you need to answer each time you go — it's specific to each activity. Mostly, I'd say no, but I know many mountaineers are driven to climb regardless of the risk.

There's a saying: there are old mountaineers, and bold mountaineers, but no old, bold mountaineers.

Introduction
Strategically homeless

IN 2016, DISILLUSIONED WITH what Auckland had become, I left. I didn't know where I wanted to live, but I figured that packing up and going on the road would at least help me figure it out.

I was also disillusioned with the standard 40-hour-work-week approach of being chained to a desk, and I had switched jobs to a new gig where I was the only staff member in New Zealand. The rest of the company was based in Australia, so I was left on my own to get on with it. My work became entirely doable remotely, and flexibly — everything was done with my 13-inch laptop, iPad and mobile phone — and eventually it just seemed silly to stay in Auckland, with its housing and traffic challenges. (In the age of Covid-19, it now seems unthinkable, perhaps ridiculous, that we once demanded that people be tied to a specific desk, in a specific office, for a specific period of time each week.)

And so I left. I packed up my whole life — except for a tramping pack, boots and ski gear — and cut a fast track south.

For the next three years I was strategically homeless. Home became wherever I'd chosen to be at that moment. Sometimes it was an alpine club lodge, sometimes a Department of Conservation (DoC) hut, sometimes camping out in the bush or bedding down in a bivvy bag if I'd stuffed up and had nowhere to sleep. Sometimes it was a nice hotel in Sydney, when I had to travel for work, which always presented a bizarre contrast of lifestyles; I once spent the night at Rangiwahia Hut in the Ruahine Range, tramped out the next day, drove to Wellington Airport, flew to Sydney and went to bed in a hotel that night.

Strategic homelessness allowed me to be in the hills every weekend and sometimes on weeknights, too. A typical excursion would start on Friday afternoon, when I'd haul on my pack, don my boots and walk into the wilderness until Monday morning. I'd usually have until around midday before I needed to be back online; that's when my Aussie colleagues would begin to down their coffee and switch on their computers (and, possibly, wonder where I was).

To the casual social media observer, it looked like I was living a dream life — always skiing, tramping, mountaineering, with beautiful photos to show for it. What wasn't quite so obvious in the dishonest social construct that is Facebook, was that it demanded more energy, enthusiasm, time management and *work* than ever. If I stole a chunk of Monday morning tramping out of the bush, it meant a late-night Monday. If I took off camping up a stream bed on Wednesday night, it meant a long Thursday workday. It was a constant juggling act — but it was worth it.

Over those years, I tramped my way up and down the country, from the Hump Ridge to Ruapehu and across the Kaimanawa and Kaweka ranges. I destroyed three pairs of boots, two packs and four sets of gaiter straps. Countless packets of dehy food and tasty snacks were consumed. People were met. Land was traversed. Books were read.

During this time I watched my good friend and fellow journalist Rob Hosking fade from the earth after losing his battle with cancer and never getting to do all the things he'd planned. His death and these years taught me that you only get one shot at this stuff. Make sure you give it heaps.

Taking in the stars and snow on a night-time traverse of the Tongariro Alpine Crossing. We started late in the evening under a full moon, which lights up the landscape as it reflects on the snow. It was cold. Very cold.
MIKE HEYDON, JET PRODUCTIONS

Ruapehu

The ice likes to bite

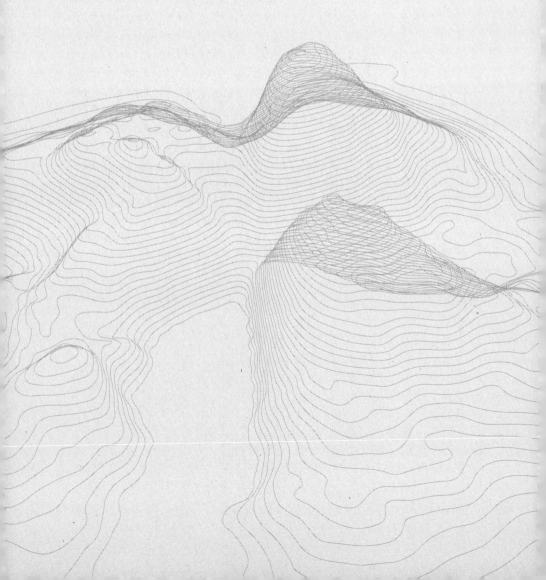

THEY SAY THERE'S more than one type of fun. In fact, there are three types. Type one is the sort of fun 'normal' people enjoy: hot tubs, beer, Netflix. It's fun at the time, requires very little effort, but isn't particularly memorable. Type two is the sort of fun only masochists enjoy: mountaineering, tough multi-day tramping, bush-bashing. It requires hard effort and it's certainly not fun at the time, but it's fun in retrospect — and it's also indelibly marked on your memory. You never forget type two fun. (Then there's type three, which is not fun at the time, not fun in retrospect, and someone probably went home in an ambulance.)

Type two fun typically involves unknown unknowns — the stuff you don't know you don't know about. I considered the concept of unknown unknowns after hearing the word 'ante-library' in an episode of *Downton Abbey*. It's the Victorian concept of a smaller, annexed library, where books that hadn't yet been read were housed. Here, in the ante-library, were one's known unknowns: knowledge you knew you were yet to acquire. The main library housed the known knowns: knowledge you were already familiar with. Presumably, bookstores were the mothership of unknown unknowns: that wide, terrifying world of things you didn't know you didn't know.

It was on a traverse of Mount Ruapehu, from the Tūroa ski field across to the Whakapapa ski area, that I converted a few unknown unknowns into known unknowns. Specifically, while sliding out of control down a steep snow face, wrenching my limbs in ways I would only properly comprehend the next day when soreness set in, frantically trying to self-arrest to prevent myself from an undignified end in the steaming crater lake. Thinking I was going to die. (Spoiler alert: I didn't.)

My tramping buddy Jen bought me an ice axe as a birthday present one year. I'd been vocal about my opinions on alpine climbing, or snow tramping; as far as I was concerned it was a silly way to expend effort and one that only Unduly Fit Types indulged in. Why spend so much time going uphill on snow when there were perfectly good chairlifts to take you up high, affording you the pleasure of zooming down, then rinse and repeat? I loved doing hot laps on my skis, and anything else was a profligate waste of the small window of winter we get each year. But having this delicious, shiny silver axe (Jen had chosen well) was a constant reminder of a challenge I hadn't been equal to. The axe glinted at me from the corner of my bedroom. 'Why haven't you used me?' it seemed to say accusingly. (I stashed it in the naughty corner of my wardrobe for a while to give me time off from all the guilt.)

Eventually I caved, as Jen had known I would. I signed up for a snowcraft course with an alpine club (not to be confused with *the* Alpine Club, the New Zealand Alpine Club) that had a lodge on Whakapapa and appeared to have a young and enthusiastic climbing contingent. I was intimidated; I'd heard stories of course attendees getting yelled at, of accidents, of bad practice. I didn't care to find out if those stories were founded; the idea of getting yelled at was enough of a deterrent.

The course included lots of rope work in a climbing gym before the practical weekend on Whakapapa. I was too inexperienced to recognise that so much rope work wasn't appropriate or useful for beginner mountaineers, and felt disappointed in my failure to master complex party-trick knots such as the Alpine Butterfly (go look it up, I'll wait here).

I was apprehensive about my chances of success on the practical weekend, but my friend Phil armed me with his climbing harness, avalanche transceiver, a good snow shovel and a few other crucial items for fooling around with on snow when you've decided to shun the chairlifts, and sort of told me to harden up. I also bought brand-new crampons, which was a committing act but one that matched Jen's ice-axe gift to me. I was all kitted out and ready to be yelled at.

I did get yelled at, and I hated it. I think this comes down to a gender difference. Stereotypically, men like the idea of the military, of hardcore instruction and toughness. Women want things explained with the opportunity to ask lots of questions, and not to feel stupid. I definitely felt stupid.

But there I was, feeling stupid, getting yelled at (for failing to move up a ridge as fast as the instructor would ideally have liked, and I still mentally give that ridge the middle finger whenever I see it), but clad in new, robust crampon-compatible boots, said brand-new crampons, and clutching a brand-new ice axe. Was I going to be one of those people who gave up after one go and put everything on Trade Me, further admitting defeat?

I brushed off the dirt from that weekend and used the skills I'd picked up to do a few alpine tramping trips with friends who were qualified to a similar level. We did a trip to the Ruapehu summit plateau, another one up Dome (2672 metres, one of Ruapehu's 12 summit peaks but very easy), and the Tongariro Alpine Crossing, which is glorious in winter.

Each came with its own micro-challenges, and I felt like I was progressing appropriately every time. Psychologist Lev Vygotsky pioneered the concept of scaffolding — you take what the learner knows and you build on it with small steps very gradually, landing you in your 'zone of proximal development'. The idea is that what you need to know next is what you already know 'plus one'. (What exactly or how much constitutes 'plus one' is undetermined, it's just a concept.) I felt that I was slowly gaining more known knowns, plus one by plus one.

But I also had a lot of unknown unknowns, and that's a dangerous place to be. My unknown unknowns were lurking, hiding behind icy outcrops and under cornices, waiting for me to slip up.

In May 1936, a man died after falling into Ruapehu's crater lake. James Gordon, a solicitor from Taumarunui, was at the crater lake with a party that included his two sons. The day was icy and the chosen site for climbing was bullish. 'The locality is very dangerous and the frozen surface is as smooth as glass,' read one media report.[1] The party had eaten an early lunch at 11.30 a.m. on the edge of the crater lake and set out to reach the summit proper, Tahurangi (then known as Ruapehu Peak), overlooking the lake. One of the party had cut only 12 steps when his instincts seized him. He turned to his companions and told them that it was too dangerous.

Downclimbing from the Great Pinnacle (aka Grand Pinnacle, 2190 metres), a distinctive peak on Whakapapa, Mount Ruapehu. I'd snapped both of my own crampons, one on each successive climbing weekend leading up to this climb, and was using a friend's pair. It felt pretty dodgy. KENT HUTCHINS

'The words were hardly out of his mouth when Gordon, who was sitting down at the time, started to slip, gained speed, and went right over the edge of the crater,' read another report.[2] His climbing companions peeked over the cliff and could see him in the water a few metres from the edge of the lake. Gordon managed to pull himself up to sit astride a small rock, but with such demanding terrain and icy conditions, and lacking an adequate rope, the party deemed it too difficult to reach him down the 'icy precipice slopes'. All except one man, Sefton Mannering, set off to Chateau Tongariro to raise the alarm.

Mannering stayed at the scene, cutting steps to help the impending rescue effort and encouraging Gordon to keep his spirits up and assuring him that help was on the way. 'All right, old man,' Gordon yelled to Mannering.[3] About waist-deep in water, he moved to another rock near the edge of the lake. Mannering couldn't reach him — the drop was simply too sheer — and after a while he saw Gordon fall back on the rock. He disappeared, and Mannering, still preparing for the rescue effort, later saw his body floating in the lake.

'Mr. Gordon [had] hung on to the rock for nearly three hours,' the *Evening Post* reported, 'battling grimly and courageously for his life. However, he weakened, probably from injuries and the cold conditions, and slipped off the rock into the water at 2.30 p.m.'[4] Carl Risberg, who was chief guide at the Chateau Tongariro at the time, achieved a speedy ascent and arrived with ropes at 3.30 p.m. but it was too late. Gordon had died in the steaming waters of the crater lake.

It was deemed too late in the day to attempt a retrieval without risking further loss of life, so the party returned to the Chateau. The next day, a 14-man team including Risberg arrived at the crater lake just after sunrise armed with long ropes, ice axes and crampons. Three of the men were lowered down into the tricky terrain, a drop of 400 feet, meaning they were at times suspended in mid-air, depending wholly on their co-rescuers to keep them safe. Gordon's body was found half-floating, face downward, just metres from the shore and close to the spot where he had originally fallen. The water wasn't deep, indicating that Gordon could have reached the shore safely, had he had sufficient strength left and not been completely exhausted.[5]

Risberg experimented two days after the accident by intentionally sliding on a similar slope, and found that ice axes did nothing to help him self-arrest, refusing to 'hold or make the slightest impression in the ice'. Even crampons and a rope didn't help in his experiments, which were carried out to see if other climbing gear and methods could have prevented a 13-stone man from sliding.[6]

They teach you how to self-arrest in snowcraft courses. You intentionally throw yourself down a steep snow slope, ice axe in hand, using the pick to brake your fall in the snow and ice. You try it first on your tummy, head uphill, and progress to doing it on your back with your head on the downhill end, which feels inordinately dangerous. You need to be able to self-arrest in every conceivable position, and you've got to be able to react quickly, because a small trip or slip will soon gain momentum and have you out of control, careening towards the Grim Reaper without a hope to grasp on to.

'You've got to keep practising not just until you can do it,' said Phil, my climbing mate who lent me his gear for the snowcraft course, 'but until you can't get it wrong.'

Self-arresting hurts — particularly if the snowpack is icy. It also wrecks your clothing and leaves your knickers full of snow. But I guess snow in his undies would have been the least of Gordon's problems on that day in 1936.

One weekend in August 2016, I had a bright idea. A few of my ski-club buddies were going around to the Tūroa side for the day. We usually skied on the Whakapapa side, and the club lodge was in National Park. This gave me transport options to execute an alpine traverse on foot from Tūroa to Whakapapa. I left a pair of skis in one of the cars at Tūroa, in case I changed my mind and decided to retreat and ski for the day instead. I had people to pick me up on Whakapapa, so long as I made it before the lifts stopped at 4 p.m. The weather forecast was stunning, with a high sitting right over the North Island. I had my shiny ice axe, still reasonably new and glinting, and I'd had enough time on crampons to feel confident going solo. It would be an adventure, scaffolded appropriately, a modest 'plus one' to challenge me just enough.

What could possibly go wrong?

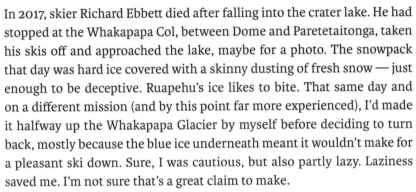

In 2017, skier Richard Ebbett died after falling into the crater lake. He had stopped at the Whakapapa Col, between Dome and Paretetaitonga, taken his skis off and approached the lake, maybe for a photo. The snowpack that day was hard ice covered with a skinny dusting of fresh snow — just enough to be deceptive. Ruapehu's ice likes to bite. That same day and on a different mission (and by this point far more experienced), I'd made it halfway up the Whakapapa Glacier by myself before deciding to turn back, mostly because the blue ice underneath meant it wouldn't make for a pleasant ski down. Sure, I was cautious, but also partly lazy. Laziness saved me. I'm not sure that's a great claim to make.

The edge of the crater lake has high walls at the Whakapapa Col side; some are as high as 80 or 100 metres (put it this way: I've seen a helicopter with a bucket on a longline completely disappear from view). Ebbett was on a different side of the lake from Gordon, but the result was the same — and just as deadly.

On the day of my bright idea and big traverse, I cheated and used my season pass and three successive chairlifts on Tūroa to gain the upper reaches of the ski field. The highest chairlift, the High Noon Express (or the Afternoon Express as many skiers call it, given it usually requires extensive de-icing in the morning and hence tends not to operate until after midday), spits you out at 2300 metres, giving you just under 500 metres of vertical ascent to stand on top of Tahurangi, the highest of Ruapehu's summit peaks at 2797 metres. It's the highest point in the North Island and I was determined to reach it. Summit fever, even at lesser altitudes, is very real. Scarcity is a common heuristic trap — the notion that you've only got this one shot to do something, to ski an untracked line even though it might be avalanche-prone, to scuba dive a particular site after a long boat ride even though a wicked current is ripping through, to do a mountain traverse because the transport opportunity isn't often there.

For a while I simply plodded across moderate snow slopes above the High Noon Express. I had people watching me, curious to see my progress, and knowing I was being observed made me nervous. A friend had advised me to take the Summit Ridge route rather than the common path straight up the snow slopes to the col beneath Tahurangi, so I angled there, at first not noticing how challenging it was for my (low) level of ability. The ridge was crusted with rime ice — a particular type of ice prone to developing on North Island snow slopes. Being a maritime climate, wet air comes in from the ocean and freezes — on chairlifts, buildings, ridges, rocks, and even people, if you're unlucky enough to be out there in the wrong conditions. Taranaki gets the worst of it, but Ruapehu's massif also gets a fair whack. (De-icing crews on the ski fields use 'Yeti sticks' — like baseball bats — to bash the ice off structures and lift lines.) Rime ice makes interesting and pretty features, but on slopes it can build up in odd ways that are tricky to navigate, especially for novice mountaineers without enough experience to know how to climb on them on steeper terrain.

And it was steep, for my ability then. I didn't realise how steep until it was too late — I was partway up the ridge navigating awkward bulges of ice in a position that made it more terrifying to turn back and try to climb down than keep going. Occasionally I looked down, but only long enough to decide that looking up was the better option. Full steam ahead.

After three hours of terror — longer than any moderately experienced climber would need to ascend Summit Ridge — I finally reached a flatter part of the ridge. It took only 10 very tame minutes to plod up the remaining easy ascent to stand atop Tahurangi. I snapped a couple of selfies, did some deep breathing and messaged Phil, who was going to ski tour up the Whakapapa Glacier to meet me at the col near the crater lake once I'd made my way down from Tahurangi and across the crater rim slopes. Texting him from the summit, I put in a special request for him to pack some chocolate biscuits. I'd definitely done enough for a MallowPuff.

Standing on Tukino Peak ready to ski down, with Te Heuheu Peak in the background. I had cramponed up from Whakapapa ski field and by this point I'd had a lot more experience and felt pretty comfortable, even solo.

One bright but windy spring day in 2018 I reached the Whakapapa Col with a group of ski-club buddies. We had ascended to the top, above the ski-field boundary, using ski-touring gear ('skins' that are furry on one side with a glued surface on the other that adheres to your skis, giving you the ability to grip on snow uphill), mostly because the ski field was crowded, we were restless, and one of the guys wanted to test out a snow kite on the flatter part of the col. Arriving at the 2600-metre mark where you first see the crater lake, we were met by a couple of snowboarders. 'Someone fell into the crater lake,' one told us. 'Looks like they're alive though — getting fished out now.' We could see the helicopter going back and forth with a sort of net on the bottom.

Sadly, they weren't. Climber Magesh Jagadeesan died after chasing runaway gear on a flat section near the crater lake. He and his companions had stopped for lunch, and gear had started to slide. Another person also fell in the chase but managed to stop himself. Jagadeesan, however, couldn't self-arrest and slid over the crater edge into the lake. He was experienced and well equipped, and a lovely guy by all accounts. It's that crater lake monster, though.

Standing at the col that day watching the rescue, and nervously watching our mate snow kiting for the first time in an area that had just proven itself to be deadly, we saw a badly equipped and inexperienced tourist slip and fall off the Dome peak. He lost his ice axe and it rocketed past me so fast I couldn't grab it. One of the others charged towards the guy to stop him from sliding further, where he would've gone into the lake. Later, we heard stories of a ski tourer on Dome who had had a similar narrow escape.

Back in 2016, on top of Tahurangi, and after celebrating the summit achievement, I descended to the Tahurangi Col using some awkward manoeuvres but clinging on with everything I had. Most of my difficulty was in having only one ice axe and not knowing how to 'front-point' — which is when you use the very front two spikes of your crampons to dig in to the snow and ice, and you face into the hill. It's much more secure than moving with crampons in a regular walking style, and it feels that way too, even though it's counter-intuitive because you have fewer spikes contacting the snow and ice. But we hadn't covered the technique of front-pointing in the snowcraft course, so I had no knowledge base to work from, nor the gear to execute it, and all the Alpine Butterfly knots in the world weren't going to help me now. (After this trip I bought a second ice axe, a semi-technical one more suited to shoving into ice, thereby further committing to the abject madness and type two fun that is mountaineering.)

The col beneath Tahurangi sits at 2620 metres and is the place usually referred to as 'the top' by non-mountaineering skiers and snowboarders who sweat their way up there each year in soft spring conditions. It affords luscious views across to Ruapehu's other summit peaks, such as Te Heuheu in the north (2732 metres, named after the chief who gifted the area),[7] Paretetaitonga on the western side (2752 metres), the aforementioned Dome (2672 metres), and the craggy Cathedral Rocks (2663 metres, also known as Matihao). Crucially, there's plenty of flat space to stop, sit down, have a rest, question your life choices, and turn around. I felt incredibly relieved to have gotten off the steep and icy summit ridge. The next step in my journey was to climb down directly from the col on the northern side and traverse the western side of the crater lake to meet Phil with his chocolate biscuits at the Whakapapa Col and from there it would be a doddle.

They say that the most dangerous time for a backcountry snow user is immediately after they've done an avalanche awareness course. That's because a little knowledge is a dangerous thing — you think you've quickly gained a lot of known knowns, and your known unknowns are neatly packaged up inside an avalanche handbook. But when it comes to snow science, there's a whole world of unknown unknowns out there. In my case, I had a plethora of unknown unknowns, and all of them were about how to judge a snowpack, and why you don't mess with a north-facing snow slope that's been baked by the sun, especially later in the day.

The first 15 steps down from the col went okay, I suppose, in that I stayed on my feet. My gut told me that things weren't going to go well and I was probably going to lose it, so I was sort of prepared for that. Each step encountered a different condition in the snowpack — some hard ice, some slush, some slush over ice. It was a lucky dip, and I had the losing ticket.

Step 16 is where the fun began. I triggered a tiny wet slide, the sort of avalanche that happens in warm conditions, and while the slide was small, the consequences had me knocked off my feet. At first I thought everything was fine. *I'd stop, wouldn't I?*

I was sliding on my bum, head uphill, the first position they teach you in self-arresting school. But I wasn't stopping, even though the snow was sticky and clumpy. Suddenly my position changed, and I'm still not sure how. My sore limbs the next day indicated that perhaps I caught a crampon and cartwheeled around, wrenching my legs. Then I was flying — at pace — down a steep snow slope, on my back with my head downhill.

'You're not going to stop if you don't do something,' I told myself. I began to give myself a serious talking-to. 'You're the only one who can do something about this right now. You have to act, or you're going to die!'

Then all the training kicked in, or perhaps just sheer self-preservation instinct. I rolled over (no mean feat when you're careening downhill) and threw the pick of my ice axe into the snow. It bit immediately and swung me in a large circle, bringing me to an abrupt stop and wrenching my arms painfully. Covered in snow, including my face, I couldn't see anything, but I knew I was neither dead nor in the crater lake. I'd ripped my pants and my underwear was full of snow.

'Are you okay?' a couple of guys yelled to me from a peak. My scuba diving training decided to kick in, and I touched my hand to my head in the long-distance dive signal that means 'I'm okay'. One of them must've also been a trained diver, because he gave me the same signal back, meaning he understood, and then did the sign for 'crayfish' — you simulate two wiggly feelers on top of your head with your two index fingers.

Out of a possible 160-metre fall from the col, I'd lost about 100 metres, and I suppose that's not a bad self-arresting effort for an idiot with far too many unknown unknowns in her back pocket. Later on, I consoled myself by examining the topo map and concluding that if I hadn't self-arrested, I probably wouldn't have ended up in the crater lake itself, but I may have had an interesting trip towards the crater lake outlet and the frozen headwaters of the Whangaehu River.

On the top of Girdlestone (Peretini, 2658 metres), one of Ruapehu's summit peaks. Note the second ice axe, acquired after the challenging day climbing Tahurangi. We took a rope, but conditions were good enough to go without.

Is it better to fall to your death knowing it's happening or being blissfully unaware?

Three years before James Gordon's fall, John Wall, a 19-year-old from Whanganui, slipped and fell over the edge of the crater lake, but he did it so quietly and unobtrusively that his climbing companions concluded he must have fainted before he fell. It was 19 May 1933, the same time of year Gordon died. The party was on a guided climb from the Chateau and stopped near the crater lake's edge to take photos. Wall had moved away slightly from the group and his companions were gazing off in a different direction at the time.

'When they looked round they could see no trace of him,' newspapers said.[8] 'At first they thought he had walked away, but on investigation they saw his body lying on broken ice about four feet from the hot lake. [His friends] think he probably fainted before falling, for they did not hear him call and did not know that he was missing until they turned round.'

Nobody could reach him — it was deemed 'humanly impossible' to get down the sheer face to the lake, as the ice conditions were very bad. It was 2 p.m., too late in the day to do anything about getting to the body, so the party left. A retrieval effort the next day involved 1000 feet of rope and a different approach angle to the lake as the glacier overhung the spot where he fell, with ice above constantly breaking away from it, creating further danger.

Wall had been educated at Wanganui Collegiate School; he was a prefect and a model student. He was due to head off to Cambridge University, and was considered to be fit, a solid tramper, and of 'marked ability'.

'Don't drop your guard on the way down.' That piece of advice, dished out to me by Phil before my silly trip traversing Ruapehu, has always stuck with me. It's echoed in the title of Kiwi climber Lydia Bradey's book *Going Up Is Easy*. Bradey was the first woman to climb Everest without oxygen, and she did it solo. Going up is easy because getting down off a mountain safely is often more of a challenge — fatigue sets in and the climber tends to be imbued with a sense of success. George Mallory and Andrew Irvine might well have been the first people to summit Mount Everest, before Sir Edmund Hillary, but they didn't make it back to camp alive. In the mountaineering world, returning safely to base camp is an essential part of being able to claim a first ascent.

As mentioned earlier, I am still alive, and I made it back on my own two feet, under my own steam and without requiring an ambulance, for which I'm eternally grateful, and a fact that allows me to categorise the outing as type two fun rather than type three. Not only that, I didn't end up going for an unplanned swim in the crater lake. My guard was definitely up as I traversed the western side of the lake to meet Phil at the col and consume an inadvisable number of chocolate biscuits. I told him about the fall and he didn't say much, which I felt was his way of communicating that he thought I was indeed a halfwit, only he was too polite to spell that out for me in such obvious terms. The rest of the day featured an uneventful snow plod back down the Whakapapa Glacier and through the ski field and getting back to the ski club lodge. When I woke up the next day I couldn't move. (Much.)

'The edge of the crater is usually safe, and visitors are frequently taken there,' said a New Zealand provincial newspaper, three days after John Wall's accident.[9]

In winter 2016, a keen Auckland man named Richard Parker ascended to Tūroa ski field and spent several hours building a snow cave near the top of one of the chairlift lines. After setting it up late at night, he went mostly unnoticed and managed to live in it for three days, with the aim of having some time away from the big smoke. It was no small undertaking; he continued working on it to build out his palace quite thoroughly. 'Inside there was a big archway and the igloo roof coming over it for the snow layers and a big entrance with a main room and an opportunity for different entranceways and it was going to have a nice window down the bottom,' he enthused. He was nearly finished building his new home when he was arrested for disorderly behaviour and resisting arrest, after a dispute involving Parker moving a bench that presumably belonged to Ruapehu Alpine Lifts, the ski-field operator. Local policeman Sergeant Mike Craig told media it was the first time police had ever had to remove someone living in a snow cave. 'I've been here for 14 years and I'm not aware of another incident quite like this.'[10]

Reading between the lines, I'd assume there's more to the story than what was publicly reported — the area is a national park with free and open access, but users do need to be mindful of the need of the ski-field operator as a concession holder to carry out operational activities. Was he perhaps a hermit looking for a place to hole up? I had aspirations to construct a hermit-style life myself, although life itself always seemed to get in the way; I suppose it doesn't help that you generally have to take an active part in society in the name of gaining a pay cheque.

A mountain ranger named Arthur Cowling spent a decade, from 1921 to 1931, largely by himself on the slopes of Ruapehu in the name of caretaking on the maunga, living in a tiny hut at around 1400 metres altitude. His lifestyle ended thanks to a government retrenchment policy, forcing Cowling into city life to look for another job.

Cowling had no company except a horse (named Kitty the Outcast) and a cat, the latter of which had strolled out of the forest one night to check out his fire and decided to stay, turning from utterly savage to quite tame once properly fed. He would roam the mountain huts at the foot of Tongariro and Ngāuruhoe on Kitty's back, delivering supplies and making sure all was well. Eventually, the horse succumbed to rheumatism, probably from spending so much time in damp, cold conditions.

Cowling was a fixture at search and rescue operations on the Central Plateau, having gained a lot of alpine experience in his youth at Aoraki/ Mount Cook, where he helped to build Mueller Hut, among others, a task requiring strenuous, back-breaking work.

I admired the tenacity, motivation and pure introversion of both the snow-cave bloke and Mr Cowling. A friend once commented to me, after learning I'd been on a nine-day solo tramp and hadn't spoken to or seen anyone for much of it, that I must be quite introverted to do something like that. I thought about that for a while; every personality test I'd ever taken (and there'd been a lot, mostly prompted by some sort of hand-

Sleeping under the stars in a bivvy bag on Ruapehu. They say you get all the peace and quiet you want once you're dead, but I don't mind some solitude while I'm alive, too.

holding exercise within corporate life) always showed me to be an 'ambivert', equally introverted and extroverted.

I didn't feel that way and so I never vibed with the results of those tests, until doing the Myers-Briggs Type Indicator, which marked me as 'INFJ' (introverted, intuitive, feeling, judging), along with luminaries such as Goethe (okay), Marie Kondo (makes sense), Mother Teresa (oooh, caring) and Lady Gaga (strange, but I suppose complimentary). Turns out, INFJ personalities are often mistaken for extroverts, or coded as ambiverts, because they're drawn to people. However, they need deeper, more meaningful connections — quality over quantity. Also turns out I'm 92 per cent introverted, a revelation that helped me finally put the conundrum to rest of why I feel so introverted but all the other personality tests in the world told me I wasn't.

I learned, also, that many INFJ types are writers — it's one of the most common career choices. Writing is the only way we can properly explain ourselves. Sometimes I have a thought and try to share it with someone, only to be interrupted, smacked down, or invalidated. 'You're wrong,' someone will say, 'this is how I see the world,' without listening to the full completeness of the thought I am trying to express. Writing that same thought down is a way of validating my own experiences in a way that's unmediated by anyone else's voice, in particular, a *male* voice. A few of those voices were always so ready and enthusiastic to correct me, explain things to me, tell me how wrong I was. For this reason I was reluctant to ever post things in the various social media forums that existed for alpine climbing and mountaineering; for fear of being ripped to pieces.

I'd witnessed it before: women being shredded online. In 2013, climber Mary Jane Walker appeared in the media after hiring crampons to ascend Mount Aspiring, which then (both) broke, leaving her unable to complete the climb. Walker wasn't impressed, particularly as she'd taken a chunk of time off work and paid to be helicoptered in. The store owner, Steve Hart, cast doubt on Walker's ability, implying the issue was her own fault and that there was nothing wrong with the crampons and perhaps it was all in her head: 'They're back on our rental shelves. There's nothing wrong with them at all. I'm quite happy to rent them out again. The only assumption I can make is that the crampons have been misused. We see it every year. People get out of their depth and go up into the mountains. I don't know what sort of climber she is.'[11]

Her climbing partner Murray Ball told the media Walker had lost her confidence after the crampons failed and could have completed the climb anyway — though he admitted the crampons were faulty and needed to be wired up. I found Ball's comments to be condescending: 'It was an unfortunate set of circumstances but not life-threatening. She's not a mountaineer. She's a tramper.' Walker's own lived experience was invalidated by two male voices in the story — amazingly, one of them was her own friend.

The brand of crampons was well known for failing, regardless of the user's level of experience, so much of the conversation hinged on the safety aspect — the company's lawyers were trigger-happy when firing off threatening letters to shut down speculation or fault claims — while a small amount of discourse went back and forth on the patronising tone of the two men quoted in the story, which positioned Walker as an ingénue in need of instruction by higher minds.

Some people on social media got stuck into Walker on a personal level: 'I had the "pleasure" of doing a snowcraft course with this particular climber about 18 months ago. Her reaction doesn't surprise me at all.'

Walker hit back: 'I am not a dickhead, I am a member of your organisation for the past 18 months and have done two courses. So hello people, I belong to your group, and I was pissed off I hired faulty gear.' And: 'I am not a dumb woman so change your attitude.'

More condescension rolled in: 'Go to bed Mary Jane.' And: 'Put the kettle on.' 'Woah . . . let's NOT descend into a debate about climbing and gender please,' said another.

A few brave women continued to put across their own views. One said she had disengaged completely from formal involvement with climbing clubs because they didn't provide a way forward for promoting climbing among women. Said another: 'Believe me, if you could spend some time as a female climber I think you would find that there is a tendency for your skills and experience to be underestimated again and again. We do live in a world where women are frequently assumed to be less competent than they are.'

I briefly delved in, got roundly smacked, and withdrew from comment, disinclined to partake further. A group of women discussed it privately, all of us agreeing that it wasn't worth trying to highlight the gendered tones in the story. Any attempt was successfully shut down by a couple of forceful voices who wanted to tell us what's what.

'I completely accept that sexism happens,' one male commenter finally conceded.

I had further encounters that made me consider the intersection between gender and confidence levels in outdoor pursuits.

A few weekends in 2017 had proven spectacular in terms of snowfall on the Bruce Road leading up the northwest flank of Ruapehu to Whakapapa. One weekend, approaching the Top of the Bruce was like being in *Ice Road Truckers*. Absolutely everything was white, and when I was forced to stop near the top car park, my car began sliding backwards, slowly, non-responsive, and I had to steer it past a line of parked cars and into a snowbank. I was quite happy with my emergency reversing skills — my experiences made me realise I could handle it.

The next weekend there was a road restriction — chains or 4WD. I drive a Subaru, which is a poor man's 4WD, so sometimes if the conditions are really bad they'll specify '4WD with good ground clearance, chains on all other vehicles' and you know the Subaru won't pass muster. But that day it was just '4WD', which indicates your Subaru will get through okay.

I saw an identical Subaru two cars in front of me go through the checkpoint. 'Have a good one, mate,' I heard the guy say to the driver. But when I got there, it was a different story.

'Is this car 4WD?' he asked.

'Yep,' I said.

'Well, I think you should put chains on it,' he said. 'It's very risky up there. Lots of snow and ice — it's dangerous.'

'So you're saying there's a restriction of chains on Subarus?' I asked.

'No, but I think you should put chains on your car. You'd be a very silly girl to go up there without chains.'

'Well, seeing as there's no restriction of chains on Subarus, I won't do that, but thanks for your advice.'

Shaken, I pulled over and questioned whether I really should continue. I watched him wave through three carloads of guys driving Subarus immediately behind me without telling them to put chains on, or that they would be 'very silly boys' to not do so. There was no difference between their cars and mine — it's not like they had some sort of magical mechanism that would somehow make their cars safer; it's just that they were men, and therefore assumed to be more competent. It was a stellar example of unconscious bias. We're socialised to see women as less capable, less knowledgeable, and unable to do complicated stuff like crevasse rescue, change lightbulbs and drive a car up a mountain road.

The weekend after this incident, I overheard two older women in my ski club asking a male clubbie to drive their 4WD up the hill for them. The car belonged to the husband of one of the women and she was convinced she was going to end up damaging it, not for any reason other than that she just assumed she wasn't competent — even though it was a clear sunny day with snow-free roads. I reminded her of 1970s second-wave feminism, that women can do anything, that she would be absolutely fine, and I did a happy dance when she decided to overcome the fear and drive it herself. (She did, and she didn't damage it, and is alive to tell the tale.) Sometimes we're so used to society telling us we're incompetent or helpless that we forget we're not.

I told a couple of female friends about this incident and they relayed their own stories in turn. One told me of being patronised when going to get a gear check for a trail marathon: 'A gear check is standard for long-distance races in remote locations. The compulsory gear list usually includes a rain jacket, thermals, gloves, hat, emergency blanket, first-aid kit, capacity to carry a certain amount of water and food — so you take your CamelBak into a shop in advance to show that you have all the bits and pieces. When I was getting my compulsory gear checked for my last trail marathon, dressed in my work clothes, I approached a staff member and asked him to check my gear. He looked me up and down (particularly my high heels) and his first words were, "What, are you going to run it in: those?" I would've walked out of the store right then if it hadn't been the only place in Auckland where I could get my gear signed off.'

Another woman, who does trail running and some very hardcore tramping, said: 'Dudes are always pretty loud when they think I can't do something. I've heard things like "Oh, you'll never make it up there before dark" and "You can't go to the summit of Mount Ollivier, it's too hard". I've never had that from another woman.' (Mount Ollivier is 1933

The Manawatu Tramping and Skiing Club lodge on Whakapapa ski field, Mount Ruapehu, under a starry winter sky. The lodge became a temporary home for me during the skiing and climbing season.

metres and an easy scramble from the tourist attraction that is Mueller Hut, in Aoraki/Mount Cook National Park.)

But the outdoors is a great equaliser. 'There are many amazing female climbers and trampers who achieve the same things that men do,' said one friend. 'My advice to any woman who experiences this sort of thing is to use it to spur herself on and to not get discouraged. I strongly encourage women to climb with other women, to organise your own trips, to buy your own gear, to encourage yourself, and your female friends, to aim high, keep pushing yourself, build your social network and supporters. And remember to out-climb that person. If someone cuts you down or underestimates you, success is the best revenge.'[12]

Aoraki/Mount Cook

Blazing a path through ignorance and convention

ACHIEVING A STATE where your underwear is filled with snow doesn't necessarily require an episode of life-threatening self-arresting. It's fairly easy to do simply from a pastime known as 'glissading', or sliding on the snow either on your bum or, for the more nimble and daring, in a standing position.

I'm heartened by historic climber Freda du Faur's love of glissading as part of the mountaineering experience. Freda was a formidable woman whose exploits include being the first woman to climb Aoraki/Mount Cook and several first ascents, and her book *The Conquest of Mount Cook and Other Climbs: An Account of Four Seasons' Mountaineering on the Southern Alps of New Zealand* reveals her to be the sort of woman to accept no nonsense from anyone.

Through reading her book, you get a sense she wasn't going to let her gender hamper her climbing escapades or get in the way of a good time. She enjoyed nothing more than a thrilling standing glissade after a tough mountain ascent. She writes of her first real mountain experience on a guided climb of Mount Sealy (2557 metres), a modest peak in Aoraki/Mount Cook National Park, when she also experienced her first glissade on a rather steep slope: 'I arrived at the bottom wrong side up, and inconveniently filled with snow. These facts, however, did not deter me from tramping back to the top just for the pleasure of doing the same thing all over again.'[1] It was on this trip that she began to seriously consider becoming a mountaineer, realising she could never be content to worship the mountains from a distance.

Did she have the physical strength, the courage, the endurance and the perseverance to achieve anything 'really worthwhile' in the mountains, she wondered? Yes, she decided, she did, and being the first woman to stand atop Aoraki/Mount Cook would be the proof.

But best not to tell anyone, lest they invalidate her plans: 'I wondered at my own presumption, and wisely decided to say nothing of my own ambitions.'[2]

Good call, Freda, good call.

I first came across Freda when trying to find information about how long it would take to reach Ball Hut, a small three-bunker on the flanks of the Tasman Glacier, and while contemplating if I could make it over Ball Pass one day. The snowcraft course instructor (not the one who yelled at me a lot, but another one) had mentioned Ball Pass as being the sort of challenge that could one day be achievable for novice mountaineers if we really concentrated on our skills and kept progressing, so I was intrigued to check out the area. Mountaineers who are really fit and fast can complete the Ball Pass trip in one very long day, but most people break it up by camping or using Ball Hut along the way.

Searching for info about the hut led me to numerous mentions of it in Freda's book. Ball Hut, historically much bigger than the current three-bunk dog box, was often used by guided parties going to and from expeditions, and the route up the side of the glacier leading to the hut became something of a highway. The Ball Hut road was once drivable the whole way to the hut (back then it was more of a lodge, really), and for a time a bus service existed to drop off skiers aiming to ascend and ski the Ball Glacier nearby. These days you need a Land Rover or similar to get in there (plus a dose of bold driving technique) and you can now only get as far as a spot called Husky Flat, which has in recent years been thoroughly washed out by storms, requiring trampers to perform a 200-metre climb as a diversion over a spur. Car rental companies usually specifically cite the Ball Hut road as a backcountry road that will nullify the car's insurance if it's taken for a drive there. (I later had the honour of driving a guiding company's Land Rover, affectionately named Tigger, up the Ball Hut road to fetch a party coming back from a mountain skills course. It was snowing and sleeting, and I was nervous my four-wheel-driving skills weren't equal to the task, but it was great fun and nobody had to make an insurance claim so I deem the trip a resounding success.)

Ball Hut is a real treat and one of my favourites. It's perched on the moraine terrace above the Tasman Glacier, with a view of De la Beche (2950 metres) and the Minarets, which can be seen in the background.

Ball Hut has gone through several incarnations in its time since Freda and friends used it and is a rather modern affair compared to its original 1891 structure. It is now bright red and very small but adequate, with spectacular views to the upper Tasman Glacier. (The original hut was swept away in an avalanche in October 1925.) Freda wrote of the last glories of the sunset, of miles and miles of pure white ice, and the view to Mount De la Beche (2950 metres) and the Minarets (3031 and 3040 metres).

I'd been eyeing up De la Beche and the Minarets from Unwin Lodge, the New Zealand Alpine Club lodge I was babysitting for a spell while the managers were away. Unwin Lodge's living-room window affords an inspirational view down the Tasman Valley and on a clear day you can see all the way to a multitude of peaks. I had been looking lustfully at the sunset bathing these peaks each evening and decided one day I would climb them, in the same way Freda decided on Aoraki/Mount Cook as her objective. De la Beche seemed like the mother peak, the 'proper' climb, while the Minarets appeared to me more as naughty younger siblings, the type who would use fake ID to get into the nightclub and party until dawn. The Minarets, I thought, would likely be much more fun to hang out with.

Freda's mentions of Ball Hut had me interested enough to opt for it as my next trip while I was staying at Aoraki/Mount Cook. Early season snow had come down, settling on the ground at the lodge, and I was reluctant to attempt any tramps higher up as a dusting of fresh snow on steep, wet tussock could be a recipe for disaster. The route into Ball Hut was meant to take three to four hours one way, was almost dead flat, and evidently still held vestiges of the old four-wheel-drive road.[3] It ticked the box for a day out that I'd find intriguing enough but that probably wouldn't result in either death or an unscheduled trip in an ambulance.

The weather cleared late the night before but the snow wasn't melting in a hurry. I left an hour before sunrise and began slogging in by headtorch in the pitch-black dark. The cold took my breath away, and as with all early starts in the name of alpine experiences, it made me question my life choices. Was it really necessary or sensible to be up at such an hour? Wouldn't a nice cosy bed be a great option? And damn it, would I ever warm up?

It took half an hour before my toes and fingers defrosted from the cold, blood circulating, swinging into the rhythm down the Ball Hut road. It was indeed very easy going until after Husky Flat and the 'big big rock' as it's known — a boulder that's bigger than a van, or perhaps a small truck. (I did wonder about my chances of ongoing longevity if one of its siblings decided suddenly to detach itself from the valley wall.) Eventually the route turns into more of a track with the occasional reassuring orange marker, and undulates slightly, requiring a bit of rock-hopping.

Longevity in Aoraki/Mount Cook National Park is a tricky thing. People fall, they succumb to hypothermia, guides and climbers are buried in avalanches. Even huts aren't safe, historically; a group of trampers perished when the hut they were staying in, Three Johns Hut at Barron Saddle, was blown clean off the mountainside.[4]

The first Pākehā to die in Aoraki/Mount Cook National Park was George Napier, a 20-something-year-old who disappeared in 1907 after leaving Ball Hut. It's assumed he slipped while crossing the Hooker River and drowned but nobody really knows as his body was never recovered. More than 240 people have died in the park to date and a handful have never been found. Occasionally, the bodies of climbers who have been missing for decades pop out of glaciers as they move slowly down the valleys.

Perhaps the most famous tragedy was in January 1930, when four women and a male guide were caught in a blizzard while en route to Ball Hut from Malte Brun Hut and perished suddenly and mysteriously on the Tasman Glacier. The group, which comprised Dorothy Smith, Helena Keane, Doris Brown and Mary Monteath, had left the hut with guide John Blomfield, while his companion guide Charles Hilgendorf said he would follow after he had cleaned up the hut. Conditions were rainy but nothing to be seriously worried about. The weather took a turn for the worse, however, and a gale sprang up while the party was in exposed terrain with nowhere to shelter. Hilgendorf soon found it to be the worst blizzard he had ever known and even though it was flat terrain he put on crampons to get traction on the glacier's ice. Lightning was all around, and his ice axe was 'hissing and spluttering to such an extent that he towed it behind him with straps rather than carry it in his hands'.[5]

Reaching De la Beche Corner on the Tasman Glacier, Hilgendorf came

Finally warming up as the sun hits the track, en route to Ball Hut. I'm not one to listen to music, but occasionally a podcast can be good company on solo missions.

across the rest of the party lying almost all together on the ice. One was face down in a hollow in the ice and had possibly been trying to shelter from the wind. Nearby, one woman's face was under the water, and another was lying on top of her — both dead and stiff. (Another guide in a later search party, Mick Bowie, described the bodies' positions differently: three of the women were together, two of whom were frozen under the water. It was thought they might have been shifted by the sheer force of the extreme wind.) The party was about 9 kilometres from reaching the shelter of Ball Hut. Hilgendorf pulled them out of the water to rest them on the ice, and continued. The wind was so strong he had to crawl on hands and knees to reach the safety of Ball Hut and raise the alarm.

Guide Blomfield was found near the women, with evidence he had also crawled on his hands and knees in an attempt to reach shelter. He had lost his possessions — hat, rucksack, ice axe — and his hands had been badly torn by the ice, including losing all the skin off the backs. Attempts to revive him by wrapping him in blankets and rubbing him proved futile.[6]

Hilgendorf stated that he thought his fate would have been the same if he had been with the party and equipped in the same way they were — which was inappropriate for the weather. 'I was equipped very differently,' he told the coroner. 'In my opinion the blizzard was at its worst a quarter of an hour before I came to the bodies.'[7] A doctor who examined the bodies and the clothing concluded they had been inadequately clad and died of exposure. However, well-known mountaineer Guy Mannering put forth the idea that the five had died from being struck by lightning — a controversial theory, published in that year's *New Zealand Alpine Journal*.[8]

Mannering claimed to have searched the existing 41 volumes of the *UK Alpine Journal*, which regularly reported climbing fatalities, and was unable to find a similar case where an entire party had died all at once, and so suddenly, from exposure. (And here he has a good point — it does indeed seem unusual.) 'I can find [no cases] where death has occurred under a period of about 12 hours, and then it is usually only one or two members of the party who have succumbed,' Mannering wrote. 'There are numerous instances of resistance for periods of 24 and 48 hours and even longer, without death resulting.' One woman had a blackened face, which some thought suggested she had been struck by lightning. However, her clothing wasn't burnt, and it was thought to be blackened due to frostbite.[9]

Another point of contention in the lightning argument was the watches the women were wearing. Several had run down, stopping later that evening, while one had stopped at 12.49 p.m. due to getting wet. It was thought by many that if the party had been struck by lightning, the watches — which were metal — would have fused. However, Hilgendorf's ice axe hissing and spluttering seemed to tally with the lightning theory, and it seemed strange at the time that guide Blomfield had three cardigans in his rucksack that the women could have put on for warmth. (On the other hand, we now know that victims of hypothermia in advanced stages often feel a rush of heat to their skin and sometimes remove clothing, to the tragic detriment of their condition.)

John Blomfield seemed to emerge as a hero of the accident, although there was some controversy at the time over the nearby Hermitage Hotel at Aoraki/Mount Cook Village using very young 'student' guides for tourist outings.[10] An extensive story in the *Evening Star* lauded 'Blomfield's heroic devotion' as he 'stripped himself to clothe the women': 'The latest details [of the tragedy] invest the death of Student-guide Blomfield with heroic glamour. His body was found, practically naked, about 150 yards from where the four women lay. He had given his clothing to them, and then had set out in the forlorn hope of regaining the Malte Brun hut and securing blankets for his charges.'

Dr Bradshaw, a climber who had come over to the Tasman Glacier from the West Coast via De la Beche, met the party en route to Ball Hut and was there later when Hilgendorf arrived with news of the tragedy. 'He was in a terrible state of exhaustion,' said Bradshaw. 'I think he had to crawl some distance down the glacier as his trousers were torn.' 'It was a wonderful performance,' commented Roy Twyneham in the story, who was at the Hermitage when Hilgendorf arrived. 'When I saw Hilgendorf at the Hermitage on his return he was all in. After the awful day he had put in, he was in the last stages of exhaustion. It was only his superb fitness and strength that enabled him to get through at all. I climbed with him a few days before, and know what he was like. . . . The weather was moderately good when they set out, but a blizzard comes on with wonderful suddenness . . . To get through a blizzard, perfect physical fitness is necessary,' continued Twyneham, insufferably, at length. 'They must have been dead within an hour and a-half of leaving the hut, as they were only four miles away when found.'[11]

In April 1931, Guy Mannering officially opened De la Beche Memorial

Refuge, a hut located at De la Beche Corner, the junction of the Tasman and Rudolf glaciers. A bivouac site existed there, and had the party made their way to it, they might have survived. The memorial hut was replaced with a new hut in 1979, but this couldn't stand up to the brutal mountain environment. It deteriorated and was removed in February 2012.[12]

The ice is shrinking and the glaciers are fast disappearing. Aoraki/Mount Cook locals, who aren't exactly elderly, can remember the days before the Tasman Glacier lake even existed — it was simply a very small body of water at the end of the ice. Older topographic maps attest to the same: the 1989 topo map shows no lake at all, and no melt holes or mini-lakes, but by the 1999 map, it was making its presence felt; one arm of the lake ran as far as Celmisia Flat and several smaller lakes were appearing within the glacier at the Murchison Valley junction. The change between 2009 and the present day, however, is dramatic and saddening.[13]

Tourists now do a short walk in the Tasman Valley to see the Blue Lakes, which are separated from the Tasman Glacier (now the lake) by a high moraine wall. The Blue Lakes were originally named for being that distinctive bright blue colour that comes from glacial melt. The glacier sat on the other side of the moraine wall, with ice higher than the lakes on the other side and down below. Water would melt from the glacier and trickle through the moraine, where the Blue Lakes were formed. Now, there's no glacier to trickle water through the moraine wall — so the lakes are more green than blue, due to algae. I did a day walk to the Blue Lakes and the melting glacier almost provoked tears, but I decided the lakes didn't need any more liquid additions. The Blue Lakes are now just a lesser tourist attraction and used by locals for swimming on a hot day.

As the glaciers shrink, access around them and onto them becomes trickier over time. Supposedly, back in Freda's time (or when the party died at De la Beche Corner) access was simply a matter of walking out onto the glacier. Skiers at Ball Hut could exit the hut straight onto the snow and ice of the Ball Glacier. Now, going from Ball Hut onto Tasman Glacier requires climbers to use 'Garbage Gully', a steep and unstable moraine gully. I'd had ideas about going for a wander from Ball Hut

Inspecting a crevasse on the upper reaches of Ball Glacier, after finally doing the Ball Pass trip. SIMON BAINBRIDGE

onto the glacier, so I started researching Garbage Gully, though I didn't find much. It's not marked on the map; it's more a case of experienced climbers knowing where it is and what it involves.

In June 1975, a young woman, Beverly McClure, had the same idea I did — going for a wander on the glacier.[14] Sitting in the sun outside Ball Hut with friends, she asked how she could get out there. Garbage Gully was by then the only way of accessing the ice, and her friends tried to talk her out of it. Off she went, 1 or 2 kilometres onto the ice. Her friends watched her through binoculars, and at last glance she seemed to be about 10 minutes' walk from the gully. She didn't reappear — it was assumed she had been put off climbing Garbage Gully again due to falling rocks, which the others had heard — but by 4 p.m. the party was worried. Through their binoculars they could see footprints in the snow heading down the glacier, back towards the track start.

Eventually they saw McClure, equal to around 2 kilometres back down the track from Ball Hut, lying on the snow on the glacier. She called to the group that she was too tired to climb up the moraine wall, and a friend advised her there was another way up the moraine further down the valley — and to keep walking. The friend reached her by 6 p.m., when McClure was exhausted and about to collapse from exposure. He soon realised he was heading towards the same state and abandoned her to get further help. Rescuers reached her by abseil at 9.30 p.m., but she was declared dead by a doctor at 2.30 a.m.

Ball Hut came into sight just as I needed a snack break. It's home to a few cheeky kea who enjoy chatting to visitors, and snatching and wrecking anything left unobserved. I do wonder how the Department of Conservation can possibly know how to construct kea-proof huts, as those sharp beaks don't seem to have a limit in terms of what they can take apart.

I stopped for a spell, happy to warm my feet after trekking in fresh snow. I had a go at following the route further along and up the ridge to Ball Pass, but a steep spot with patches made treacherously slippery by snow melting in the morning sun encouraged me to turn back in the name of self-preservation. McClure, Blomfield and others stuck in my mind. Ball Pass could definitely wait, and anyway I didn't have the gear (axe and crampons) to get me up and over it.

I sometimes wonder if I'm too conservative or hesitant. I see men taking bigger risks and setting hairy goals without any roadmap of how they'll get there, while women I know are carefully sticking to scaffolded 'plus ones'. I remember once being at a New Zealand Alpine Club meeting and listening to a young guy narrate why he and his friends were there: they'd just decided to climb Aoraki/Mount Cook. Just like that. They weren't trampers or climbers at all; they had zero experience with ice and snow. They'd decided they were going to do it, so going to an Alpine Club meeting was the logical thing to do. They got a lot of attention at that meeting for their bullishness and ambition. Meanwhile, the room was full of women who had been steadily achieving climb after climb modestly, incrementally, and with very little fanfare.

We're told the young male brain doesn't fully appreciate risk and consequences. Boffins reckon between puberty and mid-twenties, men take risks they later deem to be madness. Young women, meanwhile, don't seem to have the same problem — the assessment of risk and consequence seems to be tightly linked early on. Nature or nurture? Whichever it is, I know I'm on the conservative end of the spectrum. But I wonder, how much do I miss out on experiences, notably in the mountains, because I err on the side of caution? Could I afford to be a bit more daring and attempt things I think are scaffolded much higher or that are perhaps totally out of my reach? I usually set goals that I think I have a reasonable chance of achieving. I don't often attempt things where I suspect I might have a reasonable chance of failure. But perhaps I'm doing myself out of a world of experience, simply by being too hesitant to try.

I had actually opted for Ball Hut as I'd decided my desired mountain goal of the day was unadvisable; I'd wanted to tramp up to Sefton Bivouac as a day trip. Sefton Bivouac is one of the oldest huts in Aoraki/Mount Cook National Park, built in 1917 under the guidance of the chief guide at the Hermitage, Peter Graham — who was also Freda's guide of choice.

The bivouac had an earth floor and could sleep three people, and was situated above the junction of the Hooker and Mueller glaciers, intended to make climbs of nearby peaks more accessible. Sefton Biv, aside from being considered one of the cutest huts around,[15] is a popular shelter, well sited and evocative of the pioneering days of mountaineering.[16]

Getting up to Sefton Bivouac is technically a route (rather than a track), marked with cairns, and involves some 800 metres of steep ascent. Researching it revealed a gruesome history. One man fell to his death trying to reach Sefton Biv just moments after telling his friends he felt out of his depth on the climb. Scottish tradesman Robert Buckley, 31, was climbing with three others in February 2014. Sefton Biv was recommended by the Department of Conservation as a walk of three to four hours, but they were cautioned it was a challenging route, and harder than the nearby popular Mueller Hut route (this is absolutely true). Crucially, Buckley hadn't used crampons or an ice axe before, and when he came to an icy buttress 400 metres away from the hut, he told his friends he was 'out of his comfort zone'. Buckley fell, and was later found dead in a snow gully 270 metres below the tricky buttress.[17] Reading the account of Buckley's misadventure gave me pause.

On the other hand, even children have made it up there — as early as 1928, two boys aged 12 and 14 climbed up to it.[18] (Not only that, they used the bivouac for a successful summit trip of The Footstool (2764 metres) and Mount Sefton (3151 metres), both rigorous climbs in their own right.) So what was my problem?

Ball Hut was a gratifying trip, but it was really the result of me chickening out of doing something tougher. Like Freda, I too wondered if I had the physical strength, the courage and so on, to be a mountaineer of any worth.

The walk back from Ball Hut was uneventful but picturesque. I did the usual social media thing of loading a few pics and a description up on Facebook. Most of my non-tramping, non-climbing friends think I'm crazy; notably going out before dawn and in the snow. They think it's risky — especially doing anything outside of an urban setting by myself. In the face of social media comments about how extreme my trip looked, I knew the reality: compared to what Freda had achieved, and what so many other women climbers have done, my outing to Ball Hut wasn't even so much as a piece of lint on the hooded sweatshirt of the climbing landscape.

Returning to Ruapehu, I felt more confident in my alpine skills, but I soon hit a wall. Beyond the basic snowcraft skills, which encompass moving on snow in crampons and with an ice axe, it was proving difficult to get more experience or learn how to do more advanced roped climbing. I went along to a lot of climbing meet-ups, but it seemed to be clique-y. I found it difficult to get accepted on a trip — they were always 'full', and it appeared to be more about who you knew — or to link up with other climbers who were at my level. Organised trips catered really well to more advanced climbers, or to absolute beginners going on a snowcraft course, but I felt there was a wasteland for those in between. I began climbing alone, after reading writer-climber Paul Hersey's book *High Misadventure: New Zealand mountaineering tragedies and survival stories*,[19] in which he describes the exploits of solo climber Guy McKinnon, among other climbers and trampers.

In the book, McKinnon has a fall and survives. Although the book is partly about death in the wilderness and hence should have scared me into inaction, reading McKinnon's solo pursuits plus my predilection for tramping alone planted the seed for snow adventures by myself. I'd also long skied by myself in-bounds on Ruapehu, and felt fairly comfortable going solo, at least on my home mountain. I began heading out on the snow with ice axe and crampons to get more experience, but with parameters: an impeccably clear weather forecast and low avalanche risk, leaving intentions and a panic time with a trusted human being, and always with enough gear to dig in and save myself if something went wrong.

One quiet day on Whakapapa I decided to be lazy and use my season pass to take the chairlift up to Knoll Ridge café and start climbing from there. As a skier, I'm well used to getting on and off chairlifts, and when you're carrying climbing tools, you need to be careful of others around you so that you don't poke someone's eye out with an ice axe. So, when I went to load onto the chair, I was looking to get on one by myself. It wasn't busy at all — just two guys behind me. They were wearing jeans, sneakers and puffer jackets. No hats. No packs. No alpine gear. Clearly tourists off to have a coffee at the café. But they were trying to rush forward and get on the chair with me, and the lift operator was waving them forward too.

'Hey, I want to get on a chair by myself, I've got the sharp stuff on my pack,' I called out to the liftie, also warning the guys behind me.

'Just get on with these guys, doll, they know what they're doing,' he called back.

Doll?! He called me 'doll'?!

They jumped on with me, one either side, predictably both of them getting annoyed at having to avoid getting poked by a sharp implement for the next five minutes of the ride. Well, I *had* warned them.

I find it fascinating that two guys in sneakers and puffer jackets can be deemed more competent and knowledgeable than someone in well-used climbing gear. Was it simply because they're men? Do we automatically assign experience and ability on the basis of gender? Would I be held back from climbing harder stuff by hitting a wall of bias? Was I holding myself back? And, most importantly, what would Freda do?

To climb Aoraki/Mount Cook these days you need ice axes and crampons, a rope, snow anchors, a belay device . . . the list goes on. When Freda du Faur started her mountaineering journey with a view to climbing it in 1910, she needed a skirt.

There were further difficulties. Freda's first big climb was Mount Sealy, which then required a bivouac — an overnight stay in the open. As a young, unmarried woman travelling alone, she was subjected to much well-meaning hand-wringing from those who thought it inappropriate for her to bivouac with men. When she announced that she was off to climb Mount Sealy with a (male) guide but no chaperone, she found herself 'up against all the cherished conventions of the middle-aged', who informed her if she went ahead, she would lose her reputation: 'One old lady implored me with tears in her eyes not to "spoil my life for so small a thing as climbing a mountain" . . . for about ten minutes I almost succeeded in wishing that I possessed that useful appendage to a woman climber, a husband.'[20] Her guide was Peter Graham, a man known to be of unimpeachable reputation. His solution was to take a porter with them, but Freda baulked at having to incur extra expense just because of her gender and marital state.

Anyway, back to the skirt. To bow to Edwardian custom would have required her to wear a full-length skirt, but practicality called for pants. (One male climber on her trip refused to climb with her if she wore a skirt; Freda speculated that he might have previously seen a skirt sweeping rocks off a ledge onto others below. Eventually he caved, and climbed on with the party in spite of the skirt. Damned if she did, damned if she didn't; she couldn't win.)

Amid the controversy and further hand-wringing advice, she devised a compromise, and wore a knee-length skirt over knickerbockers, with puttees up to her knees.[21] For context, most women going for outings on the lower slopes would wear an ankle-length skirt. Even Freda considered the skirt to be 'brief', and when she worriedly showed it to Graham for his approval, he grinned and said: 'Skirt! I should call it a frill.' (The skirt can be seen in the commemorative photo taken of Freda in front of a boulder in the Hooker Valley after her successful climb of Aoraki/Mount Cook.)

Why the skirt at all? Freda enjoyed defying expectations of a woman climber as a 'masculine-looking female with short hair, a loud voice and large feet'. She saw a love of fresh air and exercise as not purely a masculine prerogative, and no need to change her femininity to indulge in it. 'I was the first unmarried woman who had wanted to climb in New Zealand,' she wrote, 'and in consequence I received all the hard knocks until one day when I awoke more or less famous in the mountaineering world, after which I could and did do exactly as seemed to me best.'[22]

Freda stands out as the pre-eminent woman climber of her time. However, others, too, were climbing, and even earlier than her — they just didn't have the audacity, or self-assurance, or perhaps arrogance, to write about themselves. Constance Barnicoat, who had grown up in New Zealand but travelled extensively, came back home and in 1903 was the first woman to cross Copland Pass, which connects the Aoraki/Mount Cook area with the West Coast and is a tough climb, now considered largely inaccessible due to rock shift and instability. Barnicoat, clearly giving even fewer fucks than Freda, eschewed a skirt for trousers while climbing and made trips unchaperoned with male guides in Europe.[23] A journalist wrote in the *Ashburton Guardian*: 'Miss Barnicoat's climbing dress is a novel one, and, if worn in the city, would be responsible for no small sensation. She protects her head with a large, grey felt, slouch hat; her body with a thick woollen sweater, and her legs with corduroy walking breeches and warm hose of the kind affected by the tourist.'[24] Sounds comfy; Constance Barnicoat is my kind of lady.

Barnicoat was outspoken on the impractical nature of wearing a skirt, 'even the shortest', while climbing, and refused any women's clothing for the activity. 'I had forsworn all tempestuous petticoats and dressed myself up as much like a boy as possible. I promptly sent for proper boys' boots, the heaviest procurable, with very thick soles which I have well nailed, and generally rigged myself out as much like a boy as possible with a white wool "sweater", knickers and puttees to my knees. Except in some such dress the guide flatly refused the risk of taking ladies; and he was perfectly justified,' she wrote after crossing the Copland Pass.[25]

By 1911, Barnicoat had several achievements to her name, collecting them from not only New Zealand but also the Pyrenees, the Russian Caucasus, and the Schreckhorn, a difficult peak in the Bernese Oberland.[26] 'This dangerous ascent is seldom attempted in winter,' a newspaper article narrated of Barnicoat's Schreckhorn summit achievement, 'and has only once before been made by a woman, and that was in the summer season.'[27] This trip was made in 1907, a full year before Freda even began climbing with Graham.

The North Island also had female climbers achieving peaks in the early 1900s. One of the earliest people to climb, and die, on Taranaki Maunga (Mount Taranaki) was Evelyn Oxenham, aged 22. Not only was her death notable for being the first woman to die on Taranaki — for Pākehā, anyway — it was also remarkable as she was climbing with a young man who wasn't a guide, and both were unchaperoned.[28] It was 1913, just after Freda had paved the way with her climbs.

With its symmetrical peak so alluring and so much more accessible, the Taranaki area attracted climbers as much as Aoraki/Mount Cook National Park did. A letter to the *Taranaki Herald* in 1903 from an anonymous correspondent claimed to know of a 'plucky little lady mountaineer' who had recently completed the 'almost impossible task' of climbing Paritutū (the Sugar Loaf), a 154-metre crag on the New Plymouth coast. She was accompanied 'against his will' by a gentleman, but not a guide, presumably also unchaperoned. Her achievements are unfortunately overshadowed by the condescending language, laced with surprise that a mere woman

The famous photo of Freda du Faur, taken after her climb of Aoraki/Mount Cook in 1910. Her skirt was considered scandalously short, and her guide Peter Graham called it a 'frill'. GEORGE MANNERING

could climb anything. You can almost see the raised eyebrows.[29]

By 1910, society was recognising mountaineering as an 'indispensable part of the life of a certain section of women' and it was no longer looked upon as a new fancy — but it *was* admittedly the domain of the wealthy European woman.[30] Newspapers were naming climbers such as Fanny Bullock Workman, Elizabeth Hawkins-Whitshed (aka Mrs Aubrey Le Blond) and Dorothy Keen. Constance Barnicoat was included in the usual lists of famous women climbers, but Freda only got significant recognition after publishing her book.

By the late 1920s, women were even guiding at the Hermitage in Aoraki/ Mount Cook. Sisters Hilda and Molly Haldane were early 'girl guides' who would take clients on glacier excursions.[31] But the first properly hardcore female guide was Betsy Blunden (later Anderson or Blunden-Anderson after she married), who is thought to be the world's first paid female alpine guide, employed at the Hermitage from 1928 not only as a guide but also as a piano player. She got the job partly because of her looks (she was described as 'a fine buxom-looking wench' in her interview)[32] and there is some evidence she resented the after-dinner duties she was required to perform: putting on an evening dress, entertaining guests, and arranging music and games. It was a role she was not at ease with.[33]

In 1930 Blunden had the honour of guiding Governor-General Lord Bledisloe to Ball Hut during his visit, and she climbed The Footstool (2764 metres) with her cousin Arthur Shand and guides Vic Williams and Mick Bowie. However, while Shand went on to climb Aoraki/Mount Cook with those guides, Blunden wasn't considered as a second guide on high peaks until the following season, after she'd summited the Minarets. Seven months after first being employed by the Hermitage, Blunden was joined by Betty Petre as a junior guide, the second female guide on the staff. Women were making inroads.

Perhaps Blunden's most famous climb was the all-women ascent of Mount Sefton in 1934, alongside Leila Davidson and Rosamund Harper.[34] It was hailed in the newspapers as 'a guideless climb', by three New Zealand 'girls'.[35] The climb, from the western side, was considered quite noteworthy, not just for being all-women and guideless, but also as Mount Sefton was reasonably difficult. On the way there, the trio stopped at Blunden's sister Janie's place in Greymouth. Janie was due to get married shortly after the three got back from their climb of Sefton and she put

Blunden on notice that she'd better not have short hair or tanned skin at the wedding. She didn't comply, and to make matters worse, she lost a tooth during the climb and had to avoid smiling while at the wedding dinner (she attempted to make a false tooth out of a piece of chewing gum, but it disappeared with the soup course).[36]

Betsy Blunden ceased guiding in 1931, dissatisfied with the Hermitage management and physically wrecked from carrying big loads, but continued tramping and climbing, leading parties, and being held in high esteem by many men. There is, however, some evidence that some members of the then all-male Canterbury Mountaineering Club (CMC) did not appreciate her existence.[37] Blunden climbed Mount Oates in Arthur's Pass National Park with two CMC members, who were lampooned by fellow members on the train on the way there. 'They were all roaring with laughter at John Pascoe [her climbing partner] taking a girl because they wouldn't have women in their club. Of course they didn't laugh afterwards.'[38] It was a first ascent, Mount Oates standing more than a thousand metres higher than Goat Pass, which is a decent day out in itself (and now the pinnacle of the Coast to Coast mountain run). Unusually, in the subsequent newspaper reports Blunden was named while the two male climbers, Pascoe and Brian Barrer, were either named as companions or simply described as 'members of the Canterbury Mountaineering Club'.[39] Perhaps Blunden was named because she was 'othered' as a non-member of the CMC, and again as the only woman, a curiosity even for that time.

Hermitage guide Junee Ashurst (née Mulvay), who climbed Aoraki/ Mount Cook as an equal partner with Harry Ayres in 1938, encountered some of the same discrimination, in spite of her relative fame as a highly competent woman guide. Although she'd risen in the ranks while her husband Hap Ashurst was overseas serving during World War II, she was summarily dismissed by chief guide Mick Bowie when he returned from the war in 1944. Bowie believed women couldn't make competent guides, although he'd missed the clear evidence of this during his time away; and locally it was accepted that Ashurst was actually more competent than some of the men. Ashurst eventually climbed Mount Tasman twice, Aoraki/Mount Cook twice, and climbed all the peaks above 10,000 feet in the Aoraki/Mount Cook National Park.[40] Stick that in your pipe and smoke it, Mick.

On the summit of Te Heuheu (2732 metres) on Ruapehu. In honour of Freda du Faur, I climbed in a skirt.

Inspired by Freda du Faur and her forthright audacity, I climbed Te Heuheu (2732 metres), the northernmost of the summit peaks on Ruapehu and arguably one of the most glorious on a clear day with crusts of ice on the ridge, wearing a skirt, much shorter than Freda's and probably far more practical. I was accompanied by neither a guide nor a chaperone, but by a married male friend I'd borrowed for the outing. I hoped Freda would appreciate my bucking of convention on her behalf.

In 1894, news reached New Zealand that Edward FitzGerald (an American best known for leading the expedition to the first ascent of Aconcagua in South America) and Matthias Zurbriggen (a Swiss guide) had plans to climb Aoraki/Mount Cook. It hadn't been conquered yet, although climbers Guy Mannering and Marmaduke Dixon had gotten within 60 metres of the summit in 1890. Local Kiwi climbers felt that the first ascent should rightly belong to New Zealanders, so several guides got an expedition together: Tom Fyfe, George Graham and Jack Clarke. Aoraki/Mount Cook wasn't hugely technical climbing and if conditions were good, FitzGerald and Zurbriggen would very likely be successful in their attempt. It was a race to the summit.

After a bout of extreme persistence, the Kiwi team won, reaching the summit at 1.30 p.m. on Christmas Day 1894 in bitingly cold winds. Upper-class toff FitzGerald wasn't happy, and reportedly said, 'Been beaten at the post and by a damned tinker.'[41] (Fyfe was a plumber, while FitzGerald came from a more privileged and educated background.) The weather presented such pressing challenges that the next day the Kiwi climbers simply abandoned their camp on the upper Hooker Glacier, under Harper Saddle, and bailed for the safety of the Hermitage.

Nineteen years later, in 1913, the entire camp was discovered 4 miles down the glacier, in the middle of the ice and on a line between the Hooker Hut and Ball Pass, having been covered with snow and then become part of the glacier itself. The tent was still fairly sound, although the ropes were rotten, and on the end of the ropes were the scrub branches that had been pushed into the snow to anchor it. Sleeping bags, socks and other odds and ends were found with the camp, including two cans of sardines — no longer in edible condition. The camp's ice-encased travels enabled the rate of travel of the glacier to be calculated at 33 inches per day.

Lucy Mannering, wife of climber Guy Mannering, was a serious climber in her own right and she was the one to discover the camp, spotting something within the ice and then working with her axe to chip away at the ice and dig it out. However, in 1939, when Guy Mannering wrote a lengthy piece for *The Press* about bodies — human or otherwise — being lost and rediscovered on glaciers, he took credit for the discovery, and its physical retrieval, himself. There was no mention of his wife, who was, in accordance with the practice of the time, always referred to as 'Mrs Mannering', 'the wife of the bank manager and well-known climber Guy Mannering'; her identity is lost to history.[42] Only days later she perished — not on a mountain but in the Aratiatia Rapids outside Taupō, after slipping off a rock while fishing.

I was making progress with confidence and climbing, but I kept occasionally banging my head on the wall of bias (or was it an ice ceiling?) and discovered others were frequently doing the same. A female friend wrote to me: 'I went to a club meeting with my [male] partner. One of the club leaders made a beeline for him, talked to him and ignored me, interrupting me if I tried to speak. I'm a far more advanced climber and tramper than my partner, but this guy was only interested in talking to him. I also had a female friend with me, and the leader said he was thinking of having more social events "to attract the girls" and pointed at us — he actually pointed at us! This, he said, would attract male climbers. He made it clear we were just there — in his mind, at least — as candy to attract the real climbers, the guys. I actually climb harder grades than my partner.' The bias seemed to be everywhere, but only noticeable if you happened to be on the wrong side of it.

I took another alpine course to learn how to use a rope and do more technical climbing, a five-day commitment, on and near Ruapehu. When it concluded and I was back at my ski-club lodge, I brought out a rope one night to practise knots. I was determined to master that old bastard the Alpine Butterfly, which seemed like the sort of knot you'd want to know about in a bad situation. As I began to tie the knot, a visiting climber demanded to know what, exactly, I was trying to do. 'That's not how you tie the Alpine Butterfly,' he scoffed. (I later found out it was indeed one of several methods for tying it and I was executing my chosen method quite correctly.) The next night, bringing out the rope to practise further, I had another climber take the rope off me before I could even start. It was as if to bat it out of my hands and say, 'This is not for you, young lady!'

The Alpine Butterfly, bless its heart, goes back to 1914, when it was used by linesmen due to its ability to withstand tension in any direction. Mountaineers soon picked it up for its many advantages, which include being easy to untie after it's had a load pulling on it, its ability to be tied with gloves on, and, apparently, to be tied one-handed.

I haven't quite mastered that part of the party trick yet.

I'd also noticed that the regular alpine and mountaineering Facebook pages weren't a welcoming environment. Anyone asking a question was liable to get lampooned by the ageing mountaineering contingent who evidently found beginners' questions hilarious, and who seemed to assume that their prior exploits and achievements gave them the right to ridicule others mercilessly. Not only that, it was shockingly sexist at times, with the old guard maintaining the hegemony. What I personally needed was a private space where I could ask questions without fear of being mocked. I set up a secret Facebook group, flippantly called it Secret Women's Mountain Business, and added all the hardcore women climbers and skiers I knew. It soon exploded, with those women adding others. I've since met several of the women serendipitously, in the wilderness and in action — on the top of an alpine pass, or in a remote hut.

If only Freda, Constance and co had had such a support network of other women interested in the outdoors. '[T]here was no one in the hotel who could or would climb Mount Sealy,' Freda lamented in her book; 'there was not the ghost of a climber on the premises, only women who found a two-mile walk quite sufficient for their powers.'[43]

Moreover, in 1909 when Freda started climbing, the New Zealand Alpine Club (NZAC) wasn't up to much. Formed in 1891, for five years it rolled along nicely, but then lapsed. 'It seems a thousand pities that no one can be found to set the club in working order,' she wrote.[44] The NZAC rallied, of course, but while it has always accepted women as members, in its early days it was focused on encouraging men into mountaineering and celebrating men's achievements. (By 2018, around 30 per cent of its membership was female, and women now regularly outnumber men on snowcraft courses.) Many climbers looked further afield and wanted acknowledgement from and membership to the Alpine Club in the UK. It didn't admit women (due to, and I am not joking here, supposed physical and moral deficiencies when it came to mountaineering), so the Ladies' Alpine Club was founded in London in 1907, eventually merging with the Alpine Club in 1975.

In New Zealand, a group called Women Climbing was set up in the 1980s to support the pursuit,[45] and while women could join the NZAC, the Canterbury Mountaineering Club held out until the 1980s in refusing to admit them. Kiwi climber Lydia Bradey looked to join the CMC in her early days getting into climbing, only to discover her gender excluded her. 'When I heard that my immediate reaction was, "How stupid",' Lydia writes in her book *Going Up Is Easy*. 'The Canterbury Mountaineering Club seemed to have this weird notion that women shouldn't, or couldn't, mountaineer. [But] women were admitted around 1980. I became a member, but I recall that a few of the older men weren't pleased and some of them may have resigned.'[46] Egg on their faces, then, when she went on to summit Everest without supplementary oxygen, cementing her place as arguably our country's toughest woman climber — even if her teammates kept implying she'd merely imagined the summit.

(Even the Swiss weren't progressive; women were forced to form their own alpine club in 1918, and it took until 1980 for women to be admitted to the Swiss Alpine Club.)[47]

Freda du Faur, described as highly strung, died by 'self-inflicted carbon monoxide poisoning' in 1935, six years after her partner Muriel Cadogan committed suicide, her family having forcefully separated the pair. They had both been given 'treatment' for being of 'inverted hedonistic persuasion'. She penned such a compelling narrative in her book, but the last thing Freda wrote was a suicide note.[48]

At the time of her death, Freda owned a set of flats in England, property in New Zealand, and about £400 in various banks, which she left to two friends in her will, naming fellow female climber Marie Byles — who also reached the summit of Aoraki/Mount Cook — as executrix. Her family opposed probate, her brother Bertram telling courts that she was 'very eccentric in her habits' and in his opinion 'at times insane',[49] and her will was being contested on that basis. However, documents written by Freda (letters, notes and an exercise book) examined by the coroner led to a conclusion that she was, in fact, quite thoroughly sane.

One quote from the book sticks in my mind:

> [N]ow, five years after my first fight for individual freedom, the girl climber at the Hermitage need expect nothing worse than raised eyebrows when she starts out unchaperoned and clad in climbing costume. It is some consolation to have achieved as much as this, and to have blazed one more little path through ignorance and convention, and added one tiny spark to the ever-growing beacon lighted by the women of this generation to help their fellow-travellers climb out of the dark woods and valleys of conventional tradition and gain the fresh, invigorating air and wider view-point of the mountain-tops.[50]

Kaweka and Kaimanawa ranges

Second–hand socks and snowy tops

A LIABILITY. That's what a company calls it when an employee has too much leave clocked up each financial year. It's an on-paper problem, affecting the company's balance sheet, and can be tricky if staff resign with a hefty leave allowance needing to be paid out. The company I was working for took a proactive approach to the 'problem' of too many holidays — which isn't really a problem in my book — and instead of forcing employees to take leave, management offered us an extra five 'gifted' days if we used up more than 20 leave days within the financial year. I had burned through a lot of leave, but hadn't managed to fit it neatly into the financial year, and needed to take nearly two weeks off in a hurry to qualify for my extra week.

Clearly all of this impending time away from work called for a long-distance tramp, and maybe even something 'ultra'. I've long been taken with the idea of mega-tramps — epic stretches in the bush and the hills with strategic food drops to ease the burden of carrying heavy supplies. Our conservation estate makes up more than a third of our total land in New Zealand, so most national parks, forest parks and wilderness areas afford us enough terrain to be able to tramp for a week or more without coming across pesky civilisation. And tramping for a week or more without having to talk to another human being sounded ideal to introverted me. The only question was, where to go?

Along with being fascinated by ultra-long-distance tramping, I'd also been attracted to the Kaweka Forest Park. There are more than 30 huts in the Kaweka Range, from lodge-style at Te Puia on the Mōhaka River to tiny, dog-box bivouacs that fit only two people — and no room to stand up. Most of them are painted bright orange, known (fittingly) as DoC Rescue Orange — handy for spotting the structures from a helicopter or from across the ranges as a desperate tramper searches for a home for the night. Generally built as part of the support network for the New Zealand Forest Service and deer cullers from the 1930s onwards, they're also much more alluring than many of the new barn-style frontcountry huts. I had an affinity with the park and its huts, and although it was an arduous drive from my former home of Auckland, the Kaweka Range waggled at me enticingly as the top option.

I mapped out a course: I'd go in at Helisika (helicopter charters) at Poronui Station, off the Napier–Taupō highway just south of Taupō. From there I'd hit up Oamaru Hut, Boyd Hut, Tussock Hut, Harkness Hut, Te Pukeohikarua Hut, Mangaturutu Hut, Makino Hut, Middle Hill Hut and end up, nine days later, at Makahu Saddle Hut, where there's road access. There, my friend Nate would meet me with a resupply of food, fuel and clean undies (specifically mine, not his), and we'd take off on an eight-day circuit around Rocks Ahead Hut to Manson Country and loop back. It would be a hut-bagging expedition par excellence.

What I hadn't given much thought to was the time of year and the conditions that brought with it: early June, with snow on the way and, as it would turn out, unseasonably cold temperatures. One of the drawcards of the Kaweka is the opportunity to get out on the tops — exposed country where the track runs right along the ridgelines. That also means the they are susceptible to insane winds, as the DoC website cautions: 'Care should be taken on . . . the tops. Mists throughout the year, very strong winds, and snow and ice in winter can make conditions extremely dangerous to the inexperienced visitor.'[1] (This is an understatement. Even the bright orange longdrops are secured to the ground with wire in some spots. I'll leave that particular predicament to your imagination.)

I'd been into the Kaweka Range a couple of times before. Once, I'd climbed from Mākāhu Saddle up to Kaweka J (1724 metres), where a sizeable memorial cairn stands to honour Heretaunga Tramping Club members killed in World War II. A poled route exists, zig-zagging up a rubble-covered slope. The stones are like marbles and it's easy to lose your footing. A moment's inattention can result in a fall that is incompatible with living — there's simply nothing to grab on to.

Feeling tired on day three of a planned 17-day tramping epic across the Kaimanawa and Kaweka ranges. After leaving Tussock Hut I encountered dozens of cold thigh-deep river crossings in the Harkness Valley.

By the 1940s, the State Forest Service (which was at that time transitioning to the New Zealand Forest Service) had noticed the way of the land in the Kaweka Range — claypans and steep slopes with dry scree, plus volcanic ash from the Hātepe eruption in 232 CE — and began planting the exotic species *Pinus contorta* in an attempt to stabilise the slopes and prevent erosion. (The area is prone to massive slips, which are actually just a normal part of our landscape, but back then were thought to be problematic and hence must be fixed. In fact, they're merely part of a cycle of rock renewal. Mother Nature knows best.)

The Forest Service got to the point where they were enthusiastically tipping sacks of seeds out of planes to get *Pinus contorta* to take hold. Would it grow, they wondered in the early days. As it turns out, yes, shit, does it ever. In its native Americas, contorta grows reasonably. In New Zealand, it thrives. Contorta has an admirable but unfortunate ability to seed profusely and then spread rapidly — up to 12 kilometres from its original tree. It's also domineering and will outcompete other forest species. The final nail in the coffin: it's dense, makes access almost impossible, and offers no tasty treats to sustain birdlife and insects.

Anyway, the Kaweka had already had the bash by that point. Native bush was either razed or felled to clear land for farming, then merino sheep were introduced. Pests were next — the forest park is a popular hunting area due to the prevalence of sika deer, red deer and small furry creatures, none of which do anything to help the erosion issue. And contorta — as you'd guess from its name — doesn't always grow neatly. Many trees end up messy and tangled, and once the roots have taken hold, they're a struggle to pull out. Deer rub their antlers on young contorta to shed velvet, breaking the tree trunk and causing it to grow back in a warped way, compounding the problem.[2]

It took a long time for tree boffins to realise that *Pinus contorta* was more of a problem than a solution. As early as 1900, contorta was being discussed as a species ideal for creating a weather block to prevent sand from the coast blowing onto property around Taranaki. Hailed for its density,[3] it was considered to be part of the first line of defence for shelter, able to withstand 'salt-gales' with better effect than any other pine.[4] Success!

After World War II, the New Zealand Forest Service set up an experimental station at Mākāhu Saddle, with a remit to research revegetation techniques and ways to control erosion. Later, the water and soil division of the Ministry of Works set up the Ngahere Experimental Basin to monitor hydrological data and further investigate the potential of *Pinus contorta* on the ravaged landscape. Contorta seemed like the perfect solution to the non-problem of erosion. All was going swimmingly.

In 1947, trial plantings of contorta began on the Blowhard Plateau in the Kaweka Range using seed collected from the Karioi Forest. A trial planting at Mākāhu Saddle in 1962 yielded results to crow about in a research paper seven years later: 'The ability of plants to survive on difficult mountainland sites is of fundamental importance, and the fact that for most provenances survival exceeded 70% after seven years emphasises the suitability of pinus contorta for high-altitude work.' It's almost comical to read in retrospect. Fears that deer rubbing antlers on the plants would damage contorta growth were allayed in the paper, noting that there was nothing to suggest that 'animals of any sort' influenced the survival of the plants.[5]

Scientists declared *Pinus contorta* to be successfully taking hold — with volunteer growth spreading to 'over 5000 ft [1524 metres] on Mount Ruapehu' (where it's now a big problem). Critically, they judged that cold high-altitude sites would prompt only a few inches of growth per year; in fact, the pines grow faster than humanity (or at least the human resource allocated to the problem by central government) can handle. Even as late in the piece as 1980, contorta was still considered to be a success, although questions were being raised over its propensity for spreading to undeveloped land. 'Pinus contorta is successful on most sites to 1400 metres,' a paper marvelled. (Reality check: it easily grows on the tops of the Kaweka Range, at 1600–1700 metres.) 'It spreads vigorously from natural seeding, especially in the absence of grazing.'[6]

The unfortunate beauty of *Pinus contorta* is its ability to grow wilfully on steep mountainsides. Here, DoC has taken to controlling contorta in creative ways, notably by hanging chainsaw operators from a helicopter to tackle wilding pines in areas they can't reach on foot. 'When you want to hang under the helicopter, you've sort of got to be slightly bent and not afraid of heights,' says Eddie Te Kahika, who's in charge of the mad but effective operation in the Kaweka. It's about trust, and faith in your team, pilot and the equipment, says Te Kahika.[7] 'Up here, you're going to end up in situations you don't like. We need guys who are going to keep their heads.'[8]

Much like an ever-increasing leave balance, the steadily creeping *Pinus contorta* is also a liability.

They say bad things come in threes, and I corrected two out of the three crucial things I'd forgotten for the trip before I left the car at Helisika. The first was loo paper — I'd had to turn around and drive back to Taupō to buy some. The second was underwear — thankfully I had two spare pairs (clean, even!) in the car. Three pairs for nine days . . . doable, if I was careful to wash a pair each day and hope they'd dry in time.

The third thing was socks. I always walk in a single pair no matter how long the trip — dirty or wet, just put them on again in the morning and deal with it[9] — but I also keep a clean, dry pair to keep my feet warm at the hut. I'd remembered the walking pair of course (I was wearing them) but I'd neglected to pack the second pair. This all occurred to me, fittingly, as I approached the thigh-deep crossing of the Mōhaka River just before getting to Oamaru Hut for the night. I nearly cried. It was June, already cold, and I couldn't face the prospect of nine days with bare feet in the huts. That might sound soft but I tend to get very cold hands and feet, requiring a proactive approach to managing my limbs.

I devised a strategy. The Kaimanawa and Kaweka ranges were always crawling with hunters; I'd explain my predicament to each hunter I met and ask if I could have his socks, until someone took pity on me. Heartened by at least having a strategy, albeit a cheeky one, I plunged into the freezing waters of the Mōhaka and charged across the gorse-ridden flats to Oamaru Hut. I had seen smoke from afar, so I knew there would be company. Two hunters had taken up residence for the night, but — wonder of wonders — three pairs of socks hung from the wire line under the eaves.

'Hey, are these socks yours?' I enquired after introducing myself and doing the usual dance of tramping pleasantries — where you've come from, where you're going, and are you likely to be a threat to their plans to kill stuff (no, please continue with the killing).

Overjoyed to be wearing a pair of old socks I found abandoned at Oamaru Hut on night one of the Kaimanawa/Kaweka tramp. The ground in this photo is frozen solid, a preview of the chilly weather to come.

'Not ours,' came the words I was desperate to hear.

I nabbed a pair. I should've grabbed two pairs, it occurred to me later; two of the pairs were very thin and wouldn't provide much warmth but had no holes, while the third pair weren't intact but were thicker. Still, I was stoked.

I subscribe to the theory that happiness is relative to the desperation of your needs. Abraham Maslow proposed something similar in his hierarchy of needs, published in a 1943 paper 'A Theory of Human Motivation'. The idea is that we're always sitting somewhere on a pyramid of needs, moving up and down as life happens to us. At the bottom are the physiological needs — food, water, shelter and warmth — and you move through safety, love/belonging and esteem to self-actualisation at the top.

At that moment, my needs were at the bottom of the pyramid and that holey, filthy pair of socks helped me jump up the ladder significantly. The happiness I derived from some long-forgotten hunter's pair of discarded stinky socks far outweighed what I would have milked from, say, a large-screen TV. I reckon the hierarchy of needs is a framework for seeing life as a game of snakes and ladders. Sometimes you're up the ladder, self-actualising with your large-screen TV, and sometimes you're down the snake, staring into nine days of physiological distress with cold feet.

They were lucky socks, too. I didn't see a single pair of socks — or even a single sock, or a ghost of a sock — the whole trip after that.

I'd been in to Oamaru Hut before in broad daylight and somehow lost the thread of the track between the Mōhaka River and the hut itself. A hunter was sitting on the deck watching me try to bash my way through gorse, matagouri and scrub to reach it. For want of one orange track marker (which had fallen off) to indicate the path from the river, I lost a good half-hour and spent it getting scratched up by nature.

This time, I easily followed the track the whole way to the door of the hut, wondering at how I'd lost it the previous time. That got me thinking about the location's potential for night tramping. At three to four hours, it held possibilities for walking in on a Friday night by headtorch.

That night we could see two headtorches bobbing up and down across the river valley as two hunters made their way along the benched track on their approach to the hut, further cementing my ideas of night tramping. They arrived and got friendly with the two hunters who were already there. After a lot of showing off of rifles and downing some bourbon, they decided to head out as a group and shoot things.

'Are you allowed to shoot in the dark?' I asked, having some vague idea that you weren't, and anyway it didn't sound like a sensible idea, particularly after imbibing large swallows of bourbon.

'Yeah, no worries,' one of them said, brushing off my concerns.

I stayed put. I could hear the occasional shot but no screaming, so I assumed everything was going okay. Eventually I went to bed, deeming it safer to present myself as already asleep when they came back. It's not often I feel unsafe in the wilderness. Being around four drunk men with guns doesn't help.

Later on, when I got out, I checked up on the Arms Code. The New Zealand Police takes the extraordinary measure of using not one but two exclamation marks when delivering instructions about alcohol and firearms (they 'do not mix! Ever!'). The seven basic firearms safety rules say that you should never drink or take drugs just before you go shooting or while you're shooting, and you shouldn't shoot with others who are or have been drinking or taking drugs.

It's also forbidden to shoot in the dark in a state forest, forest park or national park. This all seems like a sensible idea for everyone concerned.

Schoolteacher Rosemary Ives was shot by a 'hunter' while brushing her teeth by headtorch at a campsite in the Kaimanawa Range in 2010. I use quotation marks around the word hunter — in fact, they're sarcastic quotation marks — because the stupid young punk had been hanging off the back of a friend's ute, spotlighting in a populated area, and shot her from a road. The bullet tore through her cheek, resulting in brain injuries. I hardly think you can call that sort of idiotic behaviour 'hunting'.

Ives's partner, Adam Hyndman, spent a desperate hour and a half trying to keep her alive. The shooter, Andrew Mears, and his three 'hunter' friends didn't return to the scene of the accident to help. 'Not one of you got out of that truck and ran a few metres to give immediate first aid to my daughter,' said Margaret McFarlane, Ives's mother, in an impact statement read to media. They were, she said, part of a 'macho, arrogant shooting fraternity' that paid little heed to anyone else's safety or rights.[10]

Mears was jailed for manslaughter and released after serving just 11 months of his two-and-a-half-year sentence. It was the first time someone had been convicted of manslaughter for a hunting-related homicide in New Zealand.[11]

The next morning, one of the then-drunk-but-now-sober hunters insisted on preceding me on my walk up the Ōamaru River, waving his gun about as if I were in need of protection from wild animals hungry for snacking on a small defenceless female. I was grateful when he desisted at the first major side creek, cementing my opinion of a certain faction of New Zealand hunters who seem to enjoy flying in and out of huts for a spell of brandishing their weapons, beating their chests and consuming alcohol, rather than doing any actual walking and hunting. So long as it looks good on Facebook, I suppose.

After legging it up the valley on a straightforward track with only a few spots of scrambly windfalls to negotiate, I came to another sizeable side creek — Te Tanae Rangiharakeke Stream. Levels were up a bit compared to the previous few times I'd been in there, but it looked easily crossable — I'd maybe get the bottom of my shorts wet, so I tucked them up into my knickers.

It was only a small crossing in terms of width, but wouldn't you know it — in the middle section my foot slipped sideways and my whole ankle and boot became wedged between three rocks. It wasn't coming out, it wasn't wiggling, and I couldn't reach past the rocks to my boot laces to untie them and slip a foot out.

Panic threatened to set in. I talked myself off the ledge of terror. No way was I getting stuck in a ridiculous side creek with a name as long as my left leg, which was currently otherwise occupied. Setting off a personal locator beacon because I was held firmly in a creek would be a huge embarrassment. (I did at the time think of an incident I'd heard about where an elderly chap had a rock fall on him while climbing the Taipoiti River to Harman Pass; he wasn't injured but he couldn't move, and they had to call a helicopter to use strops to shift the rock, after which he merrily continued on his way.) I began to get really angry at the rocks, but that wasn't effective either. What I needed was a strategy.

I knew that climbers who fall into crevasses shed their packs first as a way of removing weight for extracting themselves — securing the pack to the end of the rope, of course, not chucking it down the crevasse. I didn't have a rope, but I could easily swing my pack over to the bank and still have it in reach. That was a load taken off. Then I began to dig. Using bare hands and motivated by the prospect of not having to set off a personal locator beacon for something so stupid, I worked bare-handed at clearing the rocks around the three main rocks that were clinging to me like happy limpets.

The water was chilly — it was June, after all — and every now and then I had to stop and warm my screaming hands up by drying them off and holding them under my armpits. Eventually my digging efforts freed up enough space to access my boot laces, and that led to an escaped foot. Finally, I was loose! The last piece of the puzzle was shifting one of the rocks to retrieve my boot, which was sorely abused by this point.

I fended off the first tentacles of hypothermia with an extra layer and more than my rationed allowance of snacks. Looking at the topographical map, I'd soon leave the Ōamaru River, cross the Waitawhero Stream and then need to ford the Ngaruroro River to reach Boyd Hut for the night. I'd crossed it a few times before, each time in clear weather and low flows. Even at that, it's often mid-thigh on me, but gently flowing and clear. The Ngaruroro is a river with great potential, both for adventure and for flooding with a vengeance. It winds through the Kaweka Range, exiting the forest park at Kuripapango and skirting the northern reaches of the Ruahine Forest Park before spilling into the ocean between Napier and Hastings.

If it was too high to cross, no major; I had a bivvy bag and could easily camp out until it went down. Bivvying out was all part of my plan B.

In April 1889, shipping agent D. Balharry of Napier called at a roadside hotel, wrote his last note to friends, rode to a bridge over the Ngaruroro

River, hitched up his horse, removed his coat and vest (with a gold watch in the pocket), and jumped from the bridge. His suicide note, described as 'flippant' by the *South Canterbury Times*, blamed the mental strain of debts. 'Christ died to save mankind,' he wrote. 'I die to save my creditors, and this act might be justly regarded as heroic when contrasted with the people who face Jardine [the Deputy Assignee].' Balharry instructed his friends to circulate the note and show it to the coroner. 'It might make a good par[agraph] for the [newspaper].'[12]

I charged on over Waitawhero Saddle towards the Ngaruroro River, which separated me from Boyd Hut and warmer circumstances. Immediately down from the saddle sat three Aussie hunters, parked up right on the track with guns loaded and binoculars out trying to spot wildlife to destroy. (Much like drinking and hunting, or spotlighting, shooting from tracks or huts isn't the done thing, for obvious reasons, such as shooting oncoming trampers by accident.) I stopped for the usual exchange of pleasantries, but they clearly weren't in a mood to chat, so I shifted on smartly.

Approaching the Ngaruroro River, I could see the water was clear and the flow wouldn't trouble me, so I charged on in and across without hesitation. I'm a confident water lover, I enjoy any opportunity to get into rivers, and I don't see the point of taking boots off to keep them dry.

At the hut later, the hunters were a lot friendlier. The confessed they'd watched me through binoculars to see if I would take my boots off, which is what they had done, in both directions. (One of them even had pink ugg boots as hut footwear. You can imagine how envious I was, with my cold feet.) They told me they were impressed when I charged through, and when they found out I was doing a nine-day solo with a view to tramping for 17 days straight, they began telling each other to 'Hazel the fuck up' as they'd decided I was tougher than they were.

I often find people are stunned to encounter a woman tramping by herself. People quiz me about weirdos in the wilderness but I reckon the bush is a long drive for a short day at the beach for your average sex pest. Aside from the occasional bout of fear — such as with the drunk hunters the night before — I generally find that the Kiwi male represents his gender quite well in the backcountry.

But like *Pinus contorta*, the roots of bias make it difficult to pull out the weed of gender expectations. I didn't need the bloke to clear the area for me on the way out of Oamaru Hut any more than I needed rescuing from the stream with my leg stuck, in the end. That's not to say the New Zealand backcountry isn't full of dangers. Mostly you need to be careful of your own stupidity, but there are plenty of traps just looking for a victim. The Ngaruroro is definitely one.

One of the earliest settlers to fall victim to the Ngaruroro itself was swagger Herbert Humphries, who drowned in November 1885. His companion sat down on the bank to remove some clothing before fording, but Humphries went straight into the water with his swag on his back, lost his footing and was carried away. His body was found about half a mile below where he'd slipped.[13]

Destructive floods in 1893 collapsed riverbanks in the Hawke's Bay and forced residents to evacuate. Some even had to be rescued through holes cut in roofs. The Ngaruroro eventually burst its banks, with water pouring at terrific speed through houses in the township of Clive. 'Women screamed in their fright and the terrified children cried as if in mortal agony,' read a newspaper report. 'Hundreds of cows swam about the township bellowing furiously; horses neighed, pigs screamed, fowls cackled. Then there was the howling wind and fearful din made by the rushing waters, which now held possession of the township, and rushed pell-mell, taking everything with them into the Ngaruroro River.'[14]

The objective danger of the Ngaruroro still exists, but personal locator beacons, cellphones and radios have made rescue easier. In 2018, hunter Joe Prusac fell 20 metres down a bluff, rolled a further 20 metres, then came to a stop precariously positioned on a ledge with the raging waters of the flooded Ngaruroro metres away. 'A lot of luck went my way,' Prusac said after surviving, with a broken neck. 'I should have died three or four times really.'[15]

From as early on as there have been Pākehā lurking in the area, the Ngaruroro River — and by extension, the Kaimanawa Range — was thought to contain gold, and they were desperate to get their hands on it. As early as February 1863, punters were running gold-prospecting expeditions to the country between the Ngaruroro River and the eastern slopes of the Ruahine Range. An expedition was organised, expecting to take two months and cost £10 per week, exclusive of tents and tools.[16]

Two months later, the prospectors returned empty-handed, having thoroughly examined the country around the Ngaruroro and through the Kaweka without finding any gold or 'auriferous formation'. Rumours of gold's existence abounded in nearby Napier, and the chief of an iwi party travelling in the area confirmed that small quartz pebbles (containing gold) could be found in some creeks. Meeting more tangata whenua, the prospecting party was encouraged to leave. 'We met the remainder of the Natives returning from the Ahuriri,' wrote party member Mr Sturm. 'The chief Krei told me that it was wrong for us to search their country for gold, and desired me to leave the Patea district, which of course I promised, asking him again about the quartz. He told me that we had found already the place, having seen where we had prospected.'

Slyly ignoring the request to leave, the prospectors instead set up camp in a hollow to hide, continuing on the mission the next morning. Then they noticed the grass on fire, hemming them in between the blaze and some high ranges, bare of vegetation and too rugged to climb. Luckily the rain extinguished the fire and the wind moved in an obliging direction. 'It is most likely that the Natives set fire to the grass with the intention of driving us from their district,' Sturm assumed, taking no responsibility for flouting the chief's request.

Despite extensive efforts, gold stubbornly refused to reveal itself. Said Sturm: 'I ended my exploration without having met in any part where we travelled over with the smallest speck of gold; neither is there any quartz or sign of auriferous formation.'[17]

Six years later, a prospecting party determined to milk gold from the hills hit pay dirt in the Kaimanawa Range in the form of auriferous quartz. The party had been prompted to set off exploring by the private exhibition of several specimens to a limited circle in Napier. Party members William McDonnell and Christopher Bracken found the quartz in a gully near and running into the Kaimanawa Range and a gold-prospecting committee appointed at a public meeting in Whanganui sought to put in a formal application to open up a payable goldfield and stake their claim.

They had to act urgently to beat other competitive prospectors:

> It has come within the knowledge of claimants that a prospecting party, acting on information derived from our prospectors, is on the point of setting out from Napier to the Kaimanawa Range; and lest that party have put in a prior claim and thus deprive the first discoverers of their just right, we have thought proper at this time to make application for the reward [offered by the provincial government for the discovery of gold]. The prospectors feel confident that rich quartz veins exist in this Province, and they have come back to the locality for the purpose of producing sufficient evidence to warrant the opening up of the field.[18]

Reports emerged that a further 'diminutive' piece of quartz found at the head of the Ngaruroro Gorge was brought to Napier and crushed, with three pennyweights of gold falling out.[19] These discoveries prompted a visit from Dr James Hector, the government geologist, two months later. He gave further suggestions about which localities were likely to contain gold, but nothing was found.[20]

The Hawke's Bay Gold Mining and Prospecting Company went quiet. Anyway, it was a tough man's game.

The next hunters I met were genuine, on the opposite end of the spectrum to the first group I had met. The pair spotted me coming some distance away, approaching Harkness Hut up the Harkness (Ngaawapurua) Stream. Contrary to the other hunters, these guys had actually shot something — multiple somethings — and they rushed to restring their meat in the trees rather than having it wafting (potentially offensively, I suppose) in the breeze on the front porch.

'Sorry,' said one, named Rory. 'We weren't expecting anyone to turn up. The place is a bit of a mess.'

Being a six-bunk old-school hut in the middle of nowhere, Harkness Hut doesn't get much traffic. Even though it was a weekend, they'd reckoned they were unlikely to see anyone coming through — it's at least two days' walk from any road end. There's an online system that allows hunters to see who is booked to fly into any given hut in the Kaweka and Kaimanawa ranges with the two main helicopter companies, and from that they had a reasonable degree of confidence they'd have sole run of the hut. Of course, they hadn't banked on a lone long-distance tramper in a pink jacket bailing them up and asking for a bunk.

I took a load off, apologised for encroaching on their space, and took advantage of the warm fire they were keeping burning. Through our chats, I described the previous hunters' behaviour.

'Yeah, you're not meant to shoot at night, for sure,' said the other hunter, Andrew, who came from a farm on the backblocks of Napier and was obviously experienced in killing things. 'You can spotlight on your own land. You've just got to make absolutely sure of your target. But if you're on conservation land, you can only spotlight with a permit, and that's usually for pest control.'

They took a dim view of the unhappy combination of booze and guns, saving their beer for later in the day when they were done. It was gratifying to meet real hunters. These guys had also flown in with fishing gear and were having a great deal of success catching and releasing fish in the deeper pools of the Ngaawapurua Stream. They'd originally been planning to fly camp on the tops — better for surprising the deer — but bad weather had pushed them to opt for a hut instead.

The next day I waved Rory and Andrew goodbye. I climbed a modest 500-metre ascent to the open tops of Te Pukeohikarua, where a cold mist was creeping through, and descended quickly to take shelter in Te Pukeohikarua (Te Puke) Hut. I'd intended to push on and skip Te Puke but the weather had other ideas. I'd snuggle up for the afternoon, drink herbal tea and run down some battery on my Kindle instead. But there wasn't so much as a stick of dry firewood around and the fireplace seemed cursed — I concluded that Satan was determined I would not light it — and after trying in vain for more than an hour I gave up and kept warm by enthusiastically sawing up tidy piles of different-sized firewood for the hut's next desperate inhabitant.

I should've known then that the trip was ultimately doomed and

I wouldn't make it to the full 17 days as I'd planned. The next hut, Mangaturutu, was as cold as sin with ice crusts forming on the inside of the windows overnight and bits of my sleeping bag freezing. (It did, however, afford me a very pretty sunrise over the ranges of Kaweka.) Leaving Mangaturutu Hut, I dropped down to the Makino River with the intention of finding secret Brooke-Well Hut, which is on a terrace above the Makino. Built between Christmas 1973 and Easter 1974 by hunters David Brookes and Laurie Cantwell (hence the name), it's a well-disguised spot, with those in the know sworn to secrecy. I had a poem copied out from a tramping mate, which was reportedly in the hut book.

> Long have been the trips of back breaking toil
> We have put into this hut so a billy may boil
> Untold hours of overcoming the adverse
> The weather, the flies have all been a curse
> So if you should stumble upon these fine walls
> Please do not tell a soul at all.

The hut began its life in canvas but has more recently been done up with plywood — which requires a helicopter to transport — and DoC workers use it as a base for their Kiwi Recovery Programme. So it's secret, but sort of not, if you get my drift. There's plenty of these huts and bivs around the country, particularly in the Kaweka. Rory and Andrew had given me coordinates to find one they knew of, called Hoyflaten, and showed me pics.

Secret huts would have to wait, though. The Makino River was still up and although I'd not done that route, I had intel that it required several crossings and some could be waist-deep. Instead, I legged the 500-metre ascent straight back again, aiming for nearby Makino Hut, where I'd been a long-time listener and now a first-time caller. On the way I ran into my first human since leaving Harkness Hut. A volunteer resetting the stoat traps, he was on a day walk and had the latest weather forecast: snow down to 600 metres. Makino Hut was right on the 1000-metre mark and was in for a dumping. The prospect of potentially yet another cursed fireplace on a cold night stressed me out a bit, but I had no alternative.

Not to worry. I got to Makino Hut just in time, before the snow started falling in earnest, and was able to gather up plenty of bone-dry wood and scrub to get the fire going. Being small with just six bunks and a new firebox, the hut was roasting in no time and I could unreservedly frolic outside in the snow knowing I had a warm hut to go back to. I stoked it frantically during the night and again in the morning, leaving it reluctantly as I knew the next hut, Middle Hill Hut, had an open fireplace, which by nature are also satanic and hence not to be trusted under any circumstances.

Gold was eventually found in the Kaweka Range in a reliable quantity in 1932, probably thanks to the Napier earthquakes in 1931 giving the earth a good shaking about. Five unemployed ne'er-do-wells made the discovery, spotting the glinting material while doing riverbank work as part of an enforced work scheme. The media buzzed. 'The rumoured discovery of alluvial gold in the bed of the Ngaruroro River has given rise to some excitement . . . and the rumour, combined with the apparently dependable details so far ascertainable, make it appear that there may be gold deposits in the large area of mountainous country through which the Ngaruroro River flows.'[21] The gold was reported to be a number of grain nuggets slightly larger than a pinhead, but pure gold rather than quartz specimens.

The men who found it weren't talkative, and were understandably reluctant to make the information public. It's probably fair to say that the five who found it didn't report for work again the next day.

The hut book at Makino Hut contained dire warnings of extreme windfall on the track to Middle Hill Hut. The track, known as either the 'three gorges' or the 'five gorges', drops steeply down to a stream bed, then straight up again, and repeats that three times (five times if you are really counting) in an arduous way. In places it's not really a track, just a vaguely marked route using the clear spaces of the claypans as access, and these are prohibitively slippery in snow, especially when it's melting. I spent the better part of the day sliding down the snake

ABOVE | Makahu Saddle Hut, my least favourite hut ever, where I spent the final night of my nine-day solo tramp.

BELOW | Dominie Biv, on Mākāhu Spur. Nate and I spent a night here before pulling the plug on the second leg of the expedition.

ABOVE | Cold but happy on the Tongariro Northern Circuit, which is devoid of tourists in winter. Nate and I managed to do it as a single-night trip, taking advantage of a very short weather window.

BELOW | The impossibly clear waters of the Ngaruroro River, just before Boyd Hut. The river was low enough to be benign when I crossed it, but has been known to claim lives when high.

when I was trying to go up the ladder, having snow dropped down my neck from trees shaking it loose, and throwing my pack under or over windfall and following somewhat blindly, hoping the track would pick up again on the other side. I could see the reason for all the warnings in the hut book.

I got to Middle Hill Hut just as the snow started up again, clouding the hitherto blue sky, and got straight into my sub-zero sleeping bag rather than trying to fuss with the open fireplace. I find they smoke you out unless you leave a door open, which lets in the cold, defying the point in the first place.

The next day I bypassed Kaweka Flats Bivouac, a tiny two-person structure, and made for Makahu Saddle Hut at the road end, where I would meet Nate, my friend who was travelling to join me for the second leg. It's incredible to me that an area so populated with huts and riddled with a spiderweb track network can at the same time be so devoid of human life. It's astounding that you can walk for days undisturbed by humanity. I guess that's a good thing.

Many people ask if there should be a wilderness area across the Kaimanawa and Kaweka ranges. The idea was first proposed by Federated Mountain Clubs (FMC) at a 1981 conference. FMC envisioned a large wilderness area of 47,000 hectares, including some Māori and Defence department land, and the New Zealand Forest Service was open to the idea. It didn't happen, partly because of size requirements to qualify as a wilderness area, which would have required taking the Māori land. (Successfully qualifying wilderness areas include the Olivine at 83,000 hectares and the Raukumara Conservation Park at 39,650 hectares.) A nearby Rangitikei Remote Experience Zone was set up — so-called to account for its smaller size — and helicopter pilots occasionally get prosecuted for flouting the rules and dropping hunters off inside the zone.[22]

Wilderness area expert Dr Les Molloy, who co-wrote the original paper on the topic, 'The State of Wilderness in New Zealand', and is considered to be the godfather of wilderness areas in Aotearoa, reckons the idea of a fully fledged Kaimanawa Wilderness Area is not dead and the option remains for anyone to pursue.[23] It's indicated as such in the Kaweka Forest Park Conservation Management Plan: 'The possibility of establishing a Kaimanawa Wilderness Area has not been abandoned. A remote experience classification is established over this area to prevent irreversible management decisions which would compromise any future Kaimanawa Wilderness Area option.'[24]

Even though Mākāhu Saddle is remote by city standards, once you reach the road end you realise you're definitely not in the wilderness anymore. Makahu Saddle Hut, two minutes' walk from the car park, was horrific, and hands-down the worst night I've ever spent in a backcountry hut: a level-five, full-speed house of horror. The walls were scrawled with unsavoury graffiti and penises, the hut book was littered with profanity and uneducated claims, and the ceiling constantly dripped with brown liquid filth.

Moreover, the literacy levels evident in the hut book and wall graffiti led me to worry about who might turn up, and what they might want to do when they got there. It was the coldest night of the trip yet. I woke up to discover a large part of my sleeping bag had gotten wet and subsequently frozen — thankfully only on the outside, not the inside — and at daybreak I packed up and removed myself to the car park to bake my gear in the sun and wait for Nate.

Here, the trip fell to pieces and we slid down snake after snake on the board game of tramping with no rescue ladders in sight. We made it up the Mākāhu track as far as Dominie Biv, where the cold and wind encouraged us to stay put for the night, and the next day deep snow made going further impossible. At one point I was stuck up to my bum in soft snow and had to fall over on purpose to create enough of a hole to be able to haul myself out. What on earth had possessed me to attempt a 17-day tramp across the exposed tops in June? The cheese must really have slipped off the cracker this time.

We retreated, repacked at the car and headed into the much more sheltered and sedate Mackintosh Hut for the night. More snow arrived and we were forced to admit defeat, heading back to my ski-club lodge on Ruapehu for two full days where the weather made it impossible to stand up outside, so we didn't try. The wind and snow was so fierce that if you stood in a certain corner of the kitchen, it would actually snow on your head, via a tiny crack in the walls. At that point I thanked my lucky stars we'd pulled the plug on the trip. This wasn't the sort of weather I wanted to get caught out in.

A brief weather window made it possible for us to get out of the lodge, and, feeling refreshed, we knocked off the Tongariro Northern Circuit in just over 24 hours, skipping two of the huts. Oturere Hut, where we overnighted, was full of tourists, bearing a stark contrast to the small, empty orange boxes of the Kaweka Range. I was slowly re-entering society, my plans to become a full-time hermit ruined by the need to earn a pay cheque.

Nate returned home, no doubt shaking firstly his head at my insane plans and secondly his fist for daring to rope him into such madness. I envied him having a home and knowing where his place was in the world. I also admired *Pinus contorta*'s ability to put down roots and relentlessly cling to its position. I'd been homeless for months, and while I'd managed to solve the problem of not wanting to live in Auckland, I hadn't yet figured out where I *did* want to live.

Taranaki
Fat girl slim, skeletons and missing men

WEIGHT BECOMES an issue when you're tramping; it comes with you to every hut. In climbing, it's even more pronounced. Climbers are very lean and conscious of body weight as it relates to dragging yourself up the hill or up a cliff. These are pursuits where you're constantly fighting against gravity, so the better your power-to-weight ratio, the more easily you achieve your objectives.

It's generally accepted that a body mass index (BMI) of around 20 is the ideal for gravity-resisting outdoor pursuits. When I started alpine climbing, mine sat at 29.9 — right on the tipping point between 'overweight' and 'obese'. In fact, some mornings I would wake up merely overweight, but would be clinically obese before I went to bed that night. Other days, if I was careful on the snacks, I managed to avoid obesity.

In March 1911, part-time climber, part-time businessman and full-time egotist Samuel Turner visited New Zealand shores from London on the ship *Arawa*, setting a skipping record along the way to keep himself 'in climbing trim'.[1] Turner had come to New Zealand for two purposes: to explore dairy exporting and to climb mountains, as he had done in the Andes and Siberia. He wasn't inclined to sit idle on the ship, managing to complete 10,300 skips in one hour and four and a half minutes to establish a new world record.

In December 1921 he broke his own record, again on board a ship, the SS *Tainui*. By then he was a well-known alpine climber with many summits and first attempts under his belt. Turner wrote to friends in Wellington of the potentially grave consequences of skipping as exercise: '[T]he doctor of the ship had warned me about skipping, saying that a passenger on the last voyage dropped dead while running about on the ship.' To counteract any deathly consequences, it was arranged that the doctor would time Turner, acting as judge and counter. Turner managed a new record of 10,610 skips without halting the rope and 10,100 in exactly one hour. He stopped then for a quick medical check at the doctor's request; his pulse was 'normal, 72' so he carried on to complete 12,510 skips in one hour and 23 minutes, and only finished due to the rope falling out of his hand, and because the doctor — presumably fearful that he would have a cadaver to deal with — had requested him to stop at 12,000.[2]

A photo taken in January 1906 on Aoraki/Mount Cook shows Turner flanked by guides Peter Graham and Tom Fyfe during the first traverse of the mountain.[3] He was described in newspapers as short, thickset and 'nuggety' (fat? surely not), but he himself reckoned he was 'always in good nick' and one of the most rapid step-cutters in the world.[4] Turner admitted to being 'a little man' at 5 feet 6 inches, but he took exception to the Wellington publication *The Free Lance*, when it stated that Turner 'did not impress the casual observer as a great athlete or a King of Climbers', which clearly offended his healthy ego.

Turner raced up the stairs at the publication to defend his reputation in person, informing the journalists that in recent weeks on the Hutt cricket ground he had skipped 10,550 times in one hour and 20 minutes, and then, 'still fresh as paint', he had hopped 200 times on each leg after a couple of minutes' pause. The world record for skipping was then still only 6000 skips, so Turner was regularly outdoing it with his 10,000-plus sessions, but he assured the journalists that 'skipping is not a mania' with him (though the casual observer can easily conclude he was obsessed), and it was only 'some quiet training for another big climb'. Regardless, Turner told the media he would skip any man in the world for £25 and donate it to charity. His outing, or as the *Horowhenua Chronicle* described it, his 'bone-picking ceremony', certainly smacks of small-man syndrome; he was clearly a man small of stature but large on self-regard, bristling at anything that might have belittled him.[5]

Turner *was* manic about skipping, but he was also impressively obsessed with physical fitness as it related to climbing. He made two traverses of (then) Mount Egmont's summit in eight and a half hours and was used to step-cutting for eight to nine hours without a rest. He deemed skipping in light boots 'not severe enough' and would skip in mountain boots, an exercise which, along with wood-chopping, walks, climbs, and unspecified Swedish exercises, would keep him fit. He also wore his mountaineering boots while playing golf, just to get used to the feel of them and break in each year's new pair, and prided himself on never askng anyone to slow down or to stop for a rest in the mountains. 'It shows due respect to the mountains to train thoroughly, and take mountaineering very seriously; not underestimate the powerful agencies at work to repel the most efficient mountaineer,' he wrote in his book *The Conquest of the New Zealand Alps.*[6]

Turner was bullish, announcing that he intended to be the first person to solo Aoraki/Mount Cook, inspired by its magnificence and grandeur. Peter Graham warned him against attempting the solo climb, and requested a letter of indemnification from Turner, clearing him of all blame in case something went wrong. Turner duly wrote the letter, thinking that it was Graham's way of trying to prevent him from attempting the climb. 'This episode made me feel more determined to climb Mount Cook alone,' he wrote. He thought crampons were a newfangled invention that were dangerous and would never come close to what he deemed to be a much safer method of chopping steps in the snow with an ice axe:[7] 'I have never used crampons . . . preferring the more skilful and safer step-chipping and cutting, so rare among amateurs in these crampon days.'[8]

Turner was inordinately proud of his physical ability and technical skills. 'I intend to climb until I am 50 years of age, and if the mountains don't claim me before then I will retire. In the meantime I intend to climb Mt. Cook myself without help of any kind. If any of your readers likes to go and do it before me, let him have a try, and if he does it I will abandon the idea, but I would very much like to show the mountains that one man can conquer one mountain, and that the highest in New Zealand.'[9]

Turner finally achieved his objective of being the first person to solo Aoraki/Mount Cook in 1919 after 14 attempts. He chronicles these adventures in his book, which is as full of Turner as he is of himself.[10] His last, successful attempt was just after suffering food poisoning. People warned him against attempting the climb, asking him to consider his wife and family, and guides at the Hermitage were now openly ridiculing his objective.

Turner remained somewhere between optimistic and determined, and bloody-minded. He had climbed Mont Blanc in 1898 and achieved more than one hundred summits since then around the world. Therefore: 'It was the most natural thing for me to aspire to the summit of Mount Cook . . . (alone), and, although I encountered opposition from the commencement and very bad conditions of weather for several years of attempts, I returned to the mountain each year, and sometimes twice in the same year, with the one burning desire to climb to the summit of Mount Cook alone.'[11]

He earned himself a 'Mount Cook certificate' for his climb signed by witness Edgar Williams, who watched from the Haast Ridge Hut and saw Turner plant a flag on top at 4 p.m. on the summit day. It was certified by Alfred Cowling,[12] government guide and official witness appointed by the Hermitage chief guide, and arranged for because the guides who had climbed Aoraki/Mount Cook thought it was impossible, and no person had ever attempted it solo.

I am thoroughly repulsed (and at times angered) by Samuel Turner's abundant ego but at the same time I identify with his ambition to climb solo and his philosophy of solo pursuits. He believed that achieving an objective alone outweighed the 'satisfying feeling' of achieving it with companions, and that the 'intensification of life far outweighs the personal risk'. Turner had been climbing for 24 years, which had made him 'exhaust nearly all the pleasures of the climbing craft except solitary climbing'.[13] For him, two months climbing excessively each year helped to balance out the 10 months of the year where he threw himself entirely into business. He said he needed the strenuous, all-absorbing recreation.

Being told you can't do something is often great motivation to persist and do it anyway. I began solo tramping after my friend David told me I couldn't do it. I'd been organising group tramping trips nearly every weekend and I usually carried more than my fair share of gear, figured out the route, and did the meal plans and the cooking. But there were trips I wanted to do — typically longer ones — and I couldn't find buddies who were on the same crazy page as me. Eventually it occurred to me that I'd be doing the same amount of planning, organising and carrying if I went solo. The only difference would be that I was, well, by myself.

'You couldn't do it,' David told me when I expressed my ambition to do the Ruapehu Round the Mountain Track by myself. 'There's no way you could carry all your own gear and food and make it around the track. No way.' I was overweight at the time, tipping into obesity by nightfall most days, and had low confidence in my own abilities, so this was a further blow.

I went anyway, figuring that slow and steady wins the race, even if the turtle weighs too much. I planned for six days, five nights, with the intention of stopping at most of the huts on the track: Waihohonu, Rangipo, Mangaehuehu, Mangaturuturu and Whakapapaiti. I did it in three nights, skipping Rangipo and Mangaturuturu huts. I arrived at Rangipo from Waihohonu at midday, having shaved an hour off the DoC track time, and thought I might as well continue on to the next hut. Same again at Mangaturuturu. It made for quite long days — eight or nine hours — but I felt I'd achieved. A few years later I told David I had started solo tramping because of his comment and he strenuously denied ever saying it. Maybe I seemed more competent by that point.

There were other people on the track and at all the huts. Then I soloed the Abel Tasman track; as a Great Walk it's popular and populated, and there were people everywhere there, too. Easy stuff. Then I tackled the next frontier: spending the night in a hut completely by myself. Oooooh, spooky! I had a South Island tramping bender coming up, with a month off work in between jobs, and I wanted to get over any fear of being alone in a backcountry hut before I went on that trip.

I chose Blyth Hut, which I'd done day trips to before. I have a great affinity with Blyth Hut — it's nestled just on the bushline at 1400 metres on the southern side of Ruapehu, it gets minimal traffic as it's a 30-minute detour off the Round the Mountain Track, and it's about five minutes' walk from a small, clear swimming hole that's often rather warm in summer as the snowmelt flows over hot rocks as it cascades down the hill. Another bonus: if you choose the right bunk, you not only get a view to Girdlestone (Peretini) peak on Ruapehu but also you get the sunrise for coffee in bed in the morning and to gaze at the stars at night, through a large window on the eastern side.

I freaked myself out a bit being alone in the dark with just a fading headtorch for company on my final jaunt to the longdrop before bed. But otherwise, being alone was quiet and soothing. I fell in love with Blyth Hut that trip. I'm still in love with it — I think we're looking at a lifelong affair.

Climbing aside, Samuel Turner also wrote — a lot. (He was egotistical about that, too.) He published several volumes on his climbing exploits, notably the aforementioned *The Conquest of the New Zealand Alps*[14] and *My Climbing Adventures in Four Continents*.

His writing isn't brilliant — stick to climbing, mate — and he talks himself up frequently: along with his 'skipping power' there is his ability to balance on things, or balance things on himself (he calls himself an 'equilibrist' to describe this pursuit). Turner reckoned he could balance 'any balanceable piece of furniture' up to 60 pounds in weight, a faculty that enabled him to turn a skipping rope three times in one jump and skip 200 times in a minute. (He even includes in his book the text from the certificate awarded when he set the skipping record.)[15] This equilibrist madness was verified by climber Conrad Kain in an alpine journal: 'Mr. Turner entertained us with balancing tricks, beginning with a sheet of note-paper on his nose and finishing by supporting a rock weighing about fifty pounds on his chin. It was a very pleasant evening.'[16] In *The Conquest of the New Zealand Alps* Turner includes a photo of himself standing on a pinnacle on the razor-sharp Haast Ridge overlooking the steep slopes of the Hochstetter Glacier, which he says shows his prowess as a 'highly developed equilibriumist' (that is a made-up word, by the way), and his 'absolute calm conquest of the mountains'.[17]

Although I was put off by his ego, I admired Turner's unrelenting drive to be ever fitter and to be a match for the mountains he wanted to 'conquer'. (I wanted not to conquer, but to commune and climb, so we differed there.) Turner's drive was angled towards the ultimate goal of attempting Mount Everest, which he never managed. He'd been offered a gold medal by the Royal Scottish Geographical Society if he achieved it. (Stupidly, though, like his blithe dismissal of crampons, he had written off K2 and its neighbouring peaks as impossible and unclimbable, due to

Blyth Hut, on Mount Ruapehu, offers stunning views of Girdlestone (Peretini) peak and is only a few minutes' walk from a swimming hole.

the sheer amount of step-cutting that would be required. Never mind that crampons, which he wrote off as dangerous, would make it possible . . .)

Turner admired himself for having a low pulse, probably a result of his superior fitness, and he abstained from treats and any sort of tasty snacks: 'I have found that being a life-teetotaller and non-smoker has helped me considerably. The mountaineer who does not smoke or drink, and has never done so, will have a much better chance of success.'[18] It was all for the mountain and he was in, boots and all. 'The best respect a climber can show the mountains is to keep himself in the pink of condition by all kinds of exercises when mountains are not available.'[19]

It worked, I suppose, even if it did take him 14 attempts to solo Aoraki/ Mount Cook, which shows persistence, patience, tenacity and resilience. All qualities I wanted to have, and felt I had a shot at developing through my ongoing lifestyle in the outdoors.

I was still held back by my weight and possessed nowhere in the realm of the sort of fitness Turner espoused. I watched others around me, particularly rock climbers, carefully maintain their leanness through strict nutrition while I ate haphazardly and suffered the effects. When you've been told you're overweight all your life it's hard to adjust. Hard to see yourself as a thin person, or a potentially thin person in my case. Hard to imagine that achieving a state of 'not-fat' would ever be possible.

Determined to shed some weight for an upcoming trip, I began a high-intensity interval training programme and a month committed to whole foods and no alcohol or coffee while staying with my brother, north of Auckland. Dad had recently gone into a nursing home with Lewy body dementia (a form of dementia that attacks muscle function and creates confusion in the mind) and we were in limbo, convinced most days he was going to fall off his perch. Outdoor adventures were off the cards while we dealt with the stress of our beloved father in decline.

We visited every day — my gig was to feed him breakfast, straight after my morning training session and green smoothie (frozen mango, low-cal almond milk, ginger, spinach). Dad frequently asked after the euthanasia Bill — was it legal yet, and if so, could we bump him off, please — and would that fucking bastard David Seymour pull his finger out and make it happen.[20] Sometimes he'd tell me he'd been attempting to die (this consisted of him closing his eyes for a few minutes and really concentrating on it, trying to propel himself into the afterlife, and unsurprisingly it never worked).

I felt like I was at least making the most of my time by trying to get my health sorted, even if I was stuck in one place and not getting out much. Eventually I realised I needed to move on with my life and I packed and headed south again, stopping for a soothing overnight at Blyth Hut with a soak in the pools. I hit Arthur's Pass a couple of days after leaving Auckland and Dad took a turn for the worse. Once more, we became convinced he would die, but once more, he inexplicably held on. He'd first noticed symptoms as far back as 2002 or 2003, and I credit (blame?) his longevity to an approach to alcohol and tasty treats that is similar to Turner's.

After a few months in the South Island, I flew north again for the winter. I'd dropped a couple of kilos thanks to continuing with the training programme and frequent tramping, but still wasn't hitting my goals. A BMI of 20 felt impossible. It was May; too early for winter climbing and skiing, but the days were still too short for long tramping trips. I holed up in a lodge on Ruapehu, did some work, continued training every day, and ate only salads, fruit and green juices. That strips the weight off, by the way, but your taste buds won't be delighted with the regime. You can also only do this sort of strict consumption if you're either alone and determined or surrounded by people who are willing to hop on the health wagon and support you. We've all had that one friend who's a relentless cake pusher: 'Just have a slice, it won't kill you'; 'You've gone too far, you're too thin'.

Freda du Faur was a fitness freak, but she was already climbing by the time she decided to throw her weight behind training for more serious pursuits within the realm of mountaineering. In 1910, after having climbed some less serious peaks, Freda spent three months training at the Dupain Institute of Physical Education in Sydney, before returning to Aoraki/Mount Cook in November 1910. The next month she successfully summited. Freda had harboured climbing ambitions since 1906, backed by a baseline fitness founded on rock climbing and scrambling with only a dog for company in Ku-ring-gai Chase National Park in Australia.

'She started climbing over the Cowan hills when she was about 13,' her father Frederick Eccleston du Faur told Sydney newspaper *The Sun* in 1915. 'Even then she did such venturesome things that I thought she was a little too daring, though she never came to grief.' Freda had been captured by the mountains after visiting New Zealand from Australia and making a trip up Taranaki Maunga (then Mount Egmont). After that, said her father, 'the fascination of alpine climbing held her in its grip'.[21] She trained under fitness instructor Muriel Cadogan at the Dupain Institute and they later became lovers. But as you know, that story doesn't have a happy ending.

Freda weighed just 51 kilograms when she climbed Aoraki/Mount Cook.[22] Weighing 51 kilograms wasn't anywhere in the realm of possibility for me, even though my BMI indicates that it would be an appropriate weight to suit my 162-centimetre stature and would be just under the ideal climbing BMI of 20. (Like Samuel Turner, I too am short; unlike Samuel Turner, I don't feel the need to compensate, or to yell at journalists.) But I'd managed to whittle myself down from my former 78 (or so) kilograms to hover around the 70-kilogram mark, thanks to keeping on the salads and keeping off the pies.

I took off for a long tramp by myself, buoyed by my incremental successes on shorter trips. It now felt quite natural to spend the night by myself in a hut, or even several nights. I felt bullish and mapped out a 10-day excursion. I would tramp from St Arnaud to Hanmer Springs: up the Travers River and over Travers Saddle; via the Blue Lake and Lake Constance; over Waiau Pass (it looked prodigiously steep on the topo map; I was worried); down the Waiau River; Lake Guyon and the Stanley River (about which I could only find scanty intel — it looked like there was a track, on the map, at least); rejoin the Waiau River; Charlies Saddle and the Edwards River; Peters Pass to St James Homestead; and finally, a gravel road-bash on the Tophouse Road and over Mount Isobel to triumph at Hanmer Springs.

It turns out 10 days' worth of food is heavy enough to give you blisters where your pack rubs on your skin, but I only found this out at the end of day one when it was too late and I was disinclined to turn around. That 10 days' worth of food was predicated on a lean 1600 calories each day. I ate a sachet of oats for breakfast with a teaspoon of black instant coffee and one sweetener tablet; crackers with cheese or peanut butter for lunch, carefully rationed; one small muesli bar and three jet planes each day; one line of chocolate from a family-sized block; and instant noodles with two tablespoons of dehydrated vegetables for dinner.

By day five my pants were feeling looser from the caloric burn of walking all day (over alpine passes and up hills, most days). I sliced up my two spare 'emergency' hair ties and used them to elasticate my shorts because they started falling down. I seemed to get fitter and fitter, and my 10-day tramp became nine days. I popped out of the woods and into the urban delights of Hanmer Springs after ignoring a forestry contracting sign that warned me not to continue. (They were right — the tracks had been bulldozed and it took me twice as long.)

People stared at me in Hanmer Springs. I assumed it was because I was visibly filthy and obviously smelly, at least until I got to my accommodation for the night and accessed a shower, or because my pants were falling off. Or perhaps they didn't so much stare as I was just not used to unknown men making eye contact. They tend to react differently to you when you're thin. When you're fat they sweep a gaze up your body from your feet, but drop the gaze again once they get to your fat bits. If the gaze actually makes it to your eyes, you're *enough*. You're good enough, thin enough, to warrant eye contact. Maybe even a smile or a hello. (I have particularly attractive female friends who I've seen get chased down the street.) Fat, they say, is a feminist issue. And the truth will set you free, says Gloria Steinem, but first it will piss you off.

So I got eye contact, thanks to nine days in the wilderness on 1600 calories a day. I hadn't done it for weight loss but rather to decrease the weight in my pack on a trip where scenery and challenge, not haute cuisine, were the objectives. I did it for myself — not for attention. And even though I'd spent 10 days alone, I wasn't particularly interested in having company.

It's a sharp about-face, though, for a woman who left St Arnaud 10 days prior with several extra kilograms on her face and frame. At one point a man smiled at me and said 'G'day' and I turned around — *I actually turned around* — to see if he was talking to someone behind me. Later, after I'd scrubbed and showered, I bought an eye-wateringly expensive swimsuit and headed to the hot springs where I encountered friendly, chatty men. That night I went out to dinner with my Kindle and someone wanted to buy me a drink and join me at the table. These things were, and still are, deeply unusual to me; being covered with a layer of fat means you have a cloak of invisibility and as an introvert I rather like being invisible.

I use various regular huts and tracks as measures of my baseline fitness: Blyth Hut, Whakapapaiti Hut, Waingongoro Hut. They're all around an hour and a half from the road end, so you can duck in for a quick overnighter and test your pack-carrying ability and track time, or you can do a day trip, which gives you a better measure for how light and fast you've become. (Or, how heavy and slow . . .)

I headed in to Waingongoro Hut on Taranaki and managed to hit my best time ever. It's a Lockwood-style hut, reminiscent of the era before DoC began building superhuts, built in 1986 — the same year that the minister of lands ruled that Mount Taranaki would be an alternative and equal official name to Mount Egmont. The surrounding national park would still be called Egmont National Park, until December 2019, when the Crown and Ngā Iwi o Taranaki agreed that the mountain would only be referred to as Taranaki Maunga and Egmont National Park would be renamed Te Papakura o Taranaki. The mountain was originally named Mount Egmont by Captain James Cook after John Perceval, the second Earl of Egmont, who never even set foot on it.

Taranaki Maunga is New Zealand's second deadliest mountain after Aoraki/Mount Cook. More than 84 people have died on its slopes. Locals will tell you that people, especially tourists, underestimate the sheer force of the weather and how quickly it can change. Easy access compounds the danger — you can drive to 1172 metres on the East Egmont side, or 952 metres on the more popular North Egmont side — making the summit ascent appear an achievable day trip. I was terrified of Taranaki.

However, before I knew how deadly it was, I wasn't terrified of the mountain but merely curious. I organised a group to go for a summit climb in summer. No snow, except a few small patches in the crater, easily navigated. No sharps needed. I did warn everyone they'd need to take plenty of warm clothes: a waterproof jacket and pants, long-sleeved top and bottom, a hat and gloves. It was summer but the weather had other ideas. Like a mother hen, I clucked over everyone, asking repeatedly if they'd packed all their warm things. I was one have-you-got-a-warm-hat query away from actually turning into my mother.

We left from Tahurangi Lodge on the northern side at the crack of

On Travers Saddle during a 10-day solo tramp from St Arnaud to Hanmer Springs. You can't tell, but my pants are starting to fall down at this stage. I encountered other solo trampers on this trip — such as Malcolm Hossack, who kindly snapped this photo for me.

dawn, split into two groups depending on how fast we thought people would go. Overweight and struggling, I put myself in the B group and intended to go at the back. We'd been walking for just shy of an hour, steadily uphill, when some of the A group came back down towards us. They'd ignored my warnings to take warm clothes and instead had gone out in shorts and t-shirts with just light jerseys — no warm hat or gloves. The weather a few hundred metres up the mountain was cold and windy, so they had decided (wisely) to turn back to the lodge. What they didn't know was there was snow at the crater.

I began to see why people die on Taranaki, and the fear trickled in.

On Labour Weekend, October 2013, I emerged from a multi-day tramping trip in the Whirinaki to hear that Nicole Sutton and Hiroki Ogawa had died on Taranaki during an annual New Zealand Alpine Club Auckland section trip to the mountain. Sutton, a novice mountaineer, had initially planned to climb the easier North Ridge route but her boyfriend Ogawa, an experienced climber and alpine instructor, had convinced her to go with another group on the more technical East Ridge route.

Several of the climbers in the East Ridge group lacked the experience or the correct gear for the climb. Ogawa, Sutton and two others became separated from the rest of the group. A few confident climbers had solo climbed without ropes to the top, seen the weather coming in — 'like hell on earth',[23] they said — and turned back, passing the message on to the main group, but Ogawa and Sutton's group didn't get the message and therefore had no idea how bad the weather had gotten.[24]

They continued over the summit, opting to take the easier North Ridge route back down, which they thought would save time. Exhausted and hypothermic, Sutton slipped and knocked another climber down the mountain. The other climber went to lend help. Both eventually made it to safety the next day after an excruciating night out in the open. Sutton and Ogawa were alone and didn't move any further. They bivvied out high on the mountain, digging an ice trench that only partially covered them. Ogawa died not long after; Sutton survived until rescuers reached her on Monday but then passed away.

The group who had gone up the North Ridge had a pleasant lunch on the summit and returned safely back the same way, oblivious to the tragedy unfolding on the eastern side.

'We know mountains are nasty places when things go wrong,' Sutton's father said.[25]

The first known Pākehā to perish on Taranaki was William Henry Southwood, an Australian who had immigrated several years previously and worked as a canvasser for the government life insurance department.

On 2 April 1891, Southwood borrowed a horse and set off from East Egmont to go shooting. He was from Wellington and was due back that evening to catch the train south, but after he didn't show, search parties were sent out. They found the horse, some ammunition and his pocket-book. It seemed he had climbed the mountain, discarding things — including his clothes, gun and spur — as he went. Searchers examined nearby gorges but the 'arctic severity' of the weather prevented any further efforts.[26] Eventually it was assumed he had fallen over a precipice and died.

One climber who had been on the mountain that same day, ascending from Dawson Falls, claimed to have heard a voice twice and the noise of falling stone coming from the other side of the summit cone. They couldn't get over the ice for the last few yards, so they abandoned their ascent attempt, and saw no one but reported the noises once Southwood had been confirmed missing. Still he went undiscovered.

Then in February 1892, a party out climbing on the mountain on an unfrequented track happened across his body, lying on its left side across two sharp boulders at the foot of a precipice about 9 metres high. Some reckoned he had fallen, others thought he had laid down and died from exhaustion, and evidence seemingly pointed either way depending on how you wanted to interpret it. One leg was thrust out and the other was bent under the body, as was one of the arms. One side of his face was crushed — consistent with an impact, but then, the

Impressive and rugged cliffs on the Brames Falls Track, part of Taranaki's round-the-mountain tramp. The maunga's southern side is tough country in places and takes no prisoners.

body had been there for 10 months. He was still fully clothed and his hat was lying nearby. On his person was a watch — stopped at 12.20 — papers in a pocket-book, money, cartridges, matches and a knife.

Newspaper reports gave overly grim details of the sort that would be frowned upon today: 'The flesh was in such a state of preservation that the party were of opinion that the snow had only melted off the body a couple of days, as mortification was just setting in . . . The body . . . was wonderfully preserved, the moustache even being quite intact.' A police constable told newspapers that Southwood had probably made the summit then had an accident and fallen, fatally, and it was estimated it would take eight men a day and a half to bring the body down. Yet others thought that the body's position indicated Southwood had 'deliberately laid himself down to die, after giving up all hope of getting off the summit'. As proof, it was pointed out that the hat and handkerchief were lying near the body as if they'd been placed there — the hat, on the right-hand side about the centre of the body, and the handkerchief at his feet. Further, it was assumed the bones were broken but there was no proof, and the 'crushed appearance' of one side of Southwood's face may have been due to exposure to the weather. He was also quite far from the rock itself.[27]

However, finally, a verdict of hypothermia and exhaustion was handed down. A newspaper report stated that one Dr Leatham had made a 'superficial examination' of the body that night at the morgue: 'He found nothing in the external appearance to lead him to suppose that the deceased had been subjected to any violence. The body was somewhat mummified, as he should have expected, as it had been subjected to a great degree of cold for a considerable period. He could detect no signs of wounds, nor of fractured limbs. The clothes appeared to be undisturbed. There were no marks that he could detect to lead one to suppose that [the] deceased had fallen. He thought it probable that he had lain down exhausted, and gone to sleep, and then been frozen to death.'[28]

The jury returned a verdict that Southwood was found dead on Taranaki and no marks of violence appeared on his body. He had with him a railway timetable and a ticket to Palmerston North.

My friend Nate has Had An Episode in capital letters on Taranaki. He reckons the mountain is his spiritual home. 'Taranaki is just one of those places that feels particularly "real" to me,' he wrote to me. 'Maunga Taranaki is true blue, unapologetically independent, off the beaten path and (thus) relatively unpolished and authentic, contrasting across its landscapes and in its many guises, yet so cohesive and unwaveringly grounded. Experiencing a few significant outdoorsing high and low moments there has probably helped to further elevate the significance of place a little for me. However, having spoken from time to time with folks who have lived there, there does seem to be a common appreciation of the undefinable yet palpable mana of the maunga.'

Nate once saved his own life on a ski mountaineering trip on Taranaki. It was a glorious clear weekend. On the Saturday, Nate and friends cramponed up the mountain, summited, switched to skis and enjoyed a soft ski down in nicely softened snow. It was so epic they went to repeat the experience on Sunday. However, low temperatures during the night had resulted in a hard freeze of the snow and it didn't release enough. Nate skied over some tracks that had frozen solid, popped a binding, fell and began to slide.

Taranaki's slopes are steep enough, and usually icy enough, that if you start to slide, your self-arrest technique needs to be on point and you have to act immediately. If you don't, you'll head towards (and then into) an area locally known as the Body Catcher (for obvious reasons). The consequences of a fall are sickening.

Nate picked up speed quickly but managed to use the ice pick on his ski pole to self-arrest. This all happened in a flash, though, and by the time he'd reacted, he had dropped 500 metres. He had lost one glove, and both hands and arms were pretty mashed up.

But, crucially, he'd stopped his slide just above the Body Catcher.

In February 1923, 60-year-old Reverend William Murray went missing on (then) Mount Egmont. Along with three others, Murray left Dawson Falls House at 4.45 a.m. for the summit, which they gained at 9.30 a.m., intending to descend on the other side to North Egmont House.

They had lunch at the summit and then started descending a route suggested by Murray. Visibility was bad. 'Soon the obvious difficulties and dangers it involved brought them to a halt, at which the others tried to induce Mr Murray to adopt another course. He flatly refused. The track he suggested lay down a compressed and rock-walled snowfield, heavily strewn with debris from the cliffs overhead. No arguments or appeals pointing out the evident obstacles and perils into which his hasty course would lead them had the slightest effect on his decision.'[29]

Two of the others followed for a while out of a sense of duty — they'd had a right barney on the top; they kept shouting after him and he refused to respond. The third went back to the Mountain House to alert the authorities with 'the strange situation that had arisen'.[30] The others eventually lost track of him, among the snow and scoria, and turned back. The route Murray had chosen to go down was obviously going to be almost impossible to return by. They attempted to get back to the summit, twice failing to get up steep crags, but finally managing to cut steps with their boots and axes, and regained the summit crater at 5.30 p.m., reaching Dawson Falls House around 7 p.m. They assumed Murray had made it safely to his destination, but the next day he hadn't arrived at North Egmont or any of the surrounding farms, and a search was mounted.

For the purposes of the search, Murray was described as 'a medium-sized man, of stalwart build . . . known for his determined temperament'.[31] He was known to be fit and sturdy, with feats of strength such as walking from Normanby to Eltham one evening to see a friend, returning the same night, and walking from Eltham to the Mountain House to start his ill-fated Mount Egmont climb. He had cycled from Normanby to Marton and returned the next day, and on his sixtieth birthday he rode around Mount Egmont — 110 miles (177 kilometres) — in one day.

Murray was particularly interested in nutrition. 'The amount of food necessary to keep the body in perfect health was one of his favourite topics. He claimed that the barest margin of sustenance was desirable, and that a man could endure severe physical tests for seven days without food.' He was writing a work on this topic and his trip up the mountain was intended to be part of a series of experiments on the ability of a man to survive without food. His companions on the day rejected the idea

Hangatahua Stony River on the flanks of Taranaki Maunga. It is rough, tough country, and it's believed the Reverend William Murray came to grief near here.

that his 'rash break' from the party was premeditated, but agreed that the 'enforced hardships' he would endure from having to survive on the mountain would give him plenty of material to test his theories.[32]

By the time searchers went to look for him, heavy rain was falling on the mountain, which would give anyone little chance of surviving ongoing exposure over the course of several days. One of his companions described the area where he was lost as wild and bleak, 'scattered with tough scrub in which progress could only be made by crawling along the ground in a manner painfully tedious'. Searchers tramped through the large sphagnum moss swamps between Taranaki and Pouākai, while a gale whistled straight off the sea, 'up the funnel shaped ravines between the spurs'.[33]

Searchers retraced his footsteps down the mountainside then up again to within a few hundred metres of the summit, where they were hit with a freezing storm that nearly had the search party in the same state as Murray. Their walking sticks were frozen in their hands and to drop them meant they wouldn't be recovered. One of the searchers slipped and slid on a steep snow face but managed to self-arrest by using his stick and steering himself towards a rock.

In the two days following Murray's disappearance, the searchers reached parts of the mountain they had never been on. They returned exhausted after their extreme efforts. They did find some trace of Murray: purposely broken twigs, leaves, footprints, the remains of a small fire and a piece of cord tied to some scrub. They discovered two of his camping spots. 'The lost man had evidently surmounted great obstacles with wonderful spirit,' newspapers reported.[34]

Murray had taken a route leading down a ravine at right angles to the obvious direct route to North Egmont.[35] Looking on the topo map, it's likely he went down either near the Turtle, a long bluff that angles almost west to east and extends more than 300 metres, or towards Carrington Ridge via the Sawtooth and Hammer. Taking the latter could have led him towards the spot where Holly Hut now stands and straight towards the sphagnum moss swamp. Taking the former would have led him, one way or another and via various streams, towards the Stony River, a wide open river valley that is true to its name. Most of that area, including Hidden Valley, features bluffs, gorges and tough terrain. Murray would have had his work cut out for him. Searchers straddled the middle ground and hunted around the Holly Flat area, fruitlessly, but eventually concluded he was lost near Bells Falls as he had been traced there but no further. At one point, he had walked down a stream bed that intersected with the track to Holly Hut, less than a hundred metres away, but hadn't picked up the track's existence.

Searchers found the sole of a boot, marked with indelible ink 'W.T.M. Jan. 31st' — the date he'd gone missing. 'It was tied to two rushes bent across the path, and was swinging conspicuously in the wind.'[36] It was assumed he'd met his fate either accidentally being swept over Bells Falls or trying to get below the waterfall and make his way down Stony River to the coast. The search was abandoned on 20 February.

Just over a year later, in May 1924, a group of men from the Taranaki County Council working in Stony River made a gruesome find. In the bed of the river they discovered a tweed suit, then, a few metres further down the waterway they found a boot — with a human foot inside, clad in a sock. It was assumed to be Murray's as no one else had been reported missing on the mountain since his disappearance — and he had been wearing a dark tweed suit on the climb.[37]

Incidentally, Reverend Murray was one of the founders of the first condensed milk factory in New Zealand and was manager of the initial attempt at making the Highlander brand of condensed milk in the South Island. A businessman-come-climber type; men combined the two, while women needed to be either supported by a husband or independently wealthy, like Freda.

I set out on Taranaki in search of Murray. Partly it was a fanciful idea of tracing his steps, paying homage to a dead man who endured a lot in his last days, partly also aversion therapy for my fears of Taranaki. My friend Julia, with several decades of search and rescue experience (not that I deemed that necessary — more an incidental), joined me. I neglected to tell Julia that the trip was an expedition to find the figurative bones of a dead guy, nor did I reveal my fears of Taranaki. Instead, I dropped in a few casual mentions on day one during a long but easy walk from Dawson Falls to Holly Hut on the well-tracked northern side of the mountain.

'Alright, tell me about the Reverend,' she demanded once we'd settled into the bunkroom after dinner and clean-up, clearly having had enough of my teasers. The hut was moderately full, with one too many conversations going on in the main room making it a noisy environment. We'd retreated, both of us too introverted to want to bother participating in the ruckus.

I told her everything from the beginning — Murray's strange insistence on going down an unplanned route; the discovery of the sole of the boot; his foot and jacket found in Stony River. I also filled her in on his obsession with nutrition and survival. 'Gosh he was arrogant, wasn't he?' she said. We both agreed that he probably set the whole thing up on purpose and it was an experiment gone horribly wrong.

The next day we slogged from Holly Hut around to Waiau Gorge Hut on the rugged and foreboding western side of Taranaki. You're definitely not in Guatemala any more once you leave Holly Hut; the track is reasonable for about 10 minutes, then quickly becomes a narrow trail on the edge of a gorge, before widening to reach the side trip to Bells Falls. Murray might be up there, somewhere, or part of him.

Bells Falls was in low flow the day we went — in fact, nearly all the streams we'd crossed so far were completely dry. Even so, the power of the water was evident and didn't help my fear of the mountain. The water carves a scar through the landscape, then falls from the bottom of a V cut into rock and doesn't so much cascade, but does something more violent — as if it's angry, ragefully punching into the pool at the bottom. We didn't get too close, anyway, as the rocks were covered in a thin veneer of ice and it all looked like a recipe for disaster.

The track continues through bush, momentarily easy travel, then emerges at the confluence of Pyramid Stream and Stony River — where Murray's foot was found. It's formidable country, full of boulders, rugged, and you can see how a body would get smashed to pieces.

Julia told me, from her search and rescue experience, that a body will often survive a fall intact even if all the bones break, but once the bones are broken things start to break up pretty quickly after that. She deemed it pretty unlikely that Murray would have had a hope of being found in one piece, but probably got washed, in the torrential rain, all the way down Stony River and out to the coast, where he'd be munched on by happy sharks. I guess somehow his foot managed to get lodged between rocks or similar, and hence avoided that fate.

Taranaki was initially confiscated from Māori by the New Zealand Government in 1865, then ostensibly 'returned' to the people of Taranaki via the Mount Egmont Vesting Act 1978, but as the Act immediately passed it back to the government as a 'gift to the nation', it looks like a bit of a sham. In 2017 the government and Taranaki iwi signed an agreement that would see the mountain become a legal personality, following in the footsteps of Te Urewera and the Whanganui River, with the Te Urewera Act 2014 and the Te Awa Tupua (Whanganui River Claims Settlement) Act 2017, respectively. Many of Taranaki's places have different names in Māori, more mellifluous and more meaningful than simply being named after a Pākehā man. It's a case study in colonisation through place name but also has potential to become a case study in decolonisation.

Dawson Falls, where we started the tramp, was named after Thomas Dawson, the first Pākehā man to 'discover' it in 1885. The Māori name is Te Rere o Noke (the Falls of Noke), named after a warrior who had done a great mischief and successfully hid from his pursuers behind the falls. (Another version has Noke being less successful in his escape. The legend has it that he ran away with a woman and the pair were pursued. The woman was captured and killed, while Noke was overtaken just at the head of the falls, so to escape he jumped over and was smashed on the rocks below and died.)[38]

Bells Falls is named after Sir Francis Dillon Bell, one of the local settlers who negotiated many settlements, and spoke fluent Māori. He and his party came across the falls after an extremely dangerous ascent of the mountain. He'd had an extraordinary escape from being 'precipitated' over a perpendicular cliff of 'great depth', said the account of the trip: 'For his foot slipped in passing over one of the said narrow gangways, and thence he slid down the snow covered declivity with great velocity to the very brink of the yawning gulf, when providentially he caught hold of a projecting rock, and thus saved himself from certain destruction.'[39]

It was pretty exciting, getting to be a Pākehā man in the outdoors back then. On the summit they found 'the only vestige of animal existence', the bleached skeleton of a rat. Then, returning down the mountain they encountered the now Bells Falls. It was 'a magnificent waterfall, over a precipitous bare basaltic cliff, some hundreds of feet in height', 'an object of transcendent sublimity'. They believed no European and no 'native' had previously been aware of its existence, and 'like all other newly discovered objects, it is entitled to a patronymic, therefore, as Mr. Bell was the originator and chief of the party . . . so be it known to the present generation, and by all posterity, as Dillon Bell's Cataract'.[40]

The Māori name for the falls is Te Rere a Tahurangi (the Falls of Tahurangi), named after Tahurangi, one of the iwi ancestors and the first to ascend the mountain, lighting a ceremonial fire to place his authority over the area and anchor his name to the mountain and its slopes. 'Rua' means 'cave' — Ruataranaki had dug a cave at the base of the mountain where he lived for a while. That cave became a famous burial cave, Te Ana a Tahatiti, which was used until the end of the nineteenth century. The cave is near the source of Stony River (Hangatahua River), before it goes over Te Rere a Tahurangi.[41]

Taranaki itself is wrapped in lyrical legend. It was formerly known as Pukeonaki,[42] and stood alongside Ruapehu, Tongariro, Ngāuruhoe (all males) and sexy, fern-covered Pīhanga (female). The mountains were all in love with Pīhanga and fought over her. Tongariro won, inflicting great wounds on the side of Pukeonaki, who flounced off to where Taranaki now stands, withdrawing underground and carving out the scar of the Whanganui River as he went. On resurfacing, he was drawn to the nubile Pouākai Range, which sits next to Taranaki and is now a popular tramping haunt. They hooked up and their offspring became the life forms — flora and fauna — on their slopes.

Now, when Taranaki hides himself in rainclouds (which is frequently), he's said to be crying for his lost love, Pīhanga (unsure how current squeeze Pouākai feels about this), and when the sunset is spectacular, he's showing himself off to her. Tongariro, meanwhile, erupts occasionally to warn Taranaki not to even think about returning.

In my attempts to be fitter and faster, I took serious inspiration from my friend Bryan, who is unduly fit and enthusiastic about carrying out mad pursuits in the outdoors. He's famous for biking from Te Awamutu to the start of the Tongariro Alpine Crossing, breaking down his bike and carrying it on his back over the crossing, then reassembling it and biking back to Te Awamutu again . . . in one go.

It's reminiscent of Sir Edmund Hillary's ascent of Mount Tapuae-o-Uenuku (2885 metres), the highest point in the South Island outside of the Southern Alps. Sir Ed was inspired by the idea of mountaineering but hadn't yet done much outside of Ruapehu rambling. He took off on a weekend solo climb of Tapuae-o-Uenuku in 1944 while training with the Royal New Zealand Air Force, in Marlborough, biking from RNZAF Base Woodbourne, just outside of Blenheim, to the track start at Gladstone Downs just to access it — some 85 kilometres each way. (Bryan's effort was more in the vicinity of 189 kilometres each way.) 'I'd climbed a decent mountain at last,' was Sir Ed's famous quote on summiting 'Tappy'.

Anyway, Bryan had recently done a 12-day trip in the Tararua Range carrying only a couple of kilograms of food because of the length of the trip and because he wanted to challenge himself. He's in the army and is used to what he terms 'deprivation exercises'. (He tells the tale of one exercise where someone claimed the team would get extra points if they returned their ration packs unused, but it turns out they were mistaken. The whole team got by on only one ration pack for 48 hours and got a bemused reception when they handed them back at the end.) During his Tararua trip Bryan had eaten each day:

> Breakfast: 5 tablespoons of oats with 3 tablespoons
> dried fruit
> Lunch: 1 One Square Meal bar or similar muesli bar
> Dinner: 1 soup sachet with 5 tablespoons instant polenta,
> 5 tablespoons red lentils and a snack of 8 tamari almonds

'And no snacks?' I queried.

'No snacks at all until day eight when I cracked into my reserves and had half a king-sized block of chocolate per day. Absolute luxury and I was really keyed up after that!'

'Did you add up the daily calories?'

'No, but I'm sure it's a pretty slim calculation. Not something I could count on my fingers and toes, but only just.'

I wanted to test out a similar deprivation diet on the Taranaki trip with Julia but I was a little chicken to go the full hog, as it were. I'd been dehydrating loads of food to experiment with — you can actually do it in the oven on a very low temperature with the fan going — and I had a complement of dehydrated goodies from hummus and pineapple slices to spinach, capers and canned tomatoes. I'd even dehydrated miniature gherkins and a green smoothie out of sheer curiosity.[43] The trip was an ideal time to test out not only how well my dehy experiments might perform in the field but also to almost-attempt a deprivation exercise with a robust safety net built in. My menu involved:

> Breakfast: 4 tablespoons oats, 1 tablespoon brown sugar,
> 1 tablespoon coconut, cinnamon
> Lunch: 5 crackers with dehydrated hummus
> Snacks: 1 muesli bar, 1 soup sachet, 3–4 sour gummy bears
> (they were awful and filled me with regret that I'd bothered
> carrying them)
> Dinner: Night one, pasta with dehy tomato sauce, capers
> and spinach. Nights two and three, dehy brown rice with
> vegetables, some vege stock powder and a sachet of tuna
> Reserves: 1 block white chocolate, 2 x two-minute noodles,
> 1 extra tuna sachet

It turns out I would make a terrible soldier as I broke into my reserves on night one and repeated the exercise on the following nights with a couple of lines of white chocolate after dinner. But in the vein of George Mallory attempting Everest, I only did it because it was there. I didn't feel like I needed the chocolate — my track fitness, combined with a low-speed fat-burning approach, had carried me through the days. (I didn't touch the noodles or the extra tuna sachet — they were there as emergency food in case we had an unforeseen delay.)

I wondered about forgoing the tuna and just doing the brown rice and veges. 'You need some protein, though,' someone in the hut said to me. People are mad keen on protein these days. I find it a bit odd, this fear of not getting enough protein. The number of processed items you can get these days with protein added, the way some people stuff themselves with it thinking they're being healthy while ignoring their veges, the curious habit of calling meat protein as if anything non-meat doesn't contain protein at all (um, hello beans and chickpeas). The clinical term for protein deficiency, did you know, is kwashiorkor — sufficient calorie intake but insufficient protein consumption, usually seen in areas of famine or poor food supply, not in the developed world. So you can probably put down the chicken breast and step away from the protein bars, you're not going to starve.

I decided I could repeat the deprivation exercise and actually do it properly — keep the breakfast and lunch the same, eat brown rice and veges for dinner, forgo snacks as Bryan did, and keep an emergency block of chocolate in reserve but take it a bit more seriously next time.

Bryan didn't die of protein deficiency either, by the way, and is still in ripe old health.

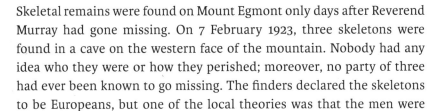

Skeletal remains were found on Mount Egmont only days after Reverend Murray had gone missing. On 7 February 1923, three skeletons were found in a cave on the western face of the mountain. Nobody had any idea who they were or how they perished; moreover, no party of three had ever been known to go missing. The finders declared the skeletons to be Europeans, but one of the local theories was that the men were tangata whenua.[44]

The news of the three skeletons prompted a yarn from 27 years earlier to make the newspapers. Stratford resident C. F. A. Volzke recalled being caught in a blizzard with two friends in 1896. They took shelter in a cave, where they found a case containing a theodolite. It was no use to them and they assumed the owner would come back to fetch it, so they put it back in the case and left. Volzke had thought about it from time to time since and reckoned he remembered perfectly where the cave was — about 2 miles from where the three skeletons were found. He told newspapers he felt confident he could go directly back to find it (though it seems that he never did).[45]

A further tale seemed to tie the skeletal remains to the theodolite. Three men, surveyors, climbed to the top of the mountain but were never seen or heard of again. Search parties found a man's tweed cap hanging on the rocks on the western peak of the crater. The cap was taken away and identified as belonging to one of the missing men, suggesting that they had reached the summit but were lost on the return.[46]

Other variations on the story emerged. Reverend R. Haddon told newspapers he recalled an incident from 1885 when three people, one or two of whom were women, set out from New Plymouth to summit the mountain and were never heard of again.[47] Yet another version features four surveyors, only one of whom survived. At the summit, one of the men left his cap there as a marker.[48] Somehow, three went missing and the surviving fourth man sent out search parties. The cap on the mountain was found, but no trace was ever discovered of the three missing men. The general thrust of the story seems to have been widely repeated in Taranaki circles over the years, with little hard evidence.

The Lands Department had no records of surveyors or members of a surveying party being lost on Mount Egmont.[49] Some staff there had more than 30 years' service in the department and still couldn't recall anything of the sort. The department also pooh-poohed Volzke's theodolite find, suggesting he had made an error in his date and that the theodolite he saw had either been thrown away or cached by one H. M. Skeet, who had been surveying the mountain in the summers between 1898 to 1900. However, Volzke's date of discovery was 1896 — two years before Skeet's surveying trips. The Lands Department also asserted that the skeletons couldn't be surveyors, as older-style theodolites included a compass, which would prevent any surveyor being lost on the mountain. That doesn't, of course, account for pure exposure — for example, the three men being caught out in a storm and taking refuge in the cave, but being under-equipped to sit out the weather.

There were also rumours of an illicit whisky still existing on the slopes of the mountain, due to wisps of smoke that would periodically emerge from the same spot for six months in 1892. The fire was suggested to have been related to the three skeletons.

Samuel Turner inserts himself into the story here, plentiful ego no doubt in tow. Turner helped with the futile search for Reverend Murray for several days after he was first announced missing, camping out at Kahui Hut on the western side of the mountain after 'heavy work' near

Taranaki Maunga as seen from a viewpoint near Hangatahua Stony River: a rare sight of the mountain without any accompanying clouds.

Bells Falls and Stony River, searching exhaustively along its banks.[50] It's unclear if they knew each other, but both seemed to have the same approach to life: stoicism; an obsession with fitness and feats of endurance; and a drive to push the boundaries, including with scant nutrition. Frankly, in Murray's case, I believe he did it all on purpose — departing from his companions on a route he knew they would not follow, in order to spend several nights in survival mode and come out triumphant.

Turner almost met the same ending as Murray, in an outing to summit the mountain years earlier, in 1916. He started from Dawson Falls at 7.20 a.m. and had a hard day of step-cutting to reach the snow-covered trig on the summit at 4 p.m. He'd expected to be able to glissade down but the slopes were frozen hard so he had to walk, carefully. Darkness fell. The track was covered with more than 6 feet of snow and he lost it in the moonless night. Turner ended up in a dry creek bed, with pools of water covered over with thick ice. Several times he fell into freezing water up to his waist, so he gave up and turned in for the night, covering himself in leaves.

'The night was calm, and I had plenty of clothes, and could have slept in comfort, but some anxious individual was calling from the track near the house, and after I answered he came down opposite where I was, about half a mile in a straight line with the house,' Turner wrote in a letter to the editor of the *Taranaki Daily News* to rebuff claims made about his trip by a rival, which really set him off. 'After this shout I made up my mind to sleep in the Mountain House that night, but after trying to get through the dense scrub from 10.30 p.m. until 2.15 a.m., I decided that if I wanted to keep my appointment at Opunake at 11 o'clock on the same morning, I would require some sleep . . .'

Turner reckoned sleeping rough was a common occurrence for him in his climbing career, and in his experience he'd had much more severe episodes than this. However, he conceded: 'I am sure that there could not be a more puzzling mountain to get off than Mt. Egmont in the dark, as the ridges are all very much like one another. . . . I am the only man who has cut his way in ice and hard snow by himself to the summit of Mt. Egmont from the Dawson's Falls side, as far as I know, [and] there is not much in the feat except to get one into training for step-cutting when I make my next attempt on Mt. Cook.'[51]

Still, newspaper reports said Turner had lost himself on the mountain, and gotten bushed. Members of a local mountaineering club went to search for him for most of the night, fearing for his safety. Turner would have hated the fears, the fuss and the doubts cast on his abilities, and it pleases me to think about that.

In the early days of the search for Murray, they bombed the pool at Bells Falls with a few charges of dynamite to see if they could dislodge the body, in case it had become entangled in something in the water.[52] To this day the body of Reverend William Murray has never been found. Or should I say, the rest of the body.

Arthur's Pass

The mystery of Miss McHaffie

I'D BEEN THINKING a lot about my own mortality and the idea that, given how much time I was spending in the wilderness, the chances of something happening to me in that setting were higher than usual.[1] Having watched an acquaintance attempt to unravel the intricacies of her husband's death (it took more than six months, at which point she was struggling to prove to her internet provider that he, as the account holder, was in fact dead and gone, and not coming back from the grave to hop online any time soon), I thought I'd be courteous to my family and get all my affairs in order sooner rather than later. Sounds morbid, I know, but I thought it was just practical.

I wrote up a document with all my details in it — bank accounts, investments, credit cards, KiwiSaver, everything I could think of — finally wrote a will, and dropped it all off to my brother. It was only when I got to Arthur's Pass, ready for a new adventure, that I found out a family member was concerned that this behaviour signified an intention to end my life (obviously, it wasn't, but I can understand that conclusion).

Arthur's Pass is hostile country. A skinny, potholed road winds through the valley and over the pass, linking Canterbury with the West Coast, intimidating to drive when trucks thunder past you. Thick bush and scrub line the steep hillsides. And there's really nothing there — fewer than 100 people (80-odd people, or 80 odd people, the local joke goes), a dairy/café with a gas pump, some rustic accommodation and an eatery called the Wobbly Kea. If you went into the hills either under-equipped or intending to get lost, you might never come out again.

I made my first visit to Arthur's Pass without big aspirations; I merely wanted to visit the new and well-appointed Hawdon Hut, three hours up the Hawdon Valley, on a track that crisscrosses Hawdon River. That time, I never made it. It had been snowing in the days leading up to my attempt and the rivers were swollen, swift and icy. I set off anyway and came to the first river crossing about five or ten minutes into the trip. Sizing it up, I could see the bottom — the river was still clear (a dirty river means trouble) — so I plunged in.

The water came up to mid-thigh and made me gasp. I recalled seeing a video about what to do if you ever fell through a frozen lake into the water: breathing is important and will help calm your system so you can gather the strength to get out. I breathed, slow and steady. In and out, in and out. Then took two more steps. My walking poles began to shudder with the flow of the water. Before I could even comprehend what I was doing, my brain had somehow instructed my body to back the hell out. I was back on the bank without consciously thinking about it . . . survival mode had kicked in and my primal instincts said, 'No way!'

I retreated to the New Zealand Alpine Club lodge in Arthur's Pass after that, dried off, and went 'finger tramping' on the topo maps to get an idea of what trips there might be around the area that didn't require river crossings. There aren't many; Arthur's Pass is famous for unbridged river tracks. I opted for ticking off the little tracks around the village instead (Devil's Punchbowl, Bealey Valley, the boringly named Arthur's Pass Walking Track, and the more incongruently named Lake Misery Track).

I only managed one 'proper' trip that time, but I'd thoroughly and irreversibly fallen in love with Arthur's Pass. When I think about a spell in the wilderness, I always itch with longing to go there.

Miss Dorothy McHaffie was 39 years old, wearing a fetching rose-pink tweed 'jumper suit', and known to be suffering from extreme mental anxiety when she disappeared in Arthur's Pass, in February 1929.

McHaffie had been training to be a midwife at St Helen's Hospital in Sydenham, Christchurch, hoping to add the last feather to her nursing cap. Her pioneering work in 'mothercraft' had already been met with acclaim at training institutions in Wellington and Invercargill, but in recent times it had all gotten too much and her nerves were shattered.

Nurses at the hospital, when interviewed by newspaper reporters, said that McHaffie was capable and professional, and she had left the hospital entirely of her own volition. She had been worried and couldn't concentrate on her study to complete her midwifery exams. She was depressed and concerned about a friend's health, but seemed to be happier at the thought of going away for a spell. She had made arrangements to stay with a friend in Kūmara, on the western side of Arthur's Pass, for a while. The hospital matron made it clear to McHaffie that she could return to nursing and her studies whenever she felt well enough.

On the morning of 16 February 1929, she boarded the West Coast Express from Christchurch to Kūmara. She was fashionably attired in her jumper suit with a crêpe de chine blouse and beige shoes, and she carried with her an amount of luggage indicative of the intention to stay for some time: two medium-sized suitcases, a black leather hat-box, a rug, a cushion, an umbrella, a fur necklet and a light-brown tweed coat. She was around 5 feet tall and slender in stature and wore her hair in two thick plaits.

Before she left, she handed over a box of jewellery to one friend for safekeeping, and said to another: 'I will come back when it is all over and then you will see how simple it all was.'

My proper trip that time was a one-night tramp on the Cass–Lagoon track. The mystery of McHaffie went around and around my head in a washing machine of thoughts as I tramped. Thoreau claimed that any time his legs began to move, his thoughts would begin to flow. I generally felt the same, but sometimes instead of the thoughts flowing away like a river, it was one particular thought persisting, and failing to be processed and spat out. I thought about Miss McHaffie going for an innocent walk in the wilderness and coming to grief. Easy to do, and the terrain and bush around the pass are brutal in parts.

In late summer 2018, a man went for a walk after taking photos at Reid Falls at Ōtira Gorge, just west of Arthur's Pass. He took a 50-metre fall, breaking some bones and bashing himself up pretty badly. Unable to walk, he crawled for three hours and eventually arrived at the top of a steep flume that carries water over the top of State Highway 6. Totally stuck, he spent the night there, and probably would have died there too, except for tourists who heard him shouting for help. He couldn't move any further — if he got properly onto the flume itself, he would slide down and drop into a rocky riverbed (certain death) — so he sat there clinging to a tree root. Rescuers couldn't use a helicopter to reach him due to fears he would be blown off by the rotor wash. He was eventually rescued by a lines team that were dropped above him and managed to secure him.

'How that man got to where he was, I've got no idea,' a Fire and Emergency rescuer told media. 'I think he would be one of the luckiest guys I've ever met.'[2]

The waterway that leads into the flume was originally called Reid's Falls, after Billy Reid, a roadman who lived in the hut at the foot of the zig-zag at Candy's Bend. Reid was returning from the pub one night at the Otira Gorge Hotel but when he reached the sharp bend in the road just before the fall, he kept walking — straight over the cliff.[3]

The truth is definitely stranger than fiction. When I read of situations like the one in 2018 — bizarre and unimaginable — I can envisage how Dorothy McHaffie might never have been found if she'd had some sort of misfortune in the bush. Though, perhaps she did it on purpose — she saw the rugged landscape and thought it an easy place to end her sorrow, and hence got off at Arthur's Pass rather than carrying on to Kūmara.

Then again, I thought, maybe it was all staged. Maybe she had something to run from in Christchurch and dropping off her effects in Arthur's Pass was a well-thought-out decoy to distract police, friends and searchers while she disappeared to another part of the South Island to start a new life, under a new name. Pregnant, perhaps, and running from the shame of being an unwed mother that was part of that time and culture.

McHaffie was bound for the Kūmara train station, several stops beyond Arthur's Pass, but for some reason that will remain known only to her, she elected to get off at Arthur's Pass instead. She checked her large collection of luggage at the Arthur's Pass station, but the railway clerk said he had no recollection of who had checked the bags other than that it was a woman.[4]

And as the Arthur's Pass station could have as many as 500 people on the platform and around the station while the east-bound and west-bound expresses crossed over, not to mention other tourists and holidaymakers, McHaffie was most unlikely to be noticed among the crowd. Drivers of service cars said that nobody fitting her description was carried between Arthur's Pass and Hokitika by cars either that day or in the past week, although a local rumour persisted that a woman answering to her description had been seen riding in a car to Kūmara that day.

All investigators knew was that she definitely got onto the train in Christchurch, and checked her bags at the Arthur's Pass station. Several days later, when she was overdue to arrive in Kūmara, a friend raised the alarm and search parties set out. Police enquired at every house in Arthur's Pass and the search extended to southern Westland. Investigators, family and reporters began to question whether she had come to harm via an accident or had intentionally hidden herself. A *NZ Truth* reporter wrote, breathless with sensation:

> Had it been Miss McHaffie's intention to hide herself in the bush country, in or near the Pass, it would be easily possible for her to do so without fear of detection as the bush in that locality is very dense, and searchers could go within a very few feet of her and not find their quarry. On the other hand, of course, it is over two weeks since Miss McHaffie disappeared, and as she was not stoutly clad, nor in the possession of food, it is very doubtful whether she could exist for long in the bush with neither food nor suitable clothing. . . . Whether, in a state of nervous prostration, she held some fearful dread of the future, whether she has lost her memory, or whether she wandered away into the silent vastness of the Southern Alps to forget the world or to obliterate some distressing memory, at present remains unsolved. . . . If she is secreted in the hills, the task of locating her might never be accomplished. One needs to travel that Great Alpine Divide to appreciate the vastness of the country and the utter futility of anything but a battalion of men engaging in the search. And then they would be puny

against the tremedous [sic] natural fortress that the Southern Alps represent to the searcher. [5]

Friends, of whom McHaffie had few, were bewildered. Neither they nor the police specifically suspected foul play, but media speculated: '[T]he theory of molestation, and a possible violent death, cannot be discounted at this stage.' Not long after her disappearance, it was said that two letters addressed to McHaffie at the Arthur's Pass Hostel disappeared from the letter rack shortly after they had been put there.

Several weeks later, police investigations turned up a new, possibly dark, piece of information. On 16 February, the date McHaffie had failed to show at her destination, two men driving from Christchurch to Arthur's Pass couldn't get over the Waimakiriri River at the Bealey and returned to nearby Cass, where they hopped on the passenger train instead. At Arthur's Pass they changed to the Christchurch-bound train and got off again at Cass, accompanied by a woman. All three were seen getting back into the car, which had been parked at the railway station, and drove off in the direction of Christchurch.[6] Still, even with this information, the case went cold.

NZ Truth, still reporting breathlessly on the case, wrote: 'As the weeks go by, the silence becomes increasingly ominous.'[7] But perhaps the answer to her disappearance lay in her gender, it was suggested: 'The complexities of the feminine mind in times of stress have accounted for more remarkable happenings than the disappearance of Miss McHaffie, but her prolonged silence, and the complete manner in which she has vanished without leaving one likely clue to her whereabouts, is most disconcerting to everyone concerned.'[8]

McHaffie's probate file, now public, contains an affidavit from one Dr W. M. Irving, who testified that the day before she travelled to Arthur's Pass he was called to attend to her. She was very upset and appeared to be in a 'highly nervous condition'. He gave her a sedative and ordered she not be disturbed but left to rest.[9] Jane Trotter, who was the matron in charge at the hospital where McHaffie was training, told the court that for several days prior to her departure for the West Coast she was not her usual self but rather in a 'nervous and neurotic condition'.[10] She was given a leave of absence and Trotter herself wrote out a telegram to the friend at Kūmara to notify her that McHaffie was coming over. Trotter charged a fellow nurse with ensuring that McHaffie was bundled onto the train. It appears her handling and departure from Christchurch was highly managed — perhaps because she wasn't in a state to manage it herself.

I chose the Cass–Lagoon track partly because of its fine appearance on the topo map; it cuts a sharp, defined zig-zag (one zig, one zag) up the side of Mount Bruce in the Bealey area, then sidles gradually to Lagoon Saddle, which (unsurprisingly) sports a small lagoon, just before reaching the first of a total of six huts on the track. That's a fair number of huts for a tramp that only takes one night to complete, so it's a lucrative option for a hut bagger.

Snow levels had receded somewhat but new snow still blanketed the tops. It was a stunning clear blue-sky day, contrasting with the white-capped mountains either side of Arthur's Pass, and the dark-green forest below. It reminded me of the Fonterra logo, although the rivers here were free of farm animals.

I'd also chosen this track because of its name. Not only did it beckon to a lagoon, its double-barrel name spoke of famous tracks around the country: Wilkin–Young, Rees–Dart, Travers–Sabine. Tracks where you got to explore one piece of terrain, ascend a saddle or pass of some sort, and be spat out into a whole new world entirely. Moreover, the sibilance of the double S in Cass, paired with the alveolar lateral approximant to launch Lagoon, delighted my inner linguist.

The zig-zag was less easy-going than it looked on the topo. I slogged through soft snow — thigh-deep towards the top — and past some impressive rockfall sidling the slopes of Mount Bruce, placated by expansive views down the Waimakiriri River and out to Mount Binser. (There's also a Mount Misery and a Mount Horrible close by; my mate Rob Hosking reckoned he had once made a list of all the dire-sounding mountains — including Mount Awful itself, Mount Terrible and Mount Sadd — and was going to do a magical misery tour.)

By the time I got to Lagoon Saddle itself, I was a bit stuffed, but determined to bag both huts — Lagoon Saddle A Frame Hut (self-descriptive, a small A-shaped structure) and Lagoon Saddle Hut (dirty and unappealing). I stopped for a cursory rest and snack break but soon had to get back on the track due to all the snow and ice and the cold that had set in. Down the Harper River to visit West Harper Hut, a historic affair with sacking bunks and corrugated-iron cladding. Losing the track and looking out for cairns and markers to try to get back on path again. And on and on, following the Harper River as it curved and twisted and turned, then two bridges in quick succession and — hurrah — Hamilton Hut, then largely empty and quiet but in recent times crawling with Te Araroa walkers who apparently don't know how to use a toilet properly (according to letters to various editors, human waste abounds around the longdrop, as tourists are too offended by a backcountry bog to actually use it so they would rather poo on the ground immediately outside. I find this astounding).

I slipped around on tree roots and frozen mud the next day as the track had turned to ice in the clear sub-zero night, where I'd admired the stars and nearly full moon. Hefting myself up and over Cass Saddle, I bagged Cass Saddle Hut (uninviting) and picked up a large, sturdy stick where the trail ends and the river crossings of the swollen Cass River began. Although the flow is always lighter at the top end of a river, towards the headwaters, the early parts of the Cass were narrow and sometimes tricky, whereas the later parts were flatter and wider, meaning I was in much shallower water. I sent my thanks out to the universe to whomever had left that stick there — presumably they'd encountered the same issue on their way up the Cass.

I stuffed up the exit entirely and instead of popping out on Grasmere Road I followed the Cass River the whole way to the highway bridge, an extra couple of kilometres. I'd left my car at the other track end, back towards Arthur's Pass, and I was planning on hitchhiking to it. Thumb out, I tried to look vulnerable enough to need a lift but tough enough that drivers should think twice about messing with me. I hadn't really hitchhiked before, except for one episode while living in France where a friend and I asked for a lift but came away with a dinner invitation for her (not me) . . . such are *les hommes français*, I suppose.

A couple of campervans went past and then long, worrying silence — what if nobody picked me up and I was still here when it got dark? A derelict-looking hatchback went flying past at top speed with an equally derelict-looking driver at the wheel — reminiscent of Doc in *Back to the Future*. Whew, glad he didn't stop, I thought. Then he screeched to a halt, pulled a violent U-turn, drove back and threw open the door. He was friendly enough, and given the choice between derelict transport and standing on the side of the road in the falling darkness I decided to jump in.

He was on his way to help a mate in Blackball, who'd just bought a property that needed cleaning up, he said, so I'd have to fold myself into the back seat next to the ladder and all the building supplies. He suggested that I put one leg on the side of the gas bottle and the other on the box of nails — she'll be right. There was no way to possibly get the seat belt on and anyway I was so wedged in that all I needed was a bit of sour cream and a dose of sweet chilli sauce and you would've been able to serve me up as a pub snack.

My new-found friend began driving at speeds I'd never experienced before. (You can't do that in the North Island — too many police — but apparently you can do it on the long straights leading into Arthur's Pass on a Tuesday night.) This is how it's going to end, I thought: in a car with a questionable character, and a 9-kilogram gas bottle going straight through my face. I'll be unrecognisable; they'll need to identify me from dental records and my name on my DoC hut pass inside my pack. That is, if the gas bottle doesn't blow up and incinerate me, obliterating all remains from the earth forever.

'That's a weird place to be hitching from, mate,' he said. 'How'd you end up there?'

'Oh well, I was meant to come out on the Cass–Lagoon track but I kept following the river and ended up climbing up from the bridge,' I explained.

'Ah right, I thought you'd been dropped off there by someone, and that'd be shitty luck so I thought I'd pick you up. Where you going — West Coast?'

'Just round the corner,' I said, hoping he would actually let me out and not abduct me and bury me underneath a recently acquired property in Blackball, never to be seen again. 'I left my car at the other track start. It's just up here actually, just pull off to the left and all good, hey thanks so much, really appreciate it, you're a legend.'

'No worries, mate, best not to hitchhike in future eh, there's a lot of weirdos out there.'

With miserable names such as Deaths Corner, Pegleg Corner and Starvation Point (along with Lake Misery itself), the terrain immediately on the western side of Arthur's Pass is rugged and ominous. Further west from the aforementioned flume of death, the Rolleston River merges with the Ōtira River to become a tumbling cascade of boulders, moss and raging water. Much like at the Gates of Haast, further south, you can imagine that anyone or anything having the misfortune to stumble into the river would simply be crunched to pieces.

It's at the Rolleston River where the 8.5-kilometre-long Ōtira tunnel was started in 1908 to allow trains access between the east and west coasts. It took until 1923 for it to be finished and finally open. The war wasn't to blame for its tardy completion — construction kept going through World War I as the government was worried the German navy might blockade the West Coast ports that were used for shipping coal. Eight people died and one firm was financially ruined during construction (after which the work was taken over by the Public Works Department, which had given the firm an optimistic five years to complete it).

The death toll was very nearly two more, after two joy-riders on a trolley had a near-death experience in April 1917. Four men, one of whom worked at the tunnel, entered surreptitiously and decided to have a ride. The acetylene light they were carrying suddenly went out and the trolley got out of control. Two of the men jumped off before things became really wild, but the other two, named Bonnington and Cowling, were stranded on it, travelling at insane speeds.

They would've died, but they got lucky — the pumps hadn't been working and a deep pool of water had formed. They hit the water at pace and the sorely abused trolley came to a sudden halt — as did its passengers, who were thrown into the dark, cold water and had to wait to be rescued, treading water. The tunnel was renowned for its severe cold, with icicles hanging from the roof and lumps of ice a frequent feature.[11] Eventually they were extracted by workmen, shaken, freezing and exhausted — it was thought that if the rescue had taken another 15 minutes, they would've been dead.[12]

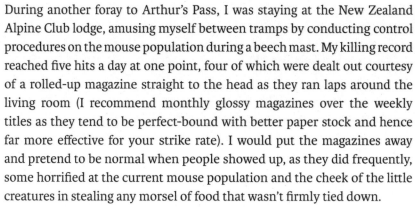

During another foray to Arthur's Pass, I was staying at the New Zealand Alpine Club lodge, amusing myself between tramps by conducting control procedures on the mouse population during a beech mast. My killing record reached five hits a day at one point, four of which were dealt out courtesy of a rolled-up magazine straight to the head as they ran laps around the living room (I recommend monthly glossy magazines over the weekly titles as they tend to be perfect-bound with better paper stock and hence far more effective for your strike rate). I would put the magazines away and pretend to be normal when people showed up, as they did frequently, some horrified at the current mouse population and the cheek of the little creatures in stealing any morsel of food that wasn't firmly tied down.

The Arthur's Pass NZAC lodge is something of a beacon for well-known climbers, and I got to know a handful whose names I'd seen on first ascent listings in the various climbing guidebooks. One day, a woman turned up who was astoundingly fit by anyone's standards. Her companion, Nina, was in my Secret Women's Mountain Business Facebook group and we had a gratifying moment of making each other's acquaintance after only knowing each other online. They were both off to climb Avalanche Peak the next day.

The fit woman was Penny Webster, whose modesty belies her life achievements. For a start, she's most recently finished a 37-year mission to bag all 24 of New Zealand's 3000-metre-plus peaks. That puts her in an elite league of only about a dozen Kiwis who've completed this challenge since the 1950s. She's also competed internationally in mogul skiing and has done nine Coast to Coast races. There's probably more that I don't know about.

Much of her mountaineering history dates back to the 1980s; she had a daughter in 1992 and put her climbing on hold, with a vow to take it up again when her daughter turned 18. In 2010 she reappeared on the mountaineering scene. That year was also the centenary of Freda du Faur's pioneering climb of Aoraki/Mount Cook, so to honour Freda, Webster dressed in similar attire and climbed it herself. (For the sixth time.)

The New Zealand Alpine Club lodge at Arthur's Pass was a welcome temporary home for me — and a delight when it snowed. While resident there, I made it a personal mission to ensure the mouse population was kept under control.

Webster says: 'I believe that we all need challenges in life, and whilst for me the 3000-metre peak challenge was going to be very demanding, I knew it was going to make my life richer. I believed that it was achievable. I am passionate about the outdoors, I like physical exercise and need goals — it keeps focus and discipline. It was competitive with the difference being that there is only one competitor — myself.'[13]

To say I was inspired by Webster was an understatement. I was endlessly impressed with how fit she was, how disciplined, and how focused towards her goals. I would consider myself a driven and motivated person, but she left me in the dust. It may be indelicate to talk about age, but seeing someone on the cusp of sixty doing big hairy climbs in a fitter state than most twenty-somethings gave me hope for what I might achieve in my next two decades.

Sometimes now, when I'm on solo trips and I feel out of my depth, unfit for the challenge or discouraged, I chant the mantra: 'I am Penny Webster, I am Penny Webster'. A friend has enquired, 'What does Penny Webster tell herself when she's in a tough spot?' Next time I see Webster, I'll ask. But I can't think of many women climbers who could outdo her.

As the lodge is a haven for the climbing fraternity (sorority?), it's a bit like a train station. It feels like a constant ebb and flow of names seen in hut books and climbing and tramping journalism. Some would arrive late at night, after a long spell in the woods, while others would leave in the dead of night to make the most of their daylight hours the next day.

A couple of chaps turned up, both very fit, muscular types, wearing the right brands and taking over the space inside the lodge as if it were their home (frankly, if it were anyone's home, I could've claimed to be living there alongside the mice). They were from Christchurch so they were regulars in Arthur's Pass, and they talked the talk quite well. One sat down opposite me, quizzed me about what I was doing there and, upon finding out that I was more on the tramping side of climbing and hadn't been Climbing Big Mountains like him, dismissed me as — perhaps — too boring. But he also recognised that I was the only viable audience in the lodge that day, and he began to hold forth at length about his exploits.

He'd climbed this thing (note: quite minor) and that thing (also quite minor) and he'd almost climbed this other thing (a bit more brag-worthy, but he hadn't made it) and he had Big Aspirations to climb something else over here. I wasn't very interested, but years of social conditioning took over and I felt I needed to be polite. He dispensed to me much advice on how I should be tramping — what to wear, what to carry, how to light a fire (it went on). I nodded at regular intervals but never had the opportunity to properly interject, even to ask a question, and anything I said was constantly interrupted.

Quelle surprise. The field of sociolinguistics has plenty of studies showing that women get interrupted more often than men — even by other women. There's also something called the Transition Relevance Place, which is the spot in a sentence where there is a pause or other signal that the current speaker might give up their turn. Typically, women are liberal with the Transition Relevance Place, whereas men are more prone to 'deep interruption' — interruption at least two syllables before a potential TRP. A former sociolinguistics student, I became painfully aware of how this particular chap kept up a running monologue on his outdoors exploits without ever allowing a Transition Relevance Place to occur. I was in verbal handcuffs.

But so was another chap, an older man who'd introduced himself simply as Ray, and wasn't very forthcoming in the current climate about what he'd been up to. He'd sat quietly, listening to this other bloke. Later, when the two guys cleared out, and it was just me and Ray enjoying the relative silence, I found out Ray was Ray Button, an International Federation of Mountain Guides Associations guide (no small feat) and well known in the climbing world for putting up new routes. For context, there are around 125 New Zealand guides listed on the New Zealand Mountain Guides Association website. Ray Button is a bit of a big deal.

While these relatively inexperienced guys had been chest-beating vociferously, Button had simply sat quietly and not competed. I was taken with his quiet presence and unassuming nature.

He gave me a bit of advice about locations to visit in the area and I pumped him for information about his recent adventures in Aoraki/Mount Cook. I ended up with a laundry list of What To Do In Arthur's Pass, from reaching Barker Hut to traversing Waimakiriri Col. Meanwhile, Penny and Nina had been up Avalanche Peak but I was too wary of the name

Crow Hut, easy to reach for an overnight trip by wombling up the Waimakariri River, hanging a right and turning up Crow River. Or, for experts, you can get there by ascending Avalanche Peak and dropping down a scree chute to the Upper Crow Valley.

and the terrain to try it — even though it's now a well-worn accessible route. It's possible to ascend Avalanche Peak, traverse the range in a northerly direction, and drop down a long scree chute, losing 500 metres' altitude, towards the valley floor of the Crow headwaters, then spend the night at Crow Hut.

I opted for a foray to Crow Hut from a different direction: up the Waimakiriri River from Klondyke Corner, turning right up the Crow. It proved easy travel aside from the seemingly never-ending gravel-bash that is the Waimak. Up at Crow Hut I was alone for the night, with a view to Mount Rolleston and Crow Glacier. Looking up towards Avalanche Peak, it seemed impossible terrain to me. Was it a lack of confidence or just sensible self-preservation? I couldn't figure it out.

Returning to the Alpine Club lodge after the Crow Hut trip, I discovered that you can be lonelier when you're surrounded by other people than when it's just you. Perhaps it's a matter of perspective. Charlotte Brontë haunted me; in a letter to a friend, she wrote: 'The evils that now and then wring a groan from my heart — lie in position — not that I am a single woman and likely to remain a single woman — but because I am a lonely woman and likely to be lonely.'[14] I felt my singleness hold hands with my loneliness and walk alongside each other.

A small group of friends arrived at the lodge. They knew I was there — I'd been pretty public about my whereabouts and had even suggested on social media that I was up for trips if anyone was in the area. It soon emerged that they had plans that didn't include me, and the main one was Goat Pass, a one-night trip going up the Deception River valley, over Goat Pass and down Mingha River. I'd wanted to do it for ages, and it hurt to have to sit there quietly and smile away at a group of people who were happy to exclude you. It was somewhat understandable — one of the group I'd dated and he was there with his new wife, who he'd fallen head over heels for and, as a result, our liaison had halted abruptly. (I prefer a slight paraphrasing of Charlotte Brontë's quote — perhaps something along the lines that the issue wasn't ongoing singleness but rather, ongoing loneliness.)

Off they went to conquer Goat Pass, with plans to do a side trip to Lake Mavis and over Mount Oates. The forecast didn't look good and two days later they reappeared at the lodge, having only made it up Mingha River and back again due to the weather.

Two days later a fine spell came through and I asked a bus driver to drop me off at the Morrison Footbridge, the northern end of the Goat Pass track. The footbridge gives you a failsafe way of crossing Ōtira River, which is too deep to do on foot. And there begins the unmarked route up the Deception River valley. It's part of the Coast to Coast race and I'd read accounts from mountain runners about the river crossings, indicating that if the first crossing is problematic, it's best to turn back as they'll get worse further up. With my trusty walking poles, I managed the first mid-thigh-deep crossing and breathed a little easier — until I came to a section where a deep pool cut into a sheer bank.

There was only a rope to lower yourself down, and if you got it wrong you'd end up in the deep. That gave me the willies — it *is* an unmarked route known for drownings, after all — but I chucked my pack down onto the riverbank and trusted the rope. After I stopped shaking, I took a couple of pics so I'd remember what it was like and made for Upper Deception Hut, then on towards Goat Pass Hut. The map indicates an actual track on the last kilometre or so, but in reality it's just a clamber up a steep stream bed, with the occasional track marker to reassure you that no, you haven't gone wrong, and yes, this is the 'track'.

The next day I woke to stunning weather and a dose of snow outside delivered by the snow fairies during the night. Then it's all downhill via the Mingha River and out to Greyneys Shelter, where I'd left the car before hopping on the bus. It was easy. I felt 'achieved'. And I felt a lot less lonely being by myself and ticking off a route I'd been excluded from than if I'd gone with a group where I wasn't welcome. I think it was Jean-Paul Sartre who said, if you're lonely when you're alone, you're in bad company.

Samuel Edgar Russell probably knew what it was like to feel lonely, or at least forgotten — his body was buried under 8 feet of snow and his companions were on the train home by the time his absence was noticed. It was in 1933 and he had been buried for a week before his body was dug out. Initially the party didn't even know whether he was with them when the avalanche occurred, or if he'd been missing for longer — nobody could remember where he'd last been seen.

Russell was from Dunedin and had graduated from Otago University with an MA the year before his death. He was at teachers' training college in Christchurch, and out to climb Avalanche Peak as a day trip with a group from three tramping clubs, including the Canterbury Mountaineering Club. There were many people but it was a party with no set leadership. The weather was bad, but the 40-some trampers set out to summit anyway. The group had halved by the time they reached the snowline, due to worsening weather and visibility, and although they'd been following the ridge most of the way, closer to the top they decided to ascend the face instead, due to the strength of the wind on the ridge.

The snow was soft on top and hard underneath — prime conditions for an unconsolidated snowpack on top of a solid layer to give way, and violently. When they were about 60 metres from the summit, the avalanche hit and travelled for 140 metres into a basin. The whole group was swept off in the slide, apart from two who managed to scramble out of the way. A few party members had minor injuries and the group turned back, save for two experienced climbers who continued on to summit regardless, descending safely.

Later, after the train had left Arthur's Pass station, someone realised Russell was missing. The party had counted 18 in total at the snowline, but hadn't noticed one extra chap had joined late, so when they counted again after the avalanche and got 18, they assumed all was well.[15]

A search was mounted immediately and went on for a week, with bad weather hampering the searchers' efforts, while local guide Oscar Coberger cautioned that the body might not be found until the snow melted in spring. Eventually Russell's body was found, at the end of the avalanche's path, by this time covered by an additional metre of new snow that had fallen during the week of searching.

Climber Arthur Harper, chairman of the New Zealand Alpine Club's accident committee, wrote that parties should not assume that a low or easy peak can be treated with less respect. 'All mountains are entitled to respect, and are apt to enforce it if ignored.'[16] At the inquest, coroner E. D. Mosley concluded: 'To some people the spirit of adventure calls very loudly, and mountaineering, with its difficulties and dangers, proves an irresistible attraction.'[17]

Avalanche Peak was so-named by Coberger (father of Annelise Coberger, the alpine skier who was the first person from the southern hemisphere to win a medal at the Winter Olympics in 1992). Named after Avalanche Creek, which falls away below the peak, it funnels into a couloir that runs long, and is typical of the worst sort of avalanche terrain as it creates a trap. Avalanche Creek was initially called Snake Creek, according to a writer in *The Press* in 1934, although the name doesn't appear anywhere else on maps or in newspaper archives, and seems rather unlikely given the absence of snakes in Aotearoa.[18]

Curiously, in 1949, two trampers came across a body on Avalanche Peak. On closer inspection, the body (that of Mr Leonard McCann, 38, a railway worker from Arthur's Pass) was found to have gunshot wounds. He was out alone on a deer-stalking expedition. It wasn't thought to be suicide, but presumably he somehow managed to shoot himself.[19]

Back in Arthur's Pass, I recovered at the NZAC lodge and plotted my next mini-expedition: up the Waimakariri River (never my favourite, as it's a wide open gravel-bash and boring in the extreme) to Carrington Hut, then side trips to Barker Hut and Waimakariri Falls Hut. Buoyed by recent success and increasing fitness, I was feeling optimistic, if not bullish.

I only made it as far as Carrington Hut, after my back decided it had had enough of carrying a pack (and, more likely, working from a tiny laptop on an unergonomic set-up at the lodge for so long). I lay there in pain for two days, snarfed a handful of painkillers and turned tail for home.

At Carrington Hut I had only one other for company, and he enjoyed telling me I was wrong every time I opened my mouth (which I soon stopped doing). I'd mentioned that you can see Mount Rolleston while heading up the Crow River, but he informed me condescendingly that it was Blimit. (It isn't; Blimit is on the other side of Arthur's Pass altogether, and incidentally was controversially named — a contraction of 'the bloody limit', which was in years past deemed too risqué for words.) I'd also mentioned wanting to do the traverse over Waimakariri Col from Waimakariri Falls Hut to the Rolleston River. It seemed to me to be sensible not to go over the col itself, which is steep on the northern side, but instead to pass via a much flatter col immediately to its west.

'That's bullshit, you can't get through there,' he told me. 'You go straight over the Waimak Col — whoever has told you that is full of shit.' But according to my desk research later, you do indeed aim for the flatter col.

I felt belittled and took solace that night reading Rebecca Solnit's essay 'Men Explain Things to Me'. Solnit is widely credited with the concept of 'mansplaining' although she didn't coin the exact term itself; it refers to a man explaining something to a woman that she already knows, without a question from her or an invitation to explain it. Crucially, she pinpoints that the dynamic 'crushes young women into silence by indicating . . . that this is not their world. It trains [women] in self-doubt and self-limitation just as it exercises men's unsupported overconfidence.'[20] I was already battling self-doubt and self-limitation without the input of this sure-of-himself bloke, who I avoided after that (thankfully Carrington Hut has more than one bunkroom).

I was gratified when I met Sophie who, with a group of Auckland University Tramping Club members, breezed through the door at the NZAC lodge like a breath of fresh air. It turned out, in that very Kiwi, two-degrees-of-separation sort of way, that Sophie had actually been to my flat before I rented it out. She worked for an outdoors store and I'd run into her boss on the way into Waitawheta Hut in the Kaimai Range some time ago; he suspected he'd left his jacket at the hut and would I mind bringing it out, if it was there? It was, and I left it under a bucket on the back deck for him to pick up — Sophie was dispatched to run the errand.

The uni tramping club folk were an enthusiastic bunch and I enjoyed their stories of their mega-tramp for the past couple of weeks — yes, *weeks* — across the ranges from Nelson to Arthur's Pass. They gave me route intel and introduced me to their famous '1000-calorie snack': a Snickers bar with a layer of peanut butter on top, another layer of Nutella (both layers the same thickness of the Snickers bar), topped with a walnut. Of course they had to re-create it for my benefit, and I could see where some of their energy came from — sugar!

The battle against the determined mouse army continued and when my friend Matt arrived in Arthur's Pass ahead of a planned seven-day expedition, he announced he'd devised a system to beat the little buggers and ensure our food supplies remained unmolested. Generally I tuck my food inside a thick plastic bag, a pack liner (which doubles as an emergency shelter), then — because realistically, they can gnaw through plastic — I pull the drawstring shut, fasten the clips, and hang the pack up on a hook or similar. Hanging food seems to foil them quite successfully.

But this trip we'd potentially be camping in a couple of spots where this wouldn't be possible, and given the sheer numbers of mice (and their cunning, bolshy antics) Matt decided extra measures needed to be taken. He cut out circles from 2-litre ice-cream lids and punched tiny holes in the centre, just enough to pull string through. We would secure our food supplies inside a waterproof bag, then hang it on a tent pole, stake or pole track marker, and use the circles to prevent the mice running down the string. It was truly a thing of innovative beauty.

And it worked! Our first night we breezed past Hawdon Hut, too busy in the peak of summer, up Twin Fall Stream and over Walker Pass to set up camp on a clear windless night on the edge of the Otehake River East Branch. (As an aside, the Otehake West Branch sees less traffic than the upper East Branch, as until recently the track was legendary for its roughness — track markers missing, track fallen away in places, tree roots and boulders aplenty — and associated Otehake Hut saw only a few visitors a year as a result. DoC gives optimistic advice such as 'travel down the Otehake is much slower than the map suggests' and 'consider the weather, the state of the river and fitness of your group before venturing down the Otehake'.)[21]

I didn't have much of an appetite for the self-punishment of the Otehake (others do; I don't judge) but I remain curious about the hot springs partway up the northern end of the Otehake River proper, beyond dark Lake Kaurapataka. In 2012, two American students survived for five days while stranded by the river in new snow and freezing temperatures by sitting tight at the springs and using them to keep warm. They walked out 'a bit hungry' but none the worse for their ordeal.[22]

Anyway, the Otehake proper could wait for another time. In the East Branch, Matt used an obliging marker pole to string up our mouse-proof system while I cooked up the first of our lightweight meals, and in the morning the proof was in the (mouse-free) pudding: our food remained unmolested by man or mouse.

It was an ambitious trip — much of it categorised as 'expert: route' by the Department of Conservation, and much of it requiring navigation skills and an agile approach to boulder-hopping. We slogged our way up Tarn Col (in retrospect, I'm fairly sure we weren't on the track at all given we battled scrub the whole way up and saw few track markers); scrambled over Taruahuna Pass (a flat, wide expanse not worthy of the term 'pass', featuring endless debris and rubble from nearby Falling Mountain after an earthquake wrecked the joint in 1929); wombled down the wide Edwards River baking in the sun and missed a crucial link track on the way out of the Edwards, meaning we took our chances in deep (but refreshing) pools to get out.

That wasn't the end — only halfway. We forded the Bealey River and crossed over the highway, our first sign of civilisation in four days. We had left a food resupply with an extra gas canister in the bushes at Klondyke Corner before embarking on the trip, and Matt was hoping the mouse-proof system had held up during the days since.

Klondyke Corner now has a shelter of sorts, well used by Te Araroa through-trampers. It originally had a hut, Klondyke Hut, which was erected after the Bealey Hotel was shifted from the northern side of the Waimakariri River to the south, making it a risk for anyone who might become stranded on the wrong side, unable to reach the hotel. The hut had blankets, pots, utensils and so on, but no food (likely hungry mice have always been an issue). Legend goes that one man reached it expecting a meal and felt so hard done by that he used chalk to label it 'Starvation Hut'; the Klondike gold rush of Canada's Yukon region in the late 1800s presented a very real risk of starvation, so the link was made. (A further legend about the hut involved a 'Chinaman' who drowned in the Bealey River and was stashed in a bunk at the hut while arrangements were made. That night, during a storm, a drunkard who decided not to risk crossing the river tucked himself in next to the seemingly sleeping figure and snored until well into daylight. He then decided to wake up his sleeping companion . . .)[23]

Our food resupply was undisturbed and we faced neither the risk of starvation nor crossing a swollen river. But the next morning an earthquake shook me awake from our tent camp on the edge of Turkey Flat in the wide bed of the Waimakariri River.

'Matt! Wake up!' I shook him awake, as he seemed determined to sleep through the drama. 'Earthquake!'

The Great Pinnacle (2190 metres), one of my favourite climbs, with Ngauruhoe (2291 metres) and Tongariro (1967 metres) behind.

ABOVE | Skiing through the ice falls on the Tasman Glacier, Aoraki/Mount Cook National Park. TREV STREAT

BELOW | Travers Saddle on the Travers–Sabine Track, Nelson Lakes National Park.

ABOVE | Lake Rotomairewhenua, also known as Blue Lake, in Nelson Lakes National Park, reputed to be the clearest lake in the world.

BELOW | The stunning clear waters of the Waimakariri River in Arthur's Pass National Park.

Sunrise over Aoraki/Mount Cook, from Mueller Hut in Aoraki/Mount Cook National Park.

Brewster Hut, Mount Aspiring
National Park.

Ball Hut, Aoraki/Mount Cook
National Park.

Te Pukeohikarua Hut,
Kaweka Forest Park.

Welcome Flat Hut,
Westland Tai Poutini
National Park.

Taranaki Maunga,
Egmont National Park.

ABOVE | The Hollyford Track runs along the eastern side of Whakatipu Waitai Lake McKerrow.

BELOW | Irrepressible greenery on the Hollyford Track, Fiordland National Park.

Reflections on the Milford Track,
Fiordland National Park.

On top of Mount Holdsworth,
Tararua Forest Park.
MIKE HEYDON, JET PRODUCTIONS

Ball Glacier, under the watchful eye of Aoraki/Mount Cook.

ABOVE | Climbing underneath the Pinnacle Ridge on Whakapapa, Mount Ruapehu, Tongariro National Park.

BELOW | Looking out to the Mueller Glacier lake from Sefton Bivouac, Aoraki/Mount Cook National Park.

Instinctively I went to drop and hold, to get under a table or into a doorway, but of course all we had was a few metres of fancy lightweight tent to protect us. So we both got out of the tent, and sort of hopped around a bit, partly out of lack of knowing exactly what to do and partly because the sandflies were also up early, looking for their breakfast. Faint rumblings reached us from further up the valley — rockslides from unstable mountainsides. We broke camp in a hurry (more to escape the sandflies than out of concern for any potential after effects of the quake) and hightailed it for Carrington Hut.

There we met Greg Ross, a lean and athletic Canadian who splits his time between Canada and his second home in the New Zealand wilderness. He seemed to blend in with the landscape and looked at ease making a small fire to boil the billy for a cup of tea. He seemed resilient, very resilient, and I admired and envied him that. I didn't put two and two together until much later when I figured out he was the same Greg Ross who, in 2015, had taken a fall on a track near Hokitika, dislocated his shoulder and endured a 10-hour crawl to a hut, then waited eight days to be rescued. No stranger to the area and with 50 years of tramping under his belt, he'd in fact cut the very track where he came to grief, 31 years ago while working for the Forest Service.

Initially, when he fell and injured himself, and because he was in shock, he took his boots off, got into his sleeping bag and stayed put for two days. But he started getting dehydrated, and he knew he had to move — especially if rain set in. Using his knees and one good arm, he crawled and slid, crawled and slid, and finally made it to Frisco Hut, his originally intended destination, where he drank a lot of water and kept warm by sandwiching himself in between two mattresses while heavy rain fell outside and temperatures dropped. He'd been unable to carry his pack or even put his boots on. At the hut, he went for seven days without food — making mental lists of what he would buy when he was back in civilisation, such as peanut butter, honey and cheese. Then a rescue team turned up. Ross had left detailed intentions with a friend who raised the alarm as planned, but his one regret, he told media, was not having a personal locator beacon.

'I relied on my experience, it got me through this time, it got me through in the past, but these days with modern technology, there's no real excuse.'[24]

During his ordeal, Ross was inspired by stories of survivors; in a perusal the Reverend William Murray would have been proud of, he said: 'I've read about Jews in the Second World War who survived months and months, their bodies living off their own muscle, fat and tissue. There were also allied [sic] pilots shot down who would hide for weeks and weeks in freezing conditions.'[25]

When he was rescued, he was on his last legs, he said, and probably wasn't going to last another two or three nights as his body was starting to cool down too much. Fruit cake and muesli bars and a swift helicopter trip back to civilisation did the trick, though, and Ross is a regular within the tramping community, particularly among the volunteer hut and track maintenance group Permolat, on the West Coast.

Permolat is credited for the excellent state of Old Julia Hut, where Matt and I stayed the next night. The group became involved in 2013 and volunteers Max Dorflinger and Dick Brasier tidied it all up. Dorflinger used macrocarpa boards from his farm to tighten up gaps in the floorboards and added some neatly crafted rimu stools. There's also a new Julia Hut, but it was full — and anyway, the old hut has way more character (the new is not really that new and it has no style). I was glad to have Matt for company that night; legend has it Old Julia Hut is haunted by two girls who disappeared in the valley in the 1870s — one Julia, one Mary, after whom the nearby confluence creeks are named.

The two girls, aged eight and 11, had been sent over Taramakau River and up the Taipō to bring home cattle — it wasn't unusual in those days for young children to undertake such errands. A great storm ensued, with thunder and lightning. Too young to be able to devise shelter and survive, it was assumed they'd perished in the bush or drowned — their bodies were never found.[26] A deer culler staying in Julia Hut in the 1960s reckoned he heard a knock on the door late one night but nobody came in and he wasn't about to get up and open it!

Getting to Old Julia Hut over Harman Pass had been a hard day. There are no track markers leaving the pass until most of the way down Mary Creek, which is rugged and full of boulders to navigate and scrub to push through. At several points, due to not being able to see my feet from the scrub, I fell into holes and had to extract myself; Matt had less of an issue with this, being somehow more agile and much taller. It was a relief to drop our still-heavy packs at the hut, have a quick break (where a weka stole my jandal and took off into the bush with it in his beak — there's nothing quite like a spell of weka wrestling), and wander down to see if we could uncover the hot springs on the Taipō River.

Piping-hot water seeped out of the riverbank. Matt had had the forethought to grab a shovel from the hut and he used his might and his engineering skills to craft a pool of sorts, surrounded by smaller rocks to keep the hot water in. Somehow the sandflies decided to leave us alone — I wonder if they dislike the smell of sulphur? — and we soothed tired feet and muscles for hours, letting cold water in via a rock channel when necessary, until darkness fell and the stars came out for company. It's a moment I won't soon forget: the surreal feeling of soaking in a hot spring while the ferocious and freezing Taipō River tumbled past, surrounded by thick West Coast forest and staring at the stars.

The rest of the trip was mostly more tame (fewer earthquakes, gentler terrain, and fewer mice) as we ambled down past Mid Taipo Hut — until we had to cross Taipō River. We'd left it too late and were too far downstream, where the water gathers up more volume from side creeks and gains enthusiasm. It was flowing clear and seemed fine, but it was a push to stay upright and not get swept off our feet.

If I'd been by myself, I wouldn't have made it and it would've been a long trek back upriver to find an easier spot to cross. Taipō means 'devil' or 'evil spirit' in Māori — and the river certainly lives up to its name — but, curiously, early English settlers used the name Taipō thinking it was what the Māori called it, and Māori used it because the English did. The actual Māori name is 'Hope oka', meaning 'stab in the loins' — because of its consistently freezing temperature! Both names are accurate.

We came to a steep climb up a bank to avoid an outcrop before the track drops down to a cableway. The steep bit had been utterly destroyed by the shaking a day or two before. It was a hard grunt with the track giving way beneath us at every step, real confidence-destroying stuff, but we finally managed to top out. I had dirt underneath my fingernails from clawing at the ground to get purchase. (I later read up on the area and found one blogger stating there was a 'significant slip' that made the track 'extremely steep and suitable for experienced users only',[27] while DoC still notes it as an extremely steep route up a fresh landslide area.)

Then the cableway! Not many still exist around New Zealand and once the health and safety types twig to the ones that are left, they too will become extinct (this one has since been replaced by a three-wire bridge). Imagine a thick wire cable strung across the river with a small metal boxcar hung onto it. The boxcar is generally tethered to one side or the other, if correct etiquette is followed, and you jump in with your pack and whizz across. If you don't have the critical mass to carry you across, you'll stall in the middle, where you start using a giant crank handle to winch yourself over, or a buddy on either side can help to winch you over. It's incredibly hard work — I'm actually not sure I would've been able to do it by myself, though Matt winched himself across quite capably.

From there it really was easy going, a flat walk to Dillon Hut — new Dillon Hut, which is actually new — and nearby old Dillons Homestead Hut, which was under threat of demolition at one point and the new hut was built in anticipation but public pressure managed to retain the old structure. The new hut is a standard modern DoC affair — beige Colorsteel with red trim, plywood lining; you could be in any other new hut, anywhere — while the homestead is appropriately rustic.

Deer antlers adorn the entrance and old newspapers and pamphlets line the walls. Some care has been taken with the interior, which features hand-hewn bunks and mattresses that depart from the regulation sanitary DoC covers. Two seventies-style armchairs are positioned in front of the open fire and a sign cautions users: 'No loaded firearms in hut please'. The old homestead was home to the Dillon family until the 1930s, when the Depression forced them out. The family had mined for quartz with a small amount of success.

Upon pulling up to the old hut we met a bloke called Laurie. He was clad in a flannel shirt, short shorts paired with gaiters and a camouflage hat and had a Santa Claus-style beard, hand on one hip but lots of friendly words. He also dispenses chocolate bars to hungry (needy) trampers and gave us a lift out in his old Land Rover with the bumper sticker '1080 POISON KILLS NATIVE BIRDS'. Whizzing through the rainforest, it felt strange to suddenly be moving so fast after so many days of slow travel. And from there, we hitchhiked back to Arthur's Pass to continue our assault on the local mouse population, food stashes safely consumed, would-be food-stealing mice foiled.

Near Dillon Hut, where Seven Mile Creek joins Taipō River, the valley widens to some grassy flats in small clearings. Thankfully.

In 1939, 19-year-old pilot Lloyd Parry, who was flying a Tiger Moth plane from Christchurch to Greymouth, was reported missing, with grave fears that the plane had crashed in the mountains between the Bealey and Ōtira rivers. There were strong winds at high altitudes, so the plane was assumed to have been blown off its course. Ten planes were scheduled to run an extensive aerial search the next day.

Searchers were soon stood down when Parry emerged near Jacksons that morning at 3 a.m., wet but uninjured, after having crash-landed the plane near the Dillons Homestead clearing and walking out of the valley around 5 p.m. the night before. Parry reported normal conditions when he left Wigram, but on crossing the Main Divide the plane's engine suddenly cut out — perhaps due to water infiltrating the petrol tank. Flying at around 1500 metres, he managed to get the plane into a glide and crash-land it into a small clearing in the Taipō Valley, wings chopping at trees 13 metres high.

As a member of the Canterbury Mountaineering Society, he knew the area and its tracks well — even so, it was no small feat for him to find the track down the Taipō and emerge to the highway. Parry had met a couple of miners near the scene of his landing, but declined to stay with them and instead borrowed their lamp and hurried to make contact with the outside world, so that others would know he was safe.[28]

The plane had sustained a small amount of damage — a bent radius rod in the undercarriage, fabric torn, and propeller tips damaged — but it was still in good enough condition to be flown out by an instructor to the Greymouth Aero Club (presumably Parry was recovering from his adventure). Several members of the club had walked into the Taipō carrying materials needed to repair the plane. Then a runway of 140 metres had to be cleared, including shifting boulders and logs. Wings from another plane were brought in to replace the damaged ones. They were packed in cradles and carried in, each by six men.[29]

It wasn't Parry's first brush with death. Two years earlier, he had crashed his motorcycle on Kaniere Road, near Hokitika, and was found by a resident who'd heard the noise. Unconscious, he was rushed to hospital and, suffering concussion, he wasn't able to remember what caused the accident.[30]

None of this deterred him, evidently, and he went on to be awarded the Distinguished Flying Cross as a Flight Lieutenant in the Royal New Zealand Air Force, No. 681 Squadron, in 1944, fighting in World War II: 'Flight Lieutenant Parry has completed numerous operational photographic reconnaissance sorties in single-engined aircraft and has invariably displayed great determination to achieve success, flying in adverse weather throughout the monsoon period. At all times this officer has set a fine example of keenness and devotion to duty.'[31] He also set a record when he flew a Douglas Dakota aircraft more than 1500 miles in seven hours 46 minutes.[32]

The New Zealand wilderness breeds them tough.

Around 1886 there was a small gold rush at Taipō River, right where Seven Mile Creek joins the Taipō itself, and where Dillon Hut and the homestead stand. A ramshackle hut known as Seven Mile Hut has been taken off the topo maps now in name, but a small black square remains on the map, as the remains of the hut are still physically in existence. (You wouldn't want to spend any time there.)

Trampers who fossick around the terraces above Dillon Hut and climb up the ridge from the confluence of Seven Mile Creek and the Taipō onto the Kelly Range will be rewarded with remnants of the gold and quartz mining from years past — traces exist of a water race and tunnels in several places, as well as a stamping battery on the Bald Range. Nearby Gold Creek and Reef Creek are dead giveaways to the history of the area. Floods were often responsible for flushing out new gold, but nobody could figure out where it was coming from.

Australian prospector and self-styled 'mining expert and geologist'

Angus McPherson wrote multiple letters to newspaper editors with long treatises on the topic of the Kelly Range and Taipō River's potential, claiming that Seven Mile Creek was probably an 'auriferous quartz field' but that access was problematic; he and others had climbed around the creek's banks, a horrible, steep and dangerous climb, with an even worse descent. But: 'I would almost stake my reputation that the pyrite lode at the Seven Mile Creek has shed the coarse gold that has been found in that stream.'

McPherson and his team had to cross and recross the creek at least 50 times, sometimes thigh-deep, and they were forced to bivvy out for the night under an overhang, trying to keep warm next to a fire. 'Hungry and exhausted I slipped while springing from one boulder to another and hurt my leg, which has been already broken twice . . . Getting too old for this game. However, I've got a kick in me yet for easier country.'[33]

I am of the opinion that McPherson did far too much talking and writing and not enough actual prospecting, if his letters are anything to go by. But even today, it seems that the area still hasn't produced the glitter; in 2012 a company named Willberg Resources was granted a two-year permit to explore the area for gold, silver, magnesium and other minerals, without affecting Arthur's Pass National Park. Nothing came of it and the company was quietly removed from the Companies Register in 2017.[34]

Back in Arthur's Pass, the mice were continuing on their beech mast-provoked rampage, even though they'd been quiet at the end of our tramping bender. I met one chap who had devised a trap using a soft-drink can, a skewer and a bucket of water — the skewer ran through the can and perched it over the water, while a dollop of tasty peanut butter acted as bait; the unsuspecting mouse would run across the skewer to the can to get to the treat and skid off, straight into the water. Due to the sheer numbers going in for the goods, the bucket had to be emptied every couple of hours.

I read up on trampers who'd gone missing in the national park. One death, that of a 20-year-old American tramper called Michael Dishnow, was described by media reports as lonely: 'His was a solitary death in a remote part of the Arthur's Pass National Park, and his body was cremated this week in Hokitika at a service without friends or family. This might have suited the young man, described by his family in Houston, Texas, as a loner who loved nature and life with gusto.'

Dishnow went missing in April 1998 after leaving Hokitika to tramp the Three Passes; his last known location was on the track at Harman Hut in mid-April. In May his decomposed body was found in a stream near the headwaters of the Arahura River, near the hut, probably after falling a couple of hundred metres down a steep bank. He would've died instantly, police said. 'He was not afraid of anything,' his mother said.[35]

I often felt I wasn't afraid of the outdoors, or afraid of anything much at all really — maybe scared of spiders and very averse to bananas, but I didn't get properly scared. I did have hesitations about some tracks and routes, and reading about Dishnow, combined with a less-than-perfect weather forecast, gave me an excuse to put off my next trip, which was to be the Three Passes — a partially unmarked and untracked route over Harman Pass, the perennial snow of Whitehorn Pass, up Browning Pass, down to Harman Hut and out via the Arahura River. Comments from a friend warning me not to do it alone also gave me pause. I was maybe a bit afraid.

I was also a wee bit afraid of loneliness.

The best way to get over a fear is to confront it, so I packed my tramping pack once again and headed out to knock off the Casey–Binser track, on the other side of Arthur's Pass and further east. Casey Hut, which was critical accommodation on the track, located near the Poulter River, was burnt down in 2015. DoC initially decided not to replace it, but in 2019 reversed the decision after two anonymous donors gave $250,000 to the cause.

I happened to be tramping during the construction of the new hut so I packed a bivvy bag to sleep out under what I hoped would be a clear sky that night. I got ambitious and walked about a third of the next day's tramp too — right past the old Casey Hut site with its charred remains and on down the Poulter River towards Mount Brown Creek. Utterly exhausted — and soaked, as I'd inadvertently walked straight through a pond much deeper and muddier than it looked — I found a spot near enough to the creek to be able to fetch water, but far enough away to be safe from sandflies. Or so I thought.

I slept reasonably well inside the bivvy bag, albeit a bit too warmly, and woke up to my alarm at 5 a.m., which I'd purposely set early so as to eat breakfast in the darkness and avoid said sandflies — all very well in theory but the little buggers must've heard my alarm. I cooked up oats and a cup of instant coffee as quickly as I could, but when I went to gulp the coffee, I discovered several thousand sandflies had decided to end themselves in the black liquid — but without any daylight it was impossible to see their discarded bodies floating in there.

Disgusted, I spat them out (I'm sure several got stuck between my teeth) and rinsed my mouth of the offending insects at the creek as best I could. Breaking camp in a hurry, I made for Binser Saddle, stopping at a clearing about a hundred metres above Pete Stream, which seemed to be sandfly-free. I sat for some time, enjoying a hot drink and chocolate cookie, thinking about life and the wilderness and loneliness some more. It seemed odd to me that I had no fear camping out in a bivvy bag in the middle of nowhere — it didn't seem lonely to me in the slightest when I actually got to doing it — but the thought of time stretching out in front of me living my life solo was sometimes, well, a bit much.

I began to conquer things that challenged me, though, starting with a repeat of the effort into Hawdon Hut, where the river crossing had caused me to turn back. This time the river levels were low and crossing was not an issue. I breezed up the valley for an overnighter in the hut, which I had all to myself, and didn't really think anything of it. Perhaps it's conditions that can make you feel safe, regardless of terrain — the right track or summit on the right day will just feel like it's meant to be.

I still had a long list of things I'd chickened out of, starting with Avalanche Peak and ranging to Sefton Bivouac in Aoraki/Mount Cook National Park. Sometimes it was tame stuff where I'd get a wobble on and turn around, only to think later that I'd pulled the plug without any real reason except self-doubt. I managed to push through one such episode at Temple Basin, a ski field that leads straight off the pass, where a memorial to Arthur Dudley Dobson stands (the explorer who forged a path through the mountains in 1864).

The expansive view out to the Waimakariri River from Binser Saddle on the Casey–Binser track in Arthur's Pass National Park.

It was summer, but a typical Arthur's Pass summer, which is basically like winter in the rest of the country. The wind was blowing, which I generally find disturbing, and rain threatened from the west, clouds bursting over the Kelly Range in the distance. I'd backed off the track before, due to the same sort of conditions and a sense of unease I couldn't put my finger on. This time I pushed forward, reasoning to myself that it was essentially a highway of a track up to the ski-field buildings to start with and I could turn around there if the feeling didn't go away.

A smooth and easy ascent of 500 metres vertical, I reached the buildings in an hour and 20 minutes, meeting several others along the way. Waterfalls cascaded in the distance and the angry clouds over the Kelly Range were holding themselves at bay for the moment. I pushed further still, around a corner to reach the final ski-field building, Pages Memorial Shelter, which is said to be haunted. Stories abound of locals who won't go near the hut, alongside other tales of trampers who bed down there only to flee in the middle of the night because of noises of ghosts walking around and rattling the doorknob. Some trampers bedding down in the hut have heard loud noises and screaming coming from underneath the floor — only it's a solid concrete base. People tend to tell the same version of the story, even if they don't realise it's been told before, and reports date back to the 1970s.[36]

I stuck my head in briefly but had no plans to stay and commune with noisy ghosts — I value my sleep too much for that sort of caper. Climbing on loose rock, I reached Temple Col — I would later come back during ski season and ride the nutcracker tow lifts all the way to the same spot, with a mate saying the only way he would ever come back to Temple Basin was in a helicopter — and ate lunch staring out at Mount Rolleston, which was becoming increasingly swathed in a cloud cap, but on a clear winter's day makes for a crisp, stunning view.

Betty Petre was the first woman to climb Mount Rolleston, in April 1927, but she is otherwise absent from climbing history — although

On the front lawn at Hawdon Hut looking up the Hawdon River to Trudge Col. Hawdon Hut is an easy trip — if the river allows you access.

it seems she was a junior guide at the Hermitage. Newspaper reports show she sat patiently at Arthur's Pass waiting for suitable climbing conditions to attempt the 2275-metre-high peak. The weather wouldn't co-operate and heavy snow fell, but eventually conditions consolidated and Petre made it to the summit to claim her prize, alongside two men who were experienced climbers and had summited Rolleston previously. 'Her performance in climbing at this late period of the season such a difficult mountain, which has foiled hundreds of good climbers, is really remarkable,' the syndicated newspaper report read. 'The back and highest peak of Rolleston, which rises from the Crow Glacier, is precipitous rock.'[37]

Mount Rolleston is one of so many peaks and places that bears the name of a Pākehā man; it was named by Arthur Dudley Dobson in 1864 after William Rolleston, the superintendent of Canterbury Province. (Incidentally, Rolleston was publicly blasted by one of his opponents in 1870 for various offences to the people, including being the nominee of the would-be aristocracy, attempting to repeal the thistle ordinance, and wanting to shut up places of entertainment at 11 p.m. Regardless, he was returned with an overwhelming majority.) What Dobson didn't know was that the mountain already had a name: Te Tara o Tama (Ahua), so called after Tama Ahua, an important Māori navigator.[38]

Back at the New Zealand Alpine Club lodge at Arthur's Pass, I met Tessa and her then partner Bryan (of the deprivation exercises), who had arrived late the previous night, after I'd gone to bed. Lodges are odd places for instantly forming connections with people — I suppose it's the common interests that bond you. Bryan bounced into the kitchen in the morning, narratives about his adventures past and future forming a constant enthusiastic patter, cooking up a hot breakfast for himself and Tessa, dishes clattering. They were off to attempt Rome Ridge, which leads up to Mount Rolleston, that day. I looked it up on the topo map and thought, no way.

I didn't see them again for some time, but we reconnected thanks to Facebook and mutual adventuring friends. They both joined up as members of my ski club for a season, and I've enjoyed multiple adventures with each of them. Bryan later told me he knew it would be a solid thing when Tessa attacked Rome Ridge with gusto. I, too, hugely admired Tessa's energy and her climbing experience in the Austrian Alps, from where she hails.

They seemed made for each other — so it came as a shock to me when eventually they parted company. I felt deflated; if they couldn't make it, who could? But, as Bryan much later reflected to me, life isn't always rainbows and unicorns.

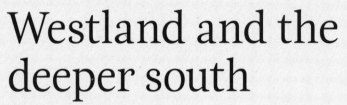

Westland and the deeper south

Pink pyjamas and taking no bullshit

STRIKING OUT for a spell of solo tramping on the West Coast, I was living at the NZAC's Fox Glacier lodge, enjoying watching the flaming fireball sunsets each night and going for the world's slowest trail runs around nearby Lake Matheson. Known for its spectacular reflections, due to organic matter from the forest colouring the water dark brown, the lake was created by the retreat of the glacier following its last significant advance 14,000 years ago, grinding out a hollow that later filled with water.

I'd been in to Welcome Flat Hut and Cedar Flat Hut, both of which have natural hot springs but are a world apart in terms of a tramping experience. Welcome Flat Hut is huge, must be booked in advance, and is stuffed to the gills with tourists most nights. There, you'll meet people from all over the world relentlessly ticking off yet another New Zealand 'must-do' experience.

The nearby hot pools run to the high fifties in temperature but hut wardens keep them down to a manageable 39 degrees or so, and the picturesque imagery you encounter on Instagram belies the disgusting truth: the bottom of the pool is in fact filled with mud, which is mixed with the discarded hair of every hirsute bather who's been in there before you. Weirdly, it looks like a very pale version of guacamole. Still, I can understand the attraction to Welcome Flat; *I* was there too, after all.

Trampers trickled in until late in the evening, many of them finding the track rougher than they'd anticipated — particularly if they were tourists used to the groomed, hard-packed, benched tracks of frontcountry Great Walks. The Welcome Flat track is easy by Westland standards, but it's at least seven hours and it's no highway. A few Europeans arrived late and were shocked to discover bedding wasn't provided, while a couple of Americans had sleeping bags but didn't have any food. The Europeans had food, while the Americans had lugged in an inadvisable amount of hard liquor, so various swaps were done and they were at least fed and watered (hic!). The warden, an obliging Kiwi guy who'd clearly seen it all before and then some, dug out a couple of emergency sleeping bags that he obviously kept hanging around for just this purpose. He rolled his eyes at me after handing them over.

I spent two nights at Welcome Flat Hut — it seemed a shame to walk in just for one night — and did a quick foray up the Copland Valley towards Douglas Rock Hut but didn't quite reach it. I got far enough to be able to stare up at what I calculated to be Du Faur Peak and Cadogan Peak (named after Freda and her lover Muriel Cadogan), humps on the skyline of the divide between Westland and Aoraki/Mount Cook. If you go over Copland Pass (which is largely not done any more due to rock instability) you end up dropping down into the Hooker Valley, a short walk from Aoraki/Mount Cook Village.

More fear and apprehension bathed me and I didn't know why. Or perhaps just a lack of impetus or drive to push up there, instead finding excuses to turn back or not even attempt it. I was still setting goals that I thought I had a reasonable chance of achieving — rather than goals I thought were a stretch or that I'd fail at. Fear of failure? Fear of trying. Maybe.

There's one hut en route to Welcome Flat called Architect Creek Hut. Pity the two women staying overnight. They were locked in by a passing gent who saw fit to slide the bolt across on the outside of the door while they were inside. The window was too high to risk jumping out of so they had to resort to using a pair of scissors and a tent peg to attack the door frame until they could work the door loose. I read about their ordeal in the hut book on the way in as I sat eating my lunch, with the door carefully propped open.[1] It occurred to me it was probably done to them on purpose, as surely you would check the inside of the hut before you took such a measure. It also occurred to me that the same thing could happen, horror of horrors, while sitting on a backcountry bog — as they nearly always have a latch on the outside to secure the door when you're done.

The Cedar Flat huts are the poor cousins to Welcome Flat Hut, in a sense. Cedar Flats is much further north and the hot pools are a more modest, rudimentary affair, accommodating only a couple of people and

Historic Cedar Flat Hut (above) and the newer hut (below). Both have their charms. And they are a world away from the bustling activity at Welcome Flat Hut.

easily missed if you aren't paying attention. The main hut is small and old but well cared for. Right next to it is an historic hut. Huts like this were built for government deer cullers from the 1930s onwards and the Cedar Flat one, resplendent in bright and cheerful DoC Rescue Orange once again, is considered to be the best surviving example on the West Coast.

Getting into Cedar Flat is easy and rugged at the same time; part of the track follows an old sawmill tram path, which makes for quick going, but another section goes along the river and requires a tramper to have the dexterity to boulder-hop, cross streams and slap sandflies all at the same time. If the river floods, this section becomes impossible to pass through.

I was lucky enough to catch a lift in with a couple of blokes in an unregistered (and probably un-WOFed) four-wheel-drive. You get a gut feeling for who you can trust and they turned out to be about right — just regular locals who didn't want me to have to walk in the rain and across boring paddocks full of cow dung. They were off for a quick hunt in another direction.

Then I met two tourists on the way in who had only negative things to say.

'The hut is so old and dirty,' the man said.

'And the hot pools are very disappointing — we did not even bother getting in,' the woman said.

'A big waste of time to come all this way,' the man reiterated.

They all but spat on the ground to express their disgust. New Zealand — who would go there?!

I didn't have any other pressing plans so I continued on regardless, expecting a dowdy, filthy hut and hot pools that were small to non-existent. So I was stunned to discover two well-kept, tidy huts (albeit not new) that I had all to myself (the peace! the quiet! the bliss!) and hot pools that I thought were rather neat. A 1-metre-high mossy cairn marked the spot at the river to scratch around for the hot springs, and good thing, too — they blended in so well with the landscape it was hard to figure out where the river ended and the warm stuff began.

Just above where Wren Creek meets the Toaroha River, a small hot pool is constructed of slabs of rock with sand cementing the cracks. The plentiful water runs clear and piping hot, steam rising into the cold, wet Westland day. Miniature cairns surround it and the rock edge borders

The natural hot pools at Welcome Flat are a major drawcard for weary walkers, more so today but also on historic trips. The bottom is muddy sludge, a bit confronting, but the bush setting is unusual and delightful.

right onto the chilly waters of Wren Creek. I couldn't understand what the tourists were complaining about, and enjoyed sitting in the hot water in the forest, looking out to the mountains shrouded in mist. Excited to have such a memorable moment, I took selfies sitting in the pool, careful not to get my phone wet, and alternated between dunking myself in the freezing creek and rewarming my body in the hot springs. I didn't linger though; the rain had picked up and the creek's flow was gradually increasing. A tangle of windfall in the middle of the creek was testament to the violence of Westland water, if it were in a bad mood.

Back at the lodge in Fox Glacier after the night in Cedar Flat's historic hut, I'd had a shower and was sitting on the deck outside the bunkrooms slicing up my blisters, feeling rather pleased with my solo adventuring efforts, when a guiding company van pulled up outside. I was wearing my pyjama bottoms — flamboyant and girly pink-checked ones — although it was far too early in the evening (okay, it was the afternoon). When the van driver got out, her first words were, 'Hi, I love your pyjamas.'

I recognised her at once, although we'd never met. It was Lydia Bradey. (Lydia Bradey loved my pyjamas! Swoon. I was fangirling hard out.) As I mentioned earlier, in 1988 she summited Mount Everest without supplementary oxygen and was the first woman to do so, but her male teammates questioned it in the media, claiming she hallucinated her summit achievement. Her team sent out a statement saying the height she had reached was uncertain and perhaps she merely 'thought' she was at the summit.

It was condescension in the extreme. Bradey writes in *Going Up Is Easy*: 'It was a statement that set out to totally belittle my achievement. I knew exactly how high I had been; there was absolutely nothing "uncertain" about it. To be subjected to such damning and chauvinistic statements . . . pissed me off.'[2] In the book, Bradey's friend and co-author Laurence Fearnley asserts: 'Women have had to fight for the right to be taken seriously as mountaineers, to participate in expeditions and be treated as equals, regardless of gender. She was determined to reach the summit of Everest and as a strong-willed, authority-questioning individual she was never going to be content playing second fiddle to a group of men with less high-altitude experience than herself.'[3]

An observer could assume Bradey's teammates were jealous of her success on Everest in the face of their own failure to summit. The book tells how she made the decision to initially head back down the mountain when a storm hit, meaning she was well positioned for the later summit attempt. Meanwhile her teammates waited out the weather higher up, but didn't make it and returned to Kathmandu as Bradey summited by herself the next day.

Bradey in real life is sparky — full of energy and enthusiasm, her zest for life evident even while fatigued from guiding clients in the mountains. Listening to me describe some of my fears around trying to find appropriate trips to do by myself, she gave me suggestions, drawing out hypothetical lines on the topo maps for me to attempt. I felt inspired to push myself further. I might never be Freda du Faur or Lydia Bradey, or Penny Webster, but then, neither is anybody else. I am just myself.

In the early 1900s, tourism was booming and places such as Milford Sound, the Chateau at Tongariro and the Hermitage at Aoraki/Mount Cook were attracting overseas visitors wanting to witness the scenic beauty of New Zealand. In 1901 the Department of Tourist and Health Resorts was formed (the first country in the world to do so) to foster tourism and one of its first acts was to establish a tramping and mountaineering route to connect the West Coast with the Hermitage. Huts were being established on the glaciers and guides were in demand. The Copland Track was constructed between 1901 and 1913 — a slow, laborious process, further dampened by the alpine weather and unstable landscape. The hot pools at Welcome Flat were a major drawcard for the track, but the department hadn't had them in its plans — they were actually discovered during the track's construction.[4]

It wasn't deemed a place for women, but they went anyway — as early as 1903, when the track was still just a thin strip blazed through the bush, rather than the pack track it became. Constance Barnicoat, who was also a journalist (in fact, the first female shorthand reporter, and known for her literary thunderbolts to the point where she was referred to as 'a first class scold'),[5] had been staying at Aoraki/Mount Cook for five weeks for mountaineering training. She had never heard of the pass or the track but caught wind of it from two West Coast women who were intending to attempt it — Ada Perkins and Jane Thomson, who were tramping buddies. 'I decided that I would go too, in any case, whether they did nor not,' she wrote in a newspaper account of her adventure. No huts existed along the track, meaning the women would sleep out each night.

The going was tough; at times Barnicoat had to get onto hands and knees, and the guides, Jack Clarke and Peter Graham, cut steps into hard ice, probing with axes to ascertain the presence of crevasses. Due to a thick mist the party had no view from the pass and it was bitterly cold and endlessly damp. Still: '[T]o me it was absolutely fascinating, going step by step, after the guide, through that snow and ice. It seems the most desirable thing in life to be able to lead a party through a Pass, poking the ice-axe into the snow and hewing out steps.' And they celebrated by toasting each other's health with whisky on the snow at the pass. Barnicoat took delight in glissading, both on snow and on mountain daisies and snowgrass — regardless of the disastrous and destructive effect it had on her knickers (yes, she noted this in her account).

The final leg of the trip was, of course, concluded with a visit to the hot springs on the way out, Barnicoat noting the curiosity of its sudden existence amongst the dense bush. Despite the mud and the sandflies: 'Under present conditions, a bathe in it, with the concomitant evils, is a doubtful joy.' And to cap it off, she rode a man's bicycle, too large for her, the last distance out to Hokitika entirely by herself, falling off multiple times due to its size. Barnicoat was complimentary of the trip, in spite of its difficulties, and dispensed the following advice to her female contemporaries who might also attempt such a thing: '[U]nless ladies are able to carry their own things, up to at least 8lb in weight, they ought to be left at home.'[6]

Buoyed by the success of the trip, she went on to climb extensively, including in Europe, where she did that famous winter ascent of the Schreckhorn (4078 metres). She wrote (and wrote, and wrote) and married another journalist and mountaineer, Julian Grande, in 1911. It was a marriage made in heaven, he said, and a year after her death in 1922 he made the first traverse of De la Beche and the Minarets from west to east, ascending and naming Mount Barnicoat in her memory.

Barnicoat, even more so than Freda, clearly took no bullshit from anyone and I like that about her. Julian Grande obviously did too. In 1907, she formed the Ladies' Alpine Club with a collection of other female mountaineers, because women weren't admitted to the all-male Alpine Club. (Women weren't admitted until 1974, shortly before the clubs merged.) Hilariously, Aubrey Le Blond, the first president of the Ladies' Alpine Club, said she didn't personally have a problem with the male conservativism — she just wanted to access the club's excellent library.

Still, Le Blond launched her thunderbolts, too: 'As a matter of fact, men do not care for women on mountains. They have a theory that women are clumsy, and have to be helped. From the very first, men have not encouraged women to climb mountains.' The most ridiculous part of the discrimination? The world height record in mountaineering was held by a woman at the time — Fanny Bullock Workman had reached 7056 metres in the Himalayas.[7]

Now, the track over the pass itself has deteriorated substantially, with erosion, loose rock and slumped terrain presenting quite serious risks as a result of the receding Hooker Glacier and thawing of glacial moraine. There's also often avalanche danger.

Language can be very revealing, although I am aware that my heightened sensitivity to bias and sexism could be leading me to draw certain conclusions. Still, language is gendered (everything is gendered, says our famous writer Eleanor Catton, from whom I am happy to accept life truths on account that she is as bad-ass as Constance Barnicoat, and all of the other women mentioned so far), but I have often observed the passive voice being used for women and the active voice for men. In researching Copland Pass I found a magazine article from 2011 that read:

> The first crossing made by a European woman occurred on
> April 4, 1902. The head guide from The Hermitage, Jack Clark
> [sic], and Peter Graham led Mrs Thompson and Miss Perkins
> of Greymouth and Miss Bandicot [sic] from London over
> the Pass.[8]

Note the passivity of the sentence here. The crossing 'occurred' — as if the women didn't fight scrub, climb a ridge, cross steep snow slopes and wade through bogs. It just *happened*. The guides led the women, apparently, whereas in male accounts of guided mountaineering, the men attack the climb, accompanied by a guide.

Maybe I am taking this all too seriously, but it's this sort of subtle undermining that also serves to undermine women's confidence. They have to be *led*, managed, like a thing to be sorted out rather than respected as active human beings with agency and autonomy and physical ability.

I recall doing the Greenstone–Caples trip with two friends, one male, one female. Greenstone–Caples is a very easy tramp but the snow had begun falling as we stomped up the Caples towards Upper Caples Hut and the next day we had fresh, thigh-deep snowdrifts going over McKellar Saddle. It's only 550 metres' vertical ascent to gain the pass but it took us nine hours in total to get over the pass and round to McKellar Hut, an hour more than the stated maximum assumed time for that section.

The track up the last section of the Caples was the worst; we were constantly hopping from tree root to rock to root again and seldom did we see a marker. The last bit involved a bush-bashing scramble right up a stream bed. The guy kept pushing us onwards, with so much self-confidence in his navigation abilities that he got angry when I asked to see the map. Nope, he wasn't getting the map out. (I now always carry my own, no matter who I'm tramping with — I like to suss out what's what around me and learn how to match up terrain features with the paper version. Again, autonomy — and independence.) He maintained the no-map policy for the whole trip.

The next day I forced a team chat about the plan for the rest of the trip, which was going to tack on the Mavora Walkway to make it a six-day epic. 'I'm planning on getting you ladies around to the next hut under the DoC time,' he said at one point. I took exception to the language used. He wasn't *getting me around* anywhere. I was on my own two legs, walking under my own steam (steam that was now coming out my ears), putting in my own effort and carrying all my own gear plus a decent swathe of group stuff! Nor was I a *thing* to be *managed* like some sort of problem for him to solve. It felt like I was denied the agency of my own body and physical effort, in the same way the women crossing Copland Pass were said to have been 'led' — it just 'occurred' — without their action or input. If only it were that easy! Then we'd all summit Mount Everest in our lunch breaks.

I went back and did Greenstone–Caples as a solo trip a few years later, to sort of cleanse the bad juju of the previous trip. It was a blast and super easy — I sliced off a third of the times on the DoC signs. Notably, the track up the upper Caples to McKellar Saddle had been significantly upgraded to a gravel highway, benched high above the old track. And now I could easily see, peering down into the valley, and the headwaters of the Caples River, that he had had us off track completely. That's why it was so hard — because his overconfident navigation was totally wrong — and why we never saw any track markers. And, come to think of it, probably why he didn't want me to look at the map.

Although the Copland Pass trip with Barnicoat was successful and publicly lauded as quite the feat, guide Jack Clarke had always had a dim view of taking women into the mountains, and later told the department the route was 'unfit for ladies'.[9]

He may have felt proven right, to an extent, when three women died while crossing the pass in 1948. But it wasn't due to their gender — they were caught in a surprise blizzard and fierce north-westerly gale while on the pass and had to hunker down in the open after one of the women became exhausted and couldn't go on. The party attempted to dig holes in the gravel and scree to get shelter and relief from the wind and snow, but that night the guide Michael Sullivan awoke to discover that all three women — Joan Bust, Christine Sullivan and Thelma Jefcoate — had died of hypothermia. The crossing is largely devoid of any sort of shelter — no trees or scrub — although shelter was only a few hundred feet away for the first woman who became overwhelmed.[10]

Guide Sullivan made it back to the Hermitage, exhausted and with frost-bitten feet. The place they'd chosen to bivouac was only an hour away from a 'staging hut' en route to the Hermitage.[11]

A north-westerly storm was predicted and the rain charts showed it was due to sweep right through Fox Glacier. I bugged out, making for Wānaka to see friends and knock off the Motatapu Track. The weather wasn't due to reach that far south and I'd hopefully get a couple of clear days.

The Motatapu was purpose-built after Canadian songstress Shania Twain (aka Eileen Lange) wanted to buy 20,000 hectares of land between Wānaka and Queenstown, in 2004. That's fine, said the Overseas Investment Office, but you'll need to do the mahi and give us some treats first. To fulfil the conditions, Twain and her then husband Mutt Lange agreed to build a tramping track, now part of the Te Araroa Trail, running from near the Motatapu Station at Glendhu Bay to Macetown, just out of Arrowtown. It's considered demanding, for experienced trampers only, and its 34 kilometres had felt out of reach to me for some time, given the comments I'd heard from so many people about how hard it was. Someone had even died after falling off the track on a day walk into the first hut.

But I was feeling fit from thrashing myself in Westland, which is about the hardest tramping country you can get in New Zealand — although regular Tararua Range trampers will likely beg to differ, and it's true in a way: the Tararua Range is classic North Island mongrel bush country.

A friend dropped me off and wished me well. I was due out in four days' time and booked on a bus from Arrowtown back to Wānaka. Looking at the topo map, I anticipated it would be rough; the track goes relentlessly up and down, almost never flat. Each day had a decent ascent and descent, and the last day was a long 25 kilometres out to Macetown then endless (well, 21) river crossings down the cold Arrow River to meet Soho Creek before civilisation in Arrowtown, by which point I didn't bother following the track, I just waded straight down the river. My arrival at Arrowtown was met by multiple amazed foreign tourists taking hurried photos of me emerging from the river like a swamp thing.

Daunted, I had opted for a short three- to four-hour day into the first hut, Fern Burn Hut. Settling in with a hot drink I read some alarming comments in the hut book about a gang of overactive possums living under the hut, who came out at night to party on the deck. Hut jokes are legendary — I've seen fake light switches, mirror balls in the longdrop — so I took it with a pinch of salt. And anyway, there was no vegetation to be seen anywhere around the hut. Surely a gang of possums would have better prospects elsewhere for something to munch on?

It was no joke. I left my last loo stop until after darkness had fallen, just before I wanted to crawl into my sleeping bag. It was just me, alone in the hut. I opened the door and was confronted by a hissing noise and several sets of unblinking red eyes. No fewer than five angry possums, each with an opinion of his (or her) own, confronted me just above head height, hanging on to a rafter. One stretched out its paw and tried to swipe at me.

I retreated immediately and slammed the door shut. I was busting for a wee! So I grabbed a broom, opened the door just enough to slide the brush out, and tried to dissuade the possum posse by swiping back at them. It made them worse. Now, they were really pissed off.

I valued my head quite a lot and didn't fancy having five sharp-clawed creatures dropping down onto me. So I did what any self-respecting lady tramper would do when confronted with a dangerous situation: I peed into my aluminium billy. Then I made sure the door was definitely clicked shut to protect against the offending animals, brushed my teeth and went to bed. (Don't worry, I washed the billy well — and anyway, isn't urine supposed to be sterile?)

The Motatapu is intimidating country, the track a tiny path only just benched into the hillside enough to walk on, the landscape utterly shattered in places from erosion. It's bald — seldom are there trees for shade — and plastered in bleached tussock. Early settlers, even those excited by the prospect of finding gold, must have found it uneasy, even threatening. With so much dull brown country, the landscape feels at times colourless, but in places where the water feeds it, it bursts into brilliance — the bright yellow and burnt orange leaves of a Central Otago autumn contrasted with whatever small amount of green grass might grow, thanks to an impossibly clear blue-green waterway. People still pan for gold here and when you peer into the burns, it's easy to imagine you can see it glinting back at you.

The track technically ends at Macetown but trampers need to walk to Arrowtown, another 15 kilometres in and out of the Arrow River. Gold was in the Arrow and up the burns (the Gold Burn or Rich Burn give that away, so does the Homeward Bound Battery, other ruins, piles of stones that were once derelict huts). A stone pillar stands at Macetown with a plaque marking the site of the former settlement, which started in 1862 and drew several hundred people to the spot. By the 1920s it was all over and the town died. Now, only a few preserved historic buildings remain (one was burned down by a tramper who lit a fire in the fireplace).

The Motatapu Track takes in some spectacular landscapes, and climbs and falls relentlessly. This photo was taken at sunrise on Roses Saddle (1188 metres), looking out towards the Harris Mountains in the distance.

William Fox might be credited with discovering gold in the Arrow River in 1862, depending on whether or not you believe his accounts versus those of his detractors. That Fox isn't to be confused with Sir William Fox, second premier of New Zealand, who was rather enthusiastic about denying Māori their land rights — although to be fair to his legacy he seems to have done an about-face later in his political career. Fox Glacier is named after him, though the Māori name is more poetic: Te Moeka o Tuawe, the bed of Tuawe, a warrior who fell and died while climbing with his lover Hine Hukatere. Franz Josef should be known as Kā Roimata o Hine Hukatere, the tears of Hine, who cries for Tuawe, her tears freezing into the glacier. Perhaps she is now crying fresh tears with the impact of climate change melting the glacial ice.

Our other Fox, William Fox, had some experience on the American goldfields and had been at the Tuapeka goldfield in Otago. It was thought he had secretly followed a prospector named McGregor to a spot where he had been harvesting 20 ounces of gold per day and begun working alongside him. Fox and his party were managing 40 pounds of gold per fortnight. This went on for some time without anyone catching on or a rush setting in, but Fox then visited the Dunstan area and he was noticed, watched, and followed back to the Arrow.[12] Then it was all on and Macetown boomed, briefly.

By Fox's own account he'd been sifting around in the Arrow River for several days before he ever noticed McGregor and his companion Stewart and no sign existed of any previous work being done in the area; Fox said the idea that he had tracked McGregor to the Arrow was false. 'I still contend that I was the first man that got gold in the Wakatipu district and also the first who made a report of the same,' he wrote in a letter to a contemporary.[13]

It was the time for gold in the South Island; back at Fox Glacier, a gold rush two years later, in 1864, drew more than 16,000 prospectors to the river valleys and, later, to its black-sand beaches, with townships erupting at Ōkārito, Five Mile and Gillespies Beach on the coast. Fox himself was newly released from prison, after a punch-up in a hotel led to six months' hard labour in the Dunedin gaol, and was on the prowl for more gold. Heading to the West Coast, he struck lucky at Fox Creek in the Arahura River, north of Hokitika, and at the Fox River in today's Paparoa National Park, which led to the establishment of the Charleston goldfield. For the Fox Glacier region, the gold rush didn't last. Just 18 months later, the beach settlements had become ghost towns.

Fox, although a jailbird and a brawler, was known for his boundless energy, fortitude, self-reliance and determination. Others had confidence in him and his leadership, and when he died (from 'decay and general debility', thanks to the hard-knock life he'd led), he had a very large funeral.[14]

By 1935, the gold rush was a distant memory. The luck had run out, and in November that year it would run out also for Fox Glacier guide Tom Christie, a 30-year-old single man who'd come from Australia and had been guiding for around six years.

Christie was returning solo from a bivouac at Pioneer Ridge where a hut was to be built. He knew the area well — so well that it didn't scare him anymore, which was considered one of the reasons for the tragedy. It's a well-known heuristic trap — familiar terrain lulls you into a false sense of security. If you've climbed a slope a dozen times and it's always been stable, you expect it to remain so, even if the snowpack is in reality about to give way on you. Christie took a different route to the usual one, along a bergschrund (where perennial ice separates from rock, typically quite deep). He jumped but misjudged the distance, broke through soft snow, and plunged hundreds of metres into the crevasse. If he hadn't died immediately from impact injuries, he would soon have died from the extreme cold and exposure. Christie left scrape marks on the edge of the crevasse, from a desperate attempt to save himself. His dog, which was his faithful companion and often leaped around the glaciers with him, was never found — it's assumed he jumped in after his master.

The alarm was raised by two climbers who had approached the Pioneer bivouac expecting Christie to meet them with hot tea. But Christie's bedding was undisturbed, and at the lower Chancellor Ridge Hut his waterproof jacket and a change of clothing indicated he had expected to return. A guide and the climbers followed Christie's trail, some of it disguised by new snow but still traceable, until they came to the crevasse. There, they found marks where Christie had probed with the long shaft of his ice axe, and a hole in the snow that told the tale of his whereabouts.

The guide, Frank Alack, made a snow anchor using his skis, roped himself to the anchor and threw the tail of it down into the abyss. The rope was some 20 metres long — quite short by today's mountaineering standards — and it failed to touch the bottom. Another rope was produced, but the men realised that the overhanging ice simply wouldn't allow for a rescue or a body recovery, even if the ropes did reach. By that time Christie had been in the crevasse for more than 27 hours and it was extremely unlikely he was alive. The rescue attempt was abandoned.[15]

In December 1935, Frank Alack and climber H. K. Douglas did a first ascent of a previously unnamed peak between Mount Halcombe and Newton Pass on a ridge on the northern side of Explorer Glacier, where Christie died. They named it Mount Christie (2636 metres), in honour of Tom.[16] It's just along the ridge from Mount Barnicoat.

Mountaineers at the time noted that Fox Glacier, like Franz Josef Glacier, tended to move at a faster rate than the glaciers on the eastern side of the divide, even up to 15 feet in a day compared to mere inches for glaciers such as the Tasman, and that ice in the deeper parts of the glacier moved more rapidly than the ice at the surface. If Christie had fallen quite deeply, he might pop out sooner rather than later, it was thought. But he's been gone for more than 85 years now, much longer than the 30 years calculated by prominent climbers in 1935.

'The disappearance of the Westland alpine guide, Tom Christie, in a crevasse on the Fox Glacier means the entombment of his body in the depths of the ice for many years to come,' a correspondent wrote. 'It may be twenty years, or a century, but it will not be for ever, for sooner or later the glacier gives up its dead.'[17] Locals reckon Christie's body is due to pop out of the lower icefall of the glacier any day now.[18]

The West Coast experiences a lot of movement for a place that doesn't give you much space to move. It's really just a thin strip of land squashed in between two formidable forces: rugged mountains on the east and foaming surf on the west, perhaps raging at not being able to destroy that last bit of flat land that survives.

There's movement in the ocean, in the glaciers, in its history. It's a place where I find it difficult to sit still. Maybe it's the unsettling nature of the landscape that makes me feel always on edge, on alert, waiting for something to happen. I feel compelled to movement there, trail running up the glacier valleys, enjoying covering ground under my own steam rather than by car, or by helicopter.

People have had ideas, big ideas, about alternative transport up the glacier valleys on the West Coast pretty much forever. More recently, Skyline Enterprises, which runs gondolas in Rotorua and Queenstown, announced it was investigating the same at Franz Josef Glacier. Survey work was done to figure out the best positioning of the towers and Skyline was working on an application for a concession and resource consent.[19] The community was largely behind the idea.

But it's not new — even as far back as 1938, an aerial railway was being discussed to open up the ski fields at the head of both glaciers. Guide Peter Graham was pushing for the railway, which would create a world attraction for tourists — meaning people could ski all year round. The idea was six towers at a cost of £30,000, linking the end of the road to Goatpath (a peak at 1821 metres).[20] (The most current gondola plan would see it go slightly further, as far as Crawford Knob.)

Nature on the West Coast never lets anything happen easily, though, and the environment has always been subject to floods, earthquakes and instability. In 1965, heavy rain soaked the glacier, causing it to burst from pressure; icebergs were still intact when they hit the West Coast surf 20 kilometres away. In 2019, DoC and the NZ Transport Agency announced that the road up to Fox Glacier would be closed indefinitely due to landslides, huge erosion and instability after floods.[21] Fox Valley contains the country's largest active landslide, the Alpine Gardens Landslide, which is estimated to be 50 to 70 million cubic metres of material currently moving at around 116 millimetres per day, but reaching 700 millimetres per day during and after rainfall. Latent anger, released by movement. Water and land, both deathly.

I visited recently, just wanting to touch Sentinel Rock at Franz Josef and wander up and down the lower part of the valley, well away from the face of the glacier. In military terms a sentinel guards or watches over an

Looking up the Copland River from Welcome Flat Hut towards Douglas
Rock Hut and the now largely disused Copland Pass route — site of several
all-women trips, such as the one led by Constance Barnicoat.

area, and Sentinel Rock seems to do just that, marking the entranceway where the track leaves the car park.[22] It's next to Teichelmann Rock (named after climber Ebenezer Teichelmann) and the pair of them fulfil their KPIs, towering over tourists embarking upon their walks.

Sentinel Rock is schist bedrock that's been smoothed by the glacial ice — it was strong enough to stay the course in spite of all that relentless rubbing. Nobody knew Sentinel Rock even existed until 1865 when the glacier retreated and revealed it. Now, it seems impossibly far from the glacier's face, and while visitors were once allowed to ascend the rock on the tourist track, access was later discouraged and the area fenced off; I wasn't game to attempt breaching them.

The glaciers typify this West Coast movement, advancing and retreating across the years, even bucking the trend between 1983 and 2008 by advancing. It's a sort of dance — a tango driven by climate change. Back, forth, with that edgy, dangerous feeling.

I can never stay long on the West Coast. It's too threatening, and it's not home for me, but rather a place to go when I feel like a brush with danger.

Fiordland
Hidden secrets, missing tribes

FIORDLAND IS WET, inaccessible, rugged and sparsely populated. It rains around 200 days per year due to wet winds blowing in from the west off the Tasman Sea — and it even has its own endemic variety of the dreaded sandfly. Thanks to its extreme terrain, it's never been logged, and the effects of humans on the land are minimal. Animals roam untroubled and much of Fiordland has never been properly explored. Right around on the south-western outer edges of the coast, names such as Broke-adrift Passage, Useless Bay and Cemetery Island conjure up images of frustrated explorers down on their luck.

Also due to its extreme terrain, and extreme weather, more than 60 people have gone missing in Fiordland and never been found. One of those is Quintin McKinnon,[1] an early explorer and guide who went missing in late 1892 without a trace except for — well, maybe — a thigh bone.

McKinnon left Te Anau for Milford by boat in late November, telling friends he would return in a few days and declining to take perishable food with him due to a favourable wind that would speed his travels on the lake, where he lived at Garden Point, just north of Te Anau township. He never made it to Milford and in time people became concerned and a search party was dispatched. His watch, gun and dog were found at his home in Garden Point, with feathers scattered around the house as his dog had been killing birds to survive. No trace was found of McKinnon in nearby huts.

Nearly a month after he had last been seen, search parties made contact with explorer Donald Sutherland at Milford Sound, who confirmed he hadn't seen McKinnon in some time. All hope of finding him was over and searchers generally held the opinion that he'd met with a watery grave.[2] Still, people continued to watch for signs of McKinnon, and in late January 1893, a sailor reported finding a locker door, tea caddy and tucker box from the boat on the lake shores.

Finally, the boat itself, the *Juliet*, was found off Lone Island in the lake, sunk in about 2 metres of water and lying on her side with the tip of the mast sticking out. McKinnon's boots, billies and other items were still in the boat so it was concluded she hadn't capsized; instead it was thought McKinnon had been knocked off the boat due to his habit of sitting on a high deck to reach the short tiller — a position where the tiniest thing might unbalance him. He was known to wear gumboots, which would've weighed him down in stormy waters. The lake had risen several feet around the time of his disappearance, so it's likely the boat drifted into the shallows, tipped onto its side and gradually let water in, filling up and sinking as the lake rose.

Where he went missing was the most exposed bit of the boat journey, nearly two thirds of the way up the lake north from Te Anau, with the flats of Te Anau Downs on the easterly side offering no protection. Searcher and friend (and later, New Zealand prime minister) Thomas Mackenzie wrote in an account of the search: 'The lake opposite the North Fiord is a most dangerous place, down that arm a wind will come sweeping like a hurricane when the wind is blowing quite steady up or down the lake.'[3]

Those who found the boat selected a small rocky outcrop near where it was found with a large white granite block sitting perfectly level, a landmark clearly seen and probably remnants of a previous glacier. They attempted to cut McKinnon's name in the stone but found they'd need better tools and returned later to inscribe it: 'Quinton M'Kinon, 1892'. For the time being they placed a cross in a cairn of stones and hung a wreath of white myrtle to commemorate the lost man.[4]

Mackenzie wrote: 'Poor M'Kinnon! His death is our loss. We grudge to see our friends cut off in the full vigour and flower of manhood, but it is a fitting ending to a life such as his — his grave the ice-dug rock, his monument the snow-clad mountain.'[5]

Mackinnon Pass on the Milford Track, the penultimate point of the experience, is named after Quintin McKinnon in honour of his achievement of blazing a trail across to Milford Sound.

The Milford Track was my first-ever overnight tramp and my first multi-day tramp at the same time. I'd done day walks but never carried a pack before — I thought it was out of my realm of ability until my friend Lisa, who is tiny, did it as an independent (i.e. non-guided) walk with friends in around 2008. I thought, if Lisa could do it and carry all her own things, surely I have a shot at achieving the same! I found some tramping buddies on the internet, ignorantly didn't bother to train for the tramp or even figure out what sort of gear I'd need to carry, and set off on the track in October 2009.

I thought I was going to die. The first day is only an hour and a half of flat walking to Clinton Hut, near the banks of the impressive Clinton River, but it felt like a slog. Day two I was filled with unwarranted optimism, but I had to make multiple stops to recover physically even though it's nearly all flat, again, aside from a gentle 100-metre ascent up to Mintaro Hut. I'd economised too much on food and felt the lack of energy. At the same time, I had no idea that it's normal in the tramping world to only take two sets of clothes: one to walk in, one dry set for the hut. I had fresh socks, underwear and clothes for each day. I'll admit it: I was a tramping numpty.

The body gets used to the abuse of tramping, though, and I managed the zig-zag track up to Mackinnon Pass and its shelter fairly well on day three. It's a 500-metre ascent — these days I'm used to at least 1000 metres' altitude gain without complaint. I was too stuffed to make it up to Sutherland Falls on a side track, a sheer 248-metre fall named after explorer Donald Sutherland. Legend has it that his friend John Mackay had won first rights to name any falls they came across in a coin toss; Mackay won and had Mackay Falls near the Arthur River named after him, a mere 25-metre waterfall, while Sutherland lost the coin toss but won the better waterfall.

Size isn't everything — I much prefer the understated, muted beauty of Mackay Falls over the thundering Sutherland Falls, which you can't properly get close to — the spray prevents close encounters and instead demands that you view the falls from further away. Mackay Falls are friendlier, softer, and more colourful; vibrant lime-green moss covers boulders, ferns spring out of wet cracks, and black rocks contain an aqua pool at the bottom. The white, fizzy water tumbling down looks like milk poured from a jug at the top.

At the last hut, Dumpling Hut, I heard stories from the warden and

Ascending to Mackinnon Pass on my third time tramping the Milford
Track — this time in much better condition than the first trip, taking less-
experienced friends and vicariously soaking up their joy. SIAN STEPHENS

other walkers about numpty trampers (I was careful to hide the fact that, given my presence and my abundance of clean socks, there was a good chance that numpties walked among them). There was one about a woman doing the Milford Track for weight-loss purposes and she'd carried in litres upon litres of fresh milk. Why? She was on the 'Special K diet' (yes, that's an actual thing — replacing a meal a day with Special K cereal). She got pretty sick.

In another, a man and his son parted ways at Quintin Lodge, where the side track to Sutherland Falls breaks off and it's a couple of hours' walk to Dumpling Hut, on day three. The son walked on ahead while the father was last seen breaking the seal on a bottle of Drambuie there at the shelter. He failed to arrive at the hut that night so the trampers formed search parties and combed the area. With no sign or sound of him, eventually everyone went to bed in the small hours, only to wake in the morning and find him wrapped up in his sleeping bag on the track right outside the hut, snoring gently.

I've been back to do the Milford Track twice more. The second time, I met my now-friend David, whose partner Maria — as it turns out — was in one of the search parties for Mr Drambuie when she did the track years before! By the third time on the track, I was well used to the rigours of tramping and had become a talented numpty-spotter myself. People have asked me, 'Isn't it boring going back and doing the same track several times over?' Not so — each time it's vastly different; I've seen the valleys in full rain, waterfalls bursting from cracks in the mountains' sides, snow on the pass, and even in baking sun after an uncharacteristic Fiordland drought. On that trip, we swam every day, even in the icy springs that feed Lake Mintaro in the upper Clinton Valley, and dunked ourselves into streams that were only just still flowing despite weeks without rain.

Kāti Mamoe (or Ngāti Mamoe, though they didn't use that spelling themselves) is an iwi now largely consigned to history. Stemming from the Hastings/Heretaunga area, they moved to the South Island and battled with Ngāi Tahu and were assimilated into the tribe through marriage and conquest. Some Māori still identify with the tribe, or as Ngāi Tahu–Ngāti Mamoe as a sort of hybrid iwi — this included writer Keri Hulme, who lived at Ōkārito on the West Coast. It has long been thought that Kāti Mamoe, having fled into the dense and forbidding terrain of Fiordland, were the 'lost tribe' of Otago, living off the land, unaware of the ongoing march of civilisation.

In 1773, Captain Cook explored the outer western edges and various channels of Fiordland, including Dusky Sound (with its Useless Islands). In his work *A Voyage Towards the South Pole*, he gives accounts of meeting natives on Indian Island, observing that they were of the same race of people as other natives he had met, with the same language and same customs. Cook wrote: 'What could induce three or four families (for I believe there are not more) to separate themselves so far from the society of the rest of their fellow-creatures, it is not easy to guess. By our meeting with inhabitants in this place, it seems probable that there are people scattered all over this southern island . . . if one may judge from appearances and circumstances, few as they are, they live not in perfect amity, one family with another.'[6]

Later, Pākehā sealers and whalers encountered Māori in the sounds around the coasts; John Dawson, captain of the schooner *Samuel*, warned others by scratching the words 'beware of the natives plenty at Preservation [Inlet]' onto a piece of slate near there.[7] Further north on the Fiordland coast, the Wild Natives River was named after a supposed 'lost tribe' at Bligh Sound by explorers in the HMS *Acheron* under Captain Stokes in 1851. Stokes concluded these people belonged to a small, isolated, unknown tribe. Moreover, early sealers gave accounts of Māori without water transportation or boat landings, caves with smoking fires that had just been abandoned as explorers pulled up, and the ability of the 'natives' to 'quietly but effectually melt into the almost impenetrable bush'.[8] Kāti Mamoe were thought to be a cunning people, able to invoke the gods and call down fog and mist to conceal themselves when pursued — hence why they can never be found. Unexplored Fiordland is dripping with mystery and enchantment.

These historic sightings of Māori, ranging along the Fiordland coast from Bligh Sound in the north, around the coast to Dusky Sound and Preservation Inlet, and even along the south coast to Te Waewae Bay, may not seem curious by today's standards of distance — but considering the extreme and rugged nature of the country, the idea that they were wandering tribes seems impossible. Māori historian Canon Stack wrote: 'Having suffered so cruelly from Ngāi Tahu, the survivors of the persecuted tribe seem to be always in a state of flight, imagining that their ancient foes are still in pursuit. Though the country has of late years been well explored by "prospecting" parties without any people being found, it is just possible that a small remnant may still remain secreted in the recesses of that inaccessible region.'[9]

Footprints were often seen on wet sandy beaches in the Fiordland region, which only added to the mystery of the lost tribe. One account, sent to the *Auckland Star* by a writer known only as 'Skipper', told of a journey into the Glaisnock Valley, off the North Fiord of Lake Te Anau, in 1925 with an artist friend. Skipper had walked ahead and sat down to wait for his friend. Watching, he saw him stop, stare at the ground in front of him, and scan the bushes until he saw his companion.

'What a clever little lad you are to think to play Man Friday to my Robinson Crusoe,' he called out. 'But you spoiled the effect of the hoax by not keeping under cover.'

Skipper denied any hoax.

'Well, you'd better get your boot on, if you haven't done so already, and we shall get on with the trek.'

Skipper, mystified, walked over and asked to be enlightened as to the 'hoax'. His friend stood at the end of a small patch of wet sand, showing a perfect, clear imprint of a bare human foot. Each toe could be clearly seen, and it must have been fresh, as recent rain would otherwise have blurred it. Skipper took off his boot and sock and made a footprint alongside it, showing that the foot was longer than his own, perhaps by two sizes.

'As we gazed in silence at the two footprints before us in that square yard of wet sand, the bush seemed danker, the valley more gloomy; and (under the cloak of anonymity) I have no shame in confessing that I derived much wholesome comfort from the feel of the high velocity rifle slung across my shoulder,' Skipper wrote.[10]

A correspondent wrote to the *Press* in response to Skipper's story. 'J. F.' had repeatedly attempted excursions from 1912 to 1915 from Lake Hauroko towards Dusky Sound. The 1914 foray was moderately successful, the objective to reach Dusky Sound by an overland route through one of the vast bits of country marked 'Unexplored' on the maps. After a month the party gave up, admitting defeat to heavy bush, fearsome gullies and ravenous sandflies. J. F. deemed it to be unexplored, but had found a stone Māori axe at Lake Hauroko, and notes that it would be easy for people to pass each other within close proximity and not know of the other's presence.[11]

Then, in 1930, a human thigh bone was found lying just outside a small cave in the bush near the Lugar Burn, which discharges into the North Fiord of Lake Te Anau, the entrance of which is not far from Lone Island, where Quintin McKinnon's boat was found. The party of deerstalkers that found the thigh bone picked it up and examined it somewhat casually, and thought no more of it until they told of their experience on returning to Invercargill and learned of the previous tale of bare footprints in a place where nobody had been known to roam. The bone itself still had a quantity of tissue adhering to it — which made it seem unlikely that it belonged to McKinnon, given he had disappeared nearly 40 years earlier. Still, it showed that modern-day society still didn't know for certain the history of the area, aside from conclusive evidence that human feet had trodden on the terrain between the Lugar Burn and the Glaisnock River.[12]

In 1905, US President Theodore Roosevelt presented the New Zealand Government with 10 wapiti deer, which were released in George Sound. Five years later, 10 moose were introduced to Supper Cove in Dusky Sound in two separate releases. The species were considered to be well suited to Fiordland, and would be prized for the potential for hunting as they were in America, bringing tourists to New Zealand for the pleasure. Opinions ran the gamut, though; moose were dangerous, said some, while others thought it a pity to turn a wonderful national park over to moose and wapiti. Yet others thought the moose wouldn't survive in such difficult country, but it was argued they would be able to adapt.

By then, moose were considered to be well established in the untracked forest areas of the sounds, penetrating far inland from where they were originally released. Yet few were seen and even fewer were shot. Moose weren't allowed to be shot until 1923, to allow for populations to grow, but nobody managed to actually get a kill until 1929. Occasional sightings were reported until 1952, when the trail went cold. The Fiordland moose population was assumed to be exhausted.

In 2012, an elderly Northland man, Fred Stewardson, produced photographs he'd taken in 1953 of several moose and confessed to having kept quiet out of fear that enthusiastic hunters would swarm the area and kill them off. As a young man he'd been hunting in Wet Jacket Arm, north of Supper Cove, with an older mentor, Eddie Young, and when they'd come across the moose, Young warned him not to shoot but to take photos instead. 'Keep your mouth shut,' Young told Stewardson. 'Don't ever tell a soul. If you do, Fiordland will have loads of trigger-happy clowns there for slaughter. Many won't give a damn if moose survive or not.'[13]

After the story was published in the media, moose history author Ken Tustin received an anonymous phone call warning him it was a hoax. Stewardson was prone to exaggerating and writing himself into stories, the caller said. Tustin called Stewardson's ex-wife in Australia, who recalled the moose photographs were taken in Canada. Tustin had had reservations about the authenticity of the photographs due to the type of vegetation shown. By then Stewardson had passed away. It's thought he was indeed in Fiordland in 1952 when the last moose was shot, but he had never visited Wet Jacket Arm.[14]

Tustin has dedicated much of his life to tracking down the elusive Fiordland moose. Chances are they're still there — DNA testing confirmed the presence of moose hair in 2002 and cameras he's set up have produced a photo, albeit blurry, of one in the wild. Still, his wild-moose chase continues — although the last shooting and last confirmed sighting was in 1952 at Herrick Creek, one was seen from a helicopter in 2020 by a pilot who had spent two seasons as a hunting guide in Canada.[15] What keeps Tustin going is the idea that New Zealand's wilderness is so vast, rugged and amazing that you can hide a big animal for 60 years.

So much is hidden in Fiordland, and so much is forgotten.

The Milford Track has 57 known avalanche paths. When you're on the track, particularly walking up the Clinton Valley, it's hard to believe any snow could collect on the mountains that provide two fearsome walls on each side — the sheer cliffs wouldn't allow it to accumulate. It's impossible to see the sloping bowls at the top of the cliffs, which provide a catchment for snow, hidden from those far below on the valley floor, until its release is triggered. The snowpack is controlled by helicopter bombing, above both the track and the nearby Homer Tunnel, which has been known to get hammered by avalanches.

Winter trampers are warned to carry avalanche rescue equipment: the 'holy trinity' of shovel, beacon and probe (considered a trinity because they are useless unless you have all three). In the event of a burial, those not buried turn their beacons to 'search' mode to pick up the buried person's transceiver signal, track the signal as close as possible, then use the probe to ascertain how deep the body lies under the snow. The next step is to dig. Many people die from impact injuries from the avalanche. Those who don't only have a short time to survive before they suffocate in their snow coffin.

When you take avalanche rescue training (I did a five-day course one winter in Central Otago and it thoroughly gave me the willies), you're told that if there are multiple burials and one is buried deeper than the other, you need to dig for the shallower one first as the other one has less chance of survival. And if a body is buried deeper than 2 metres, chances are you won't get them out in time before they suffocate — unless you've got a large party of people available to dig, and dig fast.

There are avalanche probes at the huts on the Milford Track. I was fascinated by them the first time I did the track, well before I ever did any alpine climbing, ski touring or tramping in the snow. They're kept inside a long container, a white pipe similar to plastic plumbing joinery, and hung up outside the hut with 'AVALANCHE PROBE' in red blazoned down the side. Although I had no knowledge of avalanche rescue, it seemed to me that if one of those extremely long probes should be needed, the person's soul would have departed their body long before you even got the probe out of the container. I had images in my head of people probing deep debris for bodies, pointlessly. I wonder if they've ever been used.

Jessie Reid was trying to prove herself to her six female and four male tramping companions when it all went wrong.

Reid was that very rare breed of woman for the 1920s: educated (and single and working). She had studied at Otago Girls' High School, where she won a scholarship to attend the University of Otago. There, she received a pupil teachership and graduated with a BA. She taught at several high schools and held senior positions, returning to Otago Girls' before she disappeared. Reid was intending to travel to France the next year to further her French fluency. She was, said her family, self-reliant, energetic and hard-working, with a high sense of duty.[16]

Like so many others in Fiordland, she was never seen again, and still lies out there somewhere, bones disintegrating in the bush or in a bouldery mountain stream. But most of those who have disappeared have come to grief in the waters off the coast of Fiordland or in its swollen rivers and hungry lakes. Only a small handful of people have disappeared inside its belly, in its mountains and on its land.

It was January 1920, and Reid was tramping the Milford Track. On the first day there had been discussion about her lack of fitness, so on day two, leaving Pompolona Hut, she led the party and struck out on her own, to prove she was up for it. With two women lagging slightly behind her, she began climbing Mackinnon Pass and met a party coming the other way.

The pass was blanketed in snow, and more was falling. Mackinnon Pass is the crux of the walk; a zig-zag track leads up to a narrow bench, surrounded by precipices, the only way off being a tiny path squeezed between Mount Balloon on the eastern side and drop-offs on the western side. The Roaring Burn, also known as the Roaring Meg, tumbles down the northern valley relentlessly before reaching Quintin Lodge at the valley floor.

Put simply, there wasn't really anywhere for Reid to go.

Walkers watching from Pompolona Hut in the Clinton Valley saw her go around one side of a cairn at the top of the hill, as she'd been instructed to do; she was definitely taking the correct route and had reached the far end of the pass, past the worst of the snow. An experienced tramper and a leader in the Dunedin Scramblers' Club, Reid was at home in the mountains, including navigating on untracked terrain. But that day she was not dressed for climbing, clad in long skirts down to her ankles.[17]

Two women from a party that met her coming from the other direction about half a mile from the pass warned her of the snow on the

My tramping buddy Sian at the memorial on Mackinnon Pass on the Milford Track. Despite the roasting heat we experienced in the valleys, the pass was windswept and bone-chillingly cold. We didn't stay long.

saddle and later told newspapers that she seemed exhausted: 'She told us that she was determined not to be left behind on this occasion, as she had been on the previous day, by her party, so she had gone on ahead of those with whom she had started.'[18] Their own party had been lost for about an hour on the pass, they said.

With snow falling and the climbing becoming difficult, the two women turned back and met the rest of their own party only 10 minutes away, who hurried on to catch up with her. They couldn't, though, and failed to find any trace of her. Even her tracks in the snow had been obliterated by new snow and wind.

Searchers that night were out until 4 a.m., at times in waist-deep snow, which would have made the track look wider than it actually was, creating a risk of a tramper stepping on something that wasn't backed up by solid ground. Searchers hoped she had kept tramping and reached Milford Sound, but it seemed unlikely.

Although the search for Reid had already been going for 10 days, climber Samuel Turner showed up to take charge, speaking extensively to newspaper reporters about his efforts, to the point where it was known as 'the Turner search'. He assembled a small team of guides and policemen to explore the terrain exhaustively, including searching every possible ledge of the precipices on both sides of the pass in case a body had become stuck in a fall. The men combed the terrain along the bottom of the cliffs, while Turner climbed up the cliffs themselves, to the summit bench of the pass, traversing left and right along the faces. He spent four hours on the face of each precipice while the others scoured the pass.

Still no body. The only lead left was the largest tarn at the top of Mackinnon Pass, some 10 metres deep. All other tarns on the pass had been raked for a body. It was thought that Reid lay at the bottom of the tarn, as the snow may have disguised its existence, its top being a layer of ice. There was no way to rake or drag the tarn so Turner swam out to the deepest part and dove repeatedly from ledges, touching the bottom in places and finding no body. Only one place remained unclimbed by Turner, a precipitous face on the northern side of the pass. 'I would like to be in as good climbing condition as possible before attempting that, and have decided to do this on my return from Mount Tutoko [the ascent of which he deferred to participate in this search].'[19]

It was, of course, an excellent opportunity for Turner to gain some publicity for himself, and he wasted no time supplying an account of the search — with him as the hero — to the *Evening Star* for publication.[20] It oscillated between breathless language and self-reported heroics of the tricky situations he had been compelled to navigate in attempting to find Reid. He concluded, though, that she had likely not fallen off the pass but instead walked off the track near Roaring Meg Creek (Roaring Burn) and attempted to get down to the Quintin huts via the creek — unaware of the bluffy terrain that would prevent her progress. She would likely have tired of trying to navigate huge boulders covered in snow, perhaps slipped off one, and gone to sleep in the snow, spent.

Turner's separate report to police on his search efforts 'explode[d] an idea that had some currency — that the unfortunate lady acted in a headstrong fashion, and literally ran upon her fate'.[21] He surmised that Reid in fact acted quite reasonably when she went to cross the pass on her own, even in spite of her two female companions turning back. She wasn't headstrong, he said. Jessie Reid remains hidden, more than a century on now. Said newspapers: 'No clue was found, and it must be left to time and chance to solve the enigma, or to add it to the long list of unexpounded alpine tragedies.'[22]

Yet, sometimes, Fiordland gives up its treasures. In 1925 a wedding ring was found on the Milford Track and a notice was circulated in newspapers. The ring was inscribed 'John to Mary', which rang a bell with a Dunedin resident, who recognised the names as two visitors to New Zealand from Melbourne who, as part of their honeymoon trip, had walked the track 15 years previous, the wife losing her new ring. The Reverend John and Mrs Danglow of St Kilda, Melbourne, had married on 24 November 1909 — a date that was etched on the inside of the ring. The Reverend bought his wife another ring and she had given up all hope of ever seeing the original one again.[23]

One Easter a storm — billed as a 'weather bomb' — was due to sweep the country. Weather maps showed it might bypass Fiordland, of all places, and focus on bombing the upper South Island and most of the North. I had no companions but a topo map of the Hollyford Valley, a ticket

ABOVE | A three-wire bridge on the Hollyford Track. These tend to be wobbly and slippery. Don't stuff it up!

BELOW | Lake Alabaster Hut on the Hollyford Track. From here you can choose to womble pleasantly up the Hollyford Track or, for the masochistic, up the notoriously difficult and sandfly-ridden Pyke River (I chose the former!).

to ride the jet boat back from Martins Bay in five days' time, and newly waterproofed pants and jacket. The Hollyford Track is known to be one of the easiest multi-day tramps you can do. In all of its 56 kilometres it fails to crack 100 metres altitude except for a gentle gradient to ascend Little Homer Saddle at the grand height of 143 metres.

The first day was long but easy, flat walking. I skipped the first hut, Hidden Falls Hut, only stopping for lunch and some emergency blister repairs. Hidden Falls is so-named as it's just out of sight around a corner, shimmering white spray emerging from the tall rocks the first clue of its existence. The Hollyford River thunders past, clear, green and uncrossable, broken up before its entrance into Lake McKerrow by an island at the rivermouth with a hut at just 0.3 metres above sea level. Unsurprisingly, it often floods and inhabitants of the hut have found themselves stuck on the island. Meanwhile, Lake McKerrow is almost not a lake at all but merely an extensive widening of the river before it narrows again towards Martins Bay and dumps itself into the West Coast sea.

I overnighted at Lake Alabaster Hut with several other trampers who were heading in the other direction, or, intimidated by weather reports, were only in for the one night and returning to their cars. The hut is new — a replacement, as a hut has stood there for many decades — surrounded by rainforest, and close to the white stony shores of Lake Alabaster. I snapped many photos of the tiny rocks on the shore, each so different and yet so alike, so dark and often grey when examined individually but exuding a glorious light when taken as a whole, as a shore of the still lake.

The next day the promised rain arrived and I tramped solo, feeling wary, on the Demon Trail towards Demon Trail Hut. The track is less satanic than its name would lead you to believe, but I can see how many trampers, lulled into a false sense of security by the easiness of the early part of the track, might be shocked at the rockiness and ruggedness of the trail that snakes alongside Lake McKerrow.

I was alone at Demon Trail Hut and also the next night at Hokuri Hut, where I arrived to my own surprise at having conquered the Demon Trail without much fuss at all, and certainly without becoming possessed by any evil spirits. It was quiet, the only noise the birds singing with joy at the emerging sunshine.

Although it feels like a peaceful and appropriate place to be solitary, you can feel uneasy, lonely spirits in the northern part of Lake McKerrow.

Just after leaving Hokuri Hut, I crossed the tiny rivulets in the gravel fan at the base of Hōkurī Creek. The area is known to be deadly in a flood, and a trio of hunters disappeared there in 1974, presumed drowned, the only trace of them their packs, a rifle and footprints leading into the river. I stopped for a break on the shore, lathering myself in bug spray and looked around self-consciously. It felt like I was being watched.

Those three bodies, slipping away into the cold darkness of the lake, would never be recovered.

Lake McKerrow was reassigned its te reo name thanks to the Ngāi Tahu Settlement Claims Act 1998, allocating the equivalent to be tacked on: Whakatipu Waitai. Lake Alabaster regained its title, too: Wāwāhi Waka, not to be confused with Pigeon Island of the same name in Lake Wakatipu.

Lake McKerrow was named by explorer Patrick Caples after surveyor James McKerrow, whom he met before his foray into the Hollyford, becoming the first European to cross from Lake Wakatipu to the West Coast. (Caples, a cunning Irishman, was known for hiding from Māori — he was terrified of their presence, although they were in fact quite friendly in the area — and for eating rats to survive.) Lake Alabaster was named by Captain Daniel Alabaster after, well, himself.

Captain Alabaster arrived in New Zealand from England in 1854, plying his trade as a sailmaker, general merchant and, later, gold discoverer and explorer. He entered Lake McKerrow from the sea in 1863 on board the *Aquilla* and explored the interior as far as the mountains become glacial, making a foray up the Pyke and discovering the lake, which he named after himself. He also visited Milford Sound but couldn't get through the impossibly precipitous mountains. 'I nearly lost myself here,' he wrote in an account to the Survey Office. 'The precipices are dreadful.'[24]

> NOTICE.
> I hereby give notice that I WILL NOT be RESPONSIBLE for any debts contracted by my wife, Isabella Alabaster, on and after this day.
> D. ALABASTER.
> 12th January, 1876.
> *Grey River Argus*, 13 January 1876[25]

I made it to Martins Bay Hut, at the end of the track, on day four before backtracking to the lake for a jet-boat ride the next day back to the Pyke River confluence near Lake Alabaster. Martins Bay is a trip; a long sandy spit is unreachable from the hut, as it is across a deep channel dispensing Lake McKerrow into the rough sea.

I had plenty of time to spare at the hut and walked around the tip of the coast at Long Reef as far as I dared; the waves crashing in at high tide threatened to capture me and sweep me away. I pondered a future trip up the Pyke River to Big Bay, a track known to be mud-ridden and demanding, and contemplated what sort of buildings would be attached to the rough coastline, as two structures were indicated at the southern end of Big Bay on the topo map. North of here there isn't much, just craggy hills and the occasional hut or airstrip, seldom visited, much of it unexplored.

A lot of terrain for Fiordland to keep its secrets hidden.

> CHARGE OF FAILING TO SUPPORT A WIFE.
> Daniel Alabastor [*sic*], at present residing in Christchurch, was charged with failing to contribute towards the support of his wife Isabella, living in Wellington. A communication was received from the husband, stating that he had been compelled to leave his wife owing to her adulterous conduct; and the case was postponed for a week to enable the police to institute enquiries regarding the woman's character.
> *Evening Post*, 10 May 1881[26]

> WIFE DESERTION.
> Daniel Alabastor [*sic*] was charged on remand with having deserted his wife Isabella, and left her without adequate support. The police had made enquiries concerning the woman's character, the result of which was anything but favourable to her, as it appeared she was a dissolute woman, her husband having been compelled to leave her on account of her drunken habits and immorality. The Magistrate therefore held that she was not entitled to the order she sought.
> *Evening Post*, 17 May 1881[27]

> ... Isabella Alabaster v. Daniel Alabaster — a case of assault. It
> appears that through a difference of opinion the parties have
> been living apart for some time; that on the 17th instant they
> met in Greymouth, and that the defendant then assaulted her,
> and threatened to do so again. . . . Daniel Alabaster said that he
> came to town [and] found his wife sitting in the Full and Plenty
> Hotel with a dozen other persons. He asked her what she was
> doing there, and she replied 'that was her business.' He then
> tried to drag her out, but failed, and this was the assault. . . . She
> offered to withdraw the case that morning if he allowed her to
> take her clothes. — Charles Crocker deposed that he had known
> both parties for 14 years, and that the husband had always
> treated her well. — The Magistrate stated that he would fine the
> defendant . . . the children to be returned to the husband.
> *Grey River Argus*, 25 January 1876[28]

Captain Alabaster divorced Isabella in 1891 and went on to marry Jane Elizabeth Fish the next year,[29] while Isabella went on to marry John Halloa in 1884, a marriage that turned out to be bigamous. They seemed well suited: in 1893 Halloa got drunk and used 'disgusting language' in front of a large group of children in public and was sentenced to six months in jail with hard labour.[30]

Jane Fish mourned Alabaster's death in 1920, aged 82, after a colourful career that included charges of trading without a licence on a goldfield and several further instances of assault unrelated to his first wife.[31] He was widely credited with having discovered the Stewart Island oyster beds, as well as discovering gold in the Hollyford several years before the West Coast gold rush began.[32] The children he had had with Isabella were with him when he died.

Captain Alabaster was a passenger on board the schooner *Star* in 1856 when he saved the lives of everyone on board. The ship ran into bad weather and was in peril. Alabaster, due to his knowledge of the coastline, was placed in command, and managed to navigate the vessel into Waikawa Harbour — saving the ship and her lives. The ship carried James

Macandrew, the Superintendent of Otago, who was on board to make an official visit to Invercargill. In 1892, Alabaster was awarded 5 acres of land for his timely deed.

Macandrew also had a colourful history, including doing a spell in gaol (but managing to serve his time from his residence, Carisbrook House, by arguing there was no proper place in gaol for debtors; a full investigation was held into his affairs after he was accused of misappropriating public funds). To his credit, he backed Scottish immigrant Learmonth White Dalrymple's campaign to establish Otago Girls' High School, being a staunch believer in women's education. But as an older Pākehā male with a healthy ego, Macandrew wanted to be remembered in name for his efforts at bringing Scottish settlers to New Zealand. Macandrew township was established in Southland and many street names in the area bear his name.[33] But what he really wanted was to push further into the wilds of Fiordland — namely, into the Hollyford.

Martins Bay on the west coast was already accessible by boat and Macandrew reckoned boats could continue further inland into Lake McKerrow. Supply boats could call regularly, he believed, right up to a curve on the north-eastern side of the lake that boasted a pebbly shore and plenty of flat land ripe for farming. The soil was of finest quality, deep and rich, and the land suitable for timber, with an inexhaustible water source from the lake. The bush wasn't difficult to clear, with little heavy undergrowth. To early visitors the climate felt semi-tropical in spite of the surrounding mountains and glaciers that indicate the cold temperatures it would be subjected to in the depths of winter.[34]

Macandrew's promotion of the area led to the Otago provincial government establishing a settlement on the lake in 1870. It would be named after him: Jamestown. An early map shows two rows of sections running around the curve of the lake — one row prime lakefront property, the back row second class. It had all the makings of a Fiordland paradise for immigrants.

The going was tough — too tough. Steamer *Charles Edward* was the first boat to attempt to access Jamestown, in March 1870, and struck a snag in the river. The settlers on board were safe but their cargo, while saved, was damaged.[35] Just a few months later, in July, the *Esther Ann* also came to grief, with the settlers on board losing most of their possessions, including a sawmill that was desperately needed to build their new homes.[36] Supply boats became wary of several perilous rocks in the mouth of the Hollyford River and would only go so far as dumping goods on the beach to be retrieved. The land was cleared for farming but proved unfruitful. Residents suffered and starved aside from the occasional bird or fish they caught. It was isolated and lonely, apart from the ravenous sandflies, whose mosquito cousins took over the night shift when they went to bed.

The New Zealand Railway Commission had at one point proposed to run a railway line from the mouth of the Greenstone River on Lake Wakatipu to the head of Lake McKerrow, where water transport would connect the route with Martins Bay.[37] Roads were considered, but eventually access from the Hollyford to Queenstown became just a track.

Just three years in, Jamestown's challenges were obvious. Visitor Warden Beetham wrote that the settlement was already languishing: 'The inhabitants, while they one and all spoke in the highest terms of the spot which they had chosen as their home, appeared to be in a depressed state . . . Not only have the settlers been unable to obtain regular supplies, but they have actually been reduced to the very brink of starvation . . . [T]hey look upon themselves as deserted and uncared for . . .'[38]

New settlers were disinclined to take a chance on moving to Jamestown due to the irregularity of contact with the outside world; a newcomer might have to wait six months to be picked up again. Still, Beetham concluded that given the advantages of the whole district, he predicted the settlement — if given attention — would become thickly populated and valuable.

The difficulties of Jamestown and Martins Bay and the early settlers are chronicled in the 1947 book *Pioneers of Martins Bay: The Story of New Zealand's Most Remote Settlement*, by Alice McKenzie, who lived in the area, and whose family attempted to settle at Jamestown.[39] Aged 29, she married Peter Mackenzie, and she is often credited on her works as Mrs Peter Mackenzie. She also wrote poetry — including one about the search for the missing Jessie Reid on the Milford Track.

Ten years since the first settlers arrived, Macandrew's namesake town was largely deserted, the inhabitants giving up in the face of so many hardships. Now all that remains is a plaque to mark the spot where the residents tried in vain, some items made unidentifiable by rust and entropy, and a few surviving apple trees and rose bushes.

Those who tramp the Hollyford Track, including the Demon Trail, are
rewarded with a dramatic coastline upon reaching Martins Bay.

Advocates of women's rights might learn a lesson by visiting the Bay. The daughters of the settlers may be seen fishing, shooting, and pulling their boats or canoes; and, although they are adepts at each and all of these accomplishments, the sight of girls with arms bared, seated at their oars, is scarcely one to give pleasure to the beholder.
Government representative visiting Jamestown, Warden Beetham, *Grey River Argus*, 7 January 1873[40]

Although it was Easter and the sandflies were as hungry as they'd been in the 1870s, I bared my arms (doused with strong Bushman's bug spray) as I sat on the beach at Jamestown, contemplating the peace of the environment and the naive failure of the settlement. The water was glass, the only sound an occasional bird communication. I was heartened that women could now bare their arms without judgement. So much of our backcountry history contains prescribed boundaries for women, usually dictating what they must or can't wear, how they must behave, what is constructed as 'normal'. I wonder if things would have turned out differently for Freda had she lived today, in an environment where she could bare arms, eschew the skirt and openly live as a lesbian.

Freda got a head start, for sure. The influence of her aunt, composer and musician Emmeline Woolley, is clear. Freda was a feminist because of her aunt — they both experienced women's suffrage in Australia at the same time, although they were nearly 40 years apart in age. Emmeline was a lesbian with a lifelong partner (Edith Pedley), while Freda was likely beginning to recognise that in herself, although she didn't go to any lengths to conceal her sexuality. Emmeline also bequeathed money to Freda as the sole beneficiary in her will, meaning Freda inherited enough money to be financially independent and thus able to travel to New Zealand and climb. Certainly, climbing in the early 1900s was a wealthy European person's game.

We still have constructions of what constitutes normal in the mountaineering world today, but I believe they're less overt. A female mountaineer should be thin, lithe and probably tanned. No complaints or bodily issues or excess fleshiness anywhere. One of the boys, but still appropriately feminine. No obvious make-up (I've frequently heard it described by male climbers as 'slap') but, equally, somehow mysteriously never in need of any. Strong enough to carry her own gear and the rope but gratefully accepting masculine help when offered. And never, ever letting the side down by openly expressing an inclination towards any sort of feminism.

Climbing, mountaineering, ski touring — the alpine world is still an 'othered' experience for women. All-women courses exist, with overly enthusiastic (yet sometimes patronising) names: 'Chicks With Picks', 'She's on Skis' — there's even an outing called 'She's STILL on Skis'. The names seem to come with invisible encouraging exclamation marks, as if to cement our surprise that she is out there, doing what men do, or that she is *still* doing it.

Nobody raises their eyebrows at men in the wilderness.

Mount Aspiring

Trust your instincts

MOUNT ASPIRING dominates the area around its footprint, not only visually but also as something of a rite of passage for climbers. At 3033 metres, it's our country's twenty-third-highest mountain, but it's New Zealand's highest mountain outside of the Aoraki/Mount Cook region, where the really 'serious' peaks live. Māori called it Tititea, meaning 'wedge of glittering white', 'shiny and steep white mountain peak', or 'glistening peak', after its distinctive sharp icy summit. The name 'Aspiring' was first mentioned by John Turnbull Thomson, Otago's chief surveyor, in a diary entry in 1857: 'At the head of Hawea, dist. about 40 miles, is a very lofty peak which I called Mt Aspiring.'[1] Thomson inserted a word between 'lofty' and 'peak' that is illegible in his original manuscript. Historians have settled on 'snowclad' but to me it looks rather like 'arrogant'. Other names for features in the national park are equally alluring: Stargazer, Moonraker, Cloudmaker; and sometimes, unappealing: Mount Awful, Mount Dreadful, Lucifer, The Wart.

I find the word 'aspiring' sounds like it's ascending rapidly in a spiral, at first covering great breadth and then finishing, clipped off, in the ending: /ŋ/. I was aspiring to climb Aspiring but, as ever, was intimidated by the unknown, and by historical death. It wasn't just Mount Aspiring that was laced with death and danger but the entire national park, prompting headlines such as 'Why are so many people dying in Mount Aspiring National Park?' and 'Climber grabbed at grass tufts before falling 100 metres to her death at Mt Aspiring National Park'.[2] The area includes Cascade Saddle and Rabbit Pass/Waterfall Face, both routinely attempted by tourists, both with their own objective dangers.

I had some experience of the area when I headed back as a strategically homeless person. I'd done the Routeburn Track, scenic but more or less unremarkable, except for its more recent history involving a Czech couple who were missing for more than a month before someone in their home country noticed their absence and raised the alarm. The man died on an exposed section of track in deep snow, while the woman, after abandoning his body, holed up for a month in the warden's quarters at Lake Mackenzie Hut until she was rescued. I found this scenario somehow implausible; the hut sits at 900 metres elevation and the vast majority of the benched, well-groomed track to get out to the road at The Divide is beneath the bushline. There would be some snow, sure, but the woman had told stories of how she'd attempted to fashion snow shoes to make it out.

I suppose I am unkind — in the face of surviving a trauma and having to abandon her partner's body in the deep snow, she was likely not coping and simply stayed put until someone came to her rescue. Still, wonderous media reported her being 'trapped in a remote South Island hut'[3] — which is a far cry from being traumatised and unwilling to move from the snug, well-stocked warden's quarters of a Great Walks palace. It did, however, remind me that just as media misunderstand the objective danger because they simply don't know what it's like, I might also read too much into media reports of risks and hazards at places I'm not familiar with.

Beyond the Routeburn Track, I had previously tackled the nearby Rees–Dart tramp when I first started doing solo missions. It seemed more rugged, more backcountry, to me, but in reality it's fairly mainstream and tame: up the Rees, over the Rees Saddle into Snowy Creek (a steady climb, then a 100-metre grunt up to the saddle at the end), down into the Dart Valley and out, crossing many side creeks on the way. Most of the creeks were no big deal to hop across, but one, Rough Creek, was known to flood somewhat in heavy rain. Worried, I nevertheless marched on solo, figuring I'd assess it when I got there and make a call. I found a couple of people had waited for me to make sure I got across safely, for which I was thankful; the creek's flow was strong and the woman's hand to help me across was reassuringly grippy.

Rivers are my thing, when tramping. Some people get excited about birds or plants, some people love reaching summit peaks or walking along the tops. For me, I'm happiest when thigh-deep in clear flowing water, the more blue-green the better. Most trampers don't like getting wet feet but for me it's no hardship; once your feet are wet it means there's no excuse not to get into the river again — your feet aren't getting any drier! In one episode I've never lived down, I convinced a couple of friends to come tramp into Waipakihi Hut in the Kaimanawa Range with me, initially via the Umukarikari tops but using the Waipakihi River as a route on the way out. I told them there would be 'a couple of river crossings' — meaning that there was no track, we'd just be following the river. I thought they'd figure that out for themselves by looking at the topo map, but it seemed they just trusted me blindly, and were astounded and not that pleased to discover that much of the river involved waist-deep wading. At least it was beautiful — clear, emerald-green water — and a hot summer's day.

I got the willies about rivers eventually, though. I hadn't had too many bad experiences (aside from the creek I got stuck in in the Kaimanawa Range, and a challenging solo crossing of the Waiau River on my St Arnaud to Hanmer Springs trip). But I became overconfident and too familiar with rivers, and forgot about the inherent dangers they all contain, especially when angered.

It rained on our first day of a trip in Kahurangi National Park. With plans to link up the Leslie–Karamea track with the eastern part of the Wangapeka track for a five-day trip, we made it to Salisbury Lodge under the mantle of thunder and lightning. It cleared, but day two gave us more rainy grief. In glorious hindsight we should've sat tight at Splugeons Rock Shelter, but the rain on day two simply didn't seem that bad, and we weren't crossing any big rivers, only side creeks. But side creeks can be evil, too.

It's a classic heuristic trap: get-home-itis. Or get-to-the-hut-itis. I call it 'hut lust' — it strikes when the hut is only a short way away and the alternative is camping out in the rain next to a swollen waterway, or trudging all the way back to the previous hut. The proximity to the hut, the day's destination, makes it seem like the risk is worth it.

I was with two mates, Paul and Julia, who were extremely experienced. That's another trap: 'expert halo', people more experienced than you. You'll often not speak up if you're the least experienced, because who are you to talk? And sometimes you'll automatically assign expert status to someone for one activity simply because they're competent at another one entirely. A sort of experience transfer.

We'd managed to cross one side creek, Meyer Stream, linking up for a bit of extra force and might. The next, Wilkinson Creek, seemed to have a smaller catchment area but it was running high and the water wasn't clear. We linked up and got in. I was acutely aware of the raging torrent of the Leslie River right there — and there was nothing to catch anyone who might get swept off their feet and towards the main waterway. It was hugely swollen, and angry.

'Get under me!' Julia yelled. I was frozen with fear. I didn't know what she meant and I couldn't hear, couldn't yell, couldn't move. I couldn't get words out fast enough. I felt her slipping, and stupidly, I let go (for which she later berated me, and rightly so). I slipped next, my feet being tugged out from underneath me by the insistent water. So many little droplets, but so much collaborative power. Slippery rocks put up no protest.

No time to scream or yell, all of my mental bandwidth went towards putting up the fight of my life. Shit! This is how it's going to end. No way, I thought. I'm not going down without a fight. The river, right there. *Right there.*

I fought with everything I had, arms flailing, legs pumping. I managed to roll my body over twice as I was being washed towards the river. My legs and knees bashed on rocks. A thought flashed across my mind: that bodies of river-crossing victims must be seriously smashed up. I grabbed at branches on the other bank and they slipped through my hands, but the constant friction was slowing me down. After four or five failed attempts, I caught one fast and pulled my body towards the bank. I stood up immediately, demon-driven to get out of the water and to safety before anything else could grab at me.

The creek's bank was as high as my armpits and I had a soaked multi-day pack weighing me down, but adrenaline helped to finish the job — I managed to haul myself up and onto the bank. I was wet, frozen and shaking with cold and fear. I'd ripped off multiple fingernails, torn skin everywhere and my knees and shins already had raised red bumps that would become purple-green bruises and hurt when I walked.

Later, Paul told me he thought I was a goner. He managed to grab Julia and both of them had recovered by the time I pulled myself out. We were on opposite sides of the creek, but with their combined experience and

The Matukituki River, West Branch, Mount Aspiring National Park (above), and the Waipakihi River, Kaimanawa Forest Park (below). Rivers on a hot day are my favourite tramping place to be.

steady feet they made it across without any further dramas.

I dried myself, my clothes and the contents of my soaked pack at Karamea Bend Hut that afternoon as we watched the Leslie River steadily drop and become far less threatening. I didn't want to go to bed that night, afraid of the whole episode replaying in my head while I slept — and it did.

The nightmares went on for a long time after that. I count it as one of a small handful of actual near-death experiences I've had. I still feel my heart rate rise when I think about the Leslie River and I won't argue if I never see it again.

There exist plenty of river-crossing deaths in the history of New Zealand waterways, and the Leslie River and nearby Karamea River are no different. As Karamea River discharges itself into the ocean at Karamea township on the West Coast, its history of claiming lives is bulkier than most. Historical newspaper records are littered with accounts of bodies being found (in one instance, a 13-year-old girl who had been sent to fetch mail on a horse; in another, parents who had to watch their child get swept away), all penned in colourful language that would be considered beyond the pale today.

The area, along with most stretches of the West Coast from Westport to Fox, generated great excitement at the prospect of gold in the rivers. In 1869 a rich, gold-bearing quartz reef was discovered at the Wangapeka River, and the Karamea and Leslie rivers were no strangers to the phenomenon also. Excellent specimens being produced from the Wangapeka prompted a land grab of 130 acres: 'Great expectations are formed.'[4]

It was thought that every gully and stream feeding the Leslie River carried good gold and the river would pay prospectors well. But access was difficult. A pack track ended where the Leslie met the Karamea — where Karamea Bend Hut now sits — and from there diggers had to haul their swag and make their way as best as they could. Much of the area was believed to contain gold, but it was only available to true explorers who were willing to tramp in with all their gear.[5]

It was a poor man's field, albeit one with luck readily available to those who made the effort. In January 1944, a young 20-year-old tramper from Canterbury, Stanley Williams, reaped a different sort of luck when he bumped into solitary gold fossicker Septimus J. Robinson in the Leslie

River valley. Williams had by then been lost for two days, wombling around with sunburn and extreme fatigue, and had he not met Robinson he likely would've perished. Robinson shared the last of his food with Williams — just a morsel of bread — and redirected him to the Mount Arthur Tableland, where he was met by a party of searchers from his tramping club. Williams collapsed upon meeting them but soon recovered.[6]

Although Mount Aspiring was named for its loftiness (or perhaps its arrogance), I noted that the etymology of 'aspiring' as an adjective comes from breathing, from the Latin 'aspirare': to breathe upon, blow upon, to breathe. The meaning hinges on striving for something, seeking eagerly to achieve or attain something, or to long to reach something. It means wanting to be something you currently aren't.

Social-media voyeurism is wrapped up in aspiration: we lust after images of people's lives we aspire to have, other people's lithe bodies, their lifestyles, their possessions. We view other people's lives through Instagram squares of curated, constructed half-truths, and we want those constructions to be *our* everyday lives. But nobody's real life looks like their selected presentation on Instagram. After all, everybody farts in the bath.

I looked further into the origins of 'aspiring'. One entry said the notion is of 'panting with desire' or 'perhaps of rising smoke'. Aspire, desire, panting. You know what they say: where there's smoke, there's certainly fire.

I aspired to be tougher, to tramp harder, to climb 'real' things (it felt like Ruapehu wasn't a real thing; it wasn't a South Island summit), to be more robust and always on the go. I constructed an image inside my head of what I should be like, as unrealistic as aspiring to someone else's curated life on Instagram, and always failed to achieve it. I knew that I usually set goals for myself that I had a reasonable chance of achieving, rather than stretch to goals I might not attain.

My construction of my life via social media generally had people thinking I never stopped — that I was indefatigable. After a rare post about having a bad day, one friend commented: 'So you are human,

Aspiring Hut sits on the true left of the Matukituki River West Branch, just a couple of hours' walk up the valley, and gives access to Cascade Saddle and alpine huts further into the valley.

then.' Another was thoroughly surprised to learn that I quite enjoyed the occasional lazy day wrapped up in a duvet on the couch.

I had developed a fascination with red alpine huts. They seemed to signify a level up in the sort of tramping experience or fitness you might require to make it to one. Generally speaking, frontcountry (i.e. popular) and Great Walk huts tend to be beige corrugated material, and backcountry huts (harder to get to) were in the famous DoC Rescue Orange. Beige for beginners, orange for more experienced trampers, while red seemed to me to represent huts for climbers.

There are two red huts up the Matukituki Valley, in Mount Aspiring National Park: Liverpool and French Ridge. The latter is often used for access to and from climbing Mount Aspiring itself. With a full pack carrying four days' worth of food and gear, I set off to Aspiring Hut, which is the first port of call in the Matukituki, just a couple of hours' flat walk up the valley, with the intention of bagging both red alpine huts either as overnights or day trips.

I failed. Overwhelmed by lack of confidence, and somehow cowed by the fear of the unknown, I once again talked myself out of even trying. And that was one of my major hurdles to achieving bigger goals: not actually attempting them in the first place. It wasn't as if I tried to get there and found it too difficult, or I got pipped by a swollen river or got injured. I simply failed to even try. Instead, I chickened out and spent two days at Aspiring Hut, doing a short walk up the valley to Pearl Flat, and wondering what was wrong with me.

Samuel Turner had no issues with confidence, I realised, as I worked my way through his book *Conquest of the New Zealand Alps*, my hut and camp reading material. His self-confidence fairly oozes from the pages as he narrates his dashing and dangerous exploits.

In March 1913, he led three men to do the first climb of the North West Ridge route of Mount Aspiring. Harold Hodgkinson, Jack Murrell and George Robertson were three rank amateurs who'd never been on ice and snow before but considered this no barrier. Turner got wind of their plans and wired to ask if they wanted him as their party leader and

French Ridge Hut (above) and Liverpool Hut (below) are alluring red alpine huts, a level up from the tramping I'd previously done. I initially failed to make it to either hut.

step-cutter. The idea of leading a party, notably without a guide or porter, was a drawcard, and although the three men had been warned in a letter from a guide at the Hermitage not to let Turner take leadership of their party, this only seemed to encourage them.

Turner taught the three men the basics of ice-axe work and step-cutting for their assault on what he considered to be 'one of the most inaccessible mountains in New Zealand'.[7] They battled persistent heavy rain, crevasses, avalanches, storms, and went without sleep for 70 hours to claim the summit, with Turner remarking it was the wettest climb he'd ever done. Descending from the summit and above the buttress they were benighted and had to sit tight in an emergency bivouac for the night, sheltering among rocks.

Turner believed that the 'east face' of Mount Aspiring was one of the most magnificent precipices in New Zealand, writing: 'The first climb and probably the last of Mount Aspiring east precipices was finished.'[8] His narrative, to me, is hugely puffed up and the objective dangers of the route are exaggerated. In fact, his supposed 'east precipices' were actually the now well-trodden North West Ridge — not east at all — which is the easiest and most popular route on the mountain.

'You know, Hazel,' a friend said to me one day when I described my crisis of confidence, 'what you need to do is simply conduct yourself with all the confidence of a middle-aged white guy.'

Conquering fears

Finding home

AT ONE POINT I thought I'd found a home, and a life partner. But sometimes life pulls the rug out from underneath you in the cruellest ways.

There's a bump of a hill on Acheron Road, a backcountry road that runs past Molesworth Station, between Hanmer Springs in the south and Seddon in the north. A track runs up the hill from Isolated Saddle and gains just over 200 metres in height to reach the summit. It's called Mount Augarde, named after 25-year-old Ivanhoe Stanley Augarde, whose privacy was spectacularly violated in February 1868.

Augarde discovered his betrayal by Charlie the German (last name unknown), who opened a love letter from Augarde to his girlfriend, Kate (Catherine) Gee. They'd been dating for a few years and Augarde desperately wanted to marry her, but she was having second thoughts, so Augarde — known to be a passionate man — wrote her a letter describing his ardent feelings and (stupidly) entrusted Charlie to deliver it to her. But Charlie opened it, read it, and then ensured it was circulated around the campfires up and down the Acheron. By the time the letter got to Gee, it was dirty and crumpled, their relationship defiled by the acts of a spiteful third person.

Augarde confronted Charlie, beat him up, then rode to the Rainbow area, grabbed a rifle and returned to the camp. He shot Charlie in the back below his right shoulder. The bullet came out below his heart, inflicted — said the jury in the inquest later — 'wilfully and deliberately'.[1] After killing Charlie, Augarde rode back to the Rainbow and turned the gun on himself.

The jury in the inquest returned the verdict: 'That the deceased, Ivanhoe Augarde, met his death by committing premeditated suicide, by blowing out his brains with a rifle.'[2]

Two days after having my own life upended, I put in an offer to buy a property in Ohakune. I suppose sometimes encountering a traumatic life speed bump can prompt you to finally act on something you've long dreamed about.

My property (my new home!) was appropriately Hazel-sized, one bedroom downstairs with a mezzanine floor upstairs, which I would turn into a library, thus fulfilling two long-held dreams: to own property in Ohakune and to have my own library. I figured it could also double as a wine and whisky loft when friends came to stay. I named my place the Wild Snowflake, which was sort of how I felt about myself now — a product of the winter wild, drifting around, finally settling. It was home.

Four days after moving in, I went on five weeks' leave for the summer break. I packed the car and headed to the South Island on the Cook Strait ferry for a tramping bender. It was just like the old days, only I carried a bit more baggage with me and a pressing need to heal my mind and soul. I dubbed it the 'chicken trip' — ticking off all the objectives I'd chickened out of in the past, and there was a decent laundry list of those to think about.

Empty stretches of time, marked by quietness and space, became confronting where they had once been comforting. Everything washed around inside my head, without end. I took to listening to podcasts while I drove or tramped, to have other voices to distract me and to keep me company, even though I'd been used to being on my own. After a long stretch of never having solitude, the aloneness was alienating.

My first foray into nature for a chicken objective was a failure. I attempted to get up to East Hawdon Bivouac in Arthur's Pass National Park but turned back due to elevated stream levels. At a tricky bit in the river, I could figure out three or four different ways to navigate the watercourse, but each had the same consequence if I stuffed it up: getting smashed against a huge boulder, at pace, while probably being held down by the pulsing water.

I wasn't particularly bothered by the failure of my mini-expedition, but I spent a large part of that day walking down river valleys with tears streaming down my face behind my sunglasses. I was determined not to try to get revenge and instead forgive everything immediately and just move on, but that came with its own price tag.

When in doubt, tramp it out.

Sefton Bivouac in Aoraki/Mount Cook National Park was originally just a large rock perched on a spur at 1660 metres, above the Mueller Glacier and below the Tewaewae Glacier, that offered shelter to climbers aiming for nearby Mount Sefton (3151 metres) and The Footstool (2764 metres). In 1917, Hermitage chief guide Peter Graham pioneered the building of a small hut at the rock biv site, to make climbing nearby peaks easier. It was a 1000-metre climb just to get to the bivvy site and at least a further 1000 metres to reach any peak of note from there, so the hut was pivotal for climbing success. It was made of corrugated iron with a dirt floor and slept three people. It was just big enough to stand up in — if you weren't too tall. Today the hut still stands, weathering the beatings of time and the environment, occasionally receiving a birthday brush-up thanks to various grants and volunteer work.

During my time at Aoraki/Mount Cook I'd stared at it often and wondered if I could make it up there. On the topo map it looked tricky — the contour lines are close together and there's no marked track as such, not even a route, just a couple of cairns and a rough ground trail that's essential to locate early on in order to successfully pick your way through the surrounding bluffs. I did some research and found the DoC website to be quietly discouraging: 'The route to Sefton Biv is unmarked. Route finding and moving through steep terrain (with high consequence of falls) are required to reach the biv.'[3] Other blogs and intel indicated a requirement to navigate bluffs and other places where a fall would be fatal.

Indeed. Brett Gracie, a 29-year-old climber from Dunedin, was ascending to Sefton Bivouac in June 1994 when he slipped on hard snow, about halfway up, and fell 100 metres. He died at the scene from his injuries. Another climber, 39-year-old Richard 'Bert' Willemse, came to the same end in January 2001 while descending from Sefton Biv, falling 100 metres over a bluff to his death. He had turned to talk to a friend and lost his footing on slippery grass and snow. He wasn't able to stop his fall. At that point, the terrain that was considered to be the worst of the descent was over.

Just months earlier, in September 2000, solo climber Douglas Bryant left

Aoraki/Mount Cook Village intending to climb Mount Sefton via Sefton Biv in one day. Park guides at the visitor centre advised him against it due to weather and adverse conditions, and his mother even called the Department of Conservation office asking for them to stop him. Of course, they couldn't grant the request — DoC has no authority to prevent people from entering the national park. Bryant disappeared, and his body has never been found.

Media stories about death came up high in the results when I searched for information about the route to Sefton Biv and it gave me the wobbles. While there wasn't much snow or ice around at that time, conditions were sub-zero overnight and I anticipated frozen scree or that the trail might be covered in frost and verglas, a thin coating of ice. It could be deathly. And so I never went. I never tried, no matter what the conditions were — I just looked up at the spot where the biv was perched, contemplated it, didn't go, then berated myself for not trying. Too chicken.

But now it was December, warm conditions, and I wanted to at least put on my boots and head in that direction in the name of giving it a nudge. I was staying with a mate, Simon, who'd been up there multiple times and reckoned I'd be fine; he almost seemed amused at the idea of me being too scared to go ('I never figured you to be one who fears anything in the outdoors'). My confidence was shot to pieces after the recent betrayal in my personal life. Maybe doing something a bit risky would help to get it back.

I tried getting up to the biv the day after I arrived at Aoraki/Mount Cook Village but the wind was gusting down the Hooker Valley and I was haunted by visions of being blown off the ridge. As it was, I got blown off the boardwalk on the way back, so I chalked it up as a sensible decision.

The next day delivered what the forecast had predicted: no wind and clear skies, at least in the morning. I calculated I'd need to be on the track by 7 a.m., reach the biv by 11 a.m. at the latest, and be well off the higher parts of the mountain by midday. Storming up the hard-packed touristy Hooker Track, I made the turnoff to Stocking Stream within 40 minutes. From there it's not signposted or marked, and in places it's easy to lose the trail. Which I did, blazing a creative track of my own up the lower parts of the Stocking Stream. I knew I had to ascend on the true right of the stream until a large cairn indicated where a more defined ground trail began. Smaller cairns marked the way, but in bright sunshine and dry conditions it was easy to follow.

I'd asked Sophie, from the Auckland Uni Tramping Club, about the track to the biv after running into her (again) in Arthur's Pass on my way south.

'It's totally doable,' she said. 'It's nowhere near as tricky and steep as it seems when you're looking at it on the approach.'

Her encouragement spurred me on. I knew I'd encounter more vertical sections, requiring scrambling up with hands as well as feet, walking poles dangling from my wrists by their straps, redundant on steep and technical terrain. After several hard sections, I began to worry about the descent; a sharp ridge just before the biv also gave me pause, as I elected to scramble on it rather than walking on the snow slope nearby (I was wary of crevasses — needlessly, it turned out, as it's just seasonal snow, not perennial).

After more than 900 metres of ascent, I popped over the end of the ridge and the biv was in sight, waving out to me in that bright, cheery orange shade, having been recently painted. I snapped endless photos, visited the rock bivouac behind the hut (slightly creepy) and availed myself of the thunderbox — the open-air toilet with a steel cover to stop the kea from destroying the toilet seat. Facing straight up to Mount Sefton and The Footstool, it was a loo with a view.

Sitting in the doorway of the hut staring down to the Mueller Glacier lake — where, not many years previous, the glacier itself had filled that space, right up to the old Hermitage, now the tourist car park — I had a come-to-Jesus moment. I'd recently lived through the worst period of my life. Sure, good things had happened, at least theoretically good: I'd scored a top job, paid off my Auckland mortgage, found a life partner, albeit it fleetingly. But those things hadn't made me happy. Happiness comes from peace (or at least an absence of conflict), a cadence of regular achievement, and living in harmony and balance with everything (and everyone) around you. This had all been thrown off course. I felt broken. My confidence was eroded — or perhaps, the top of it had been knocked off, much like Aoraki/Mount Cook itself in the 1991 rock avalanche.[4] But climbing to Sefton Biv, finally conquering something that had embedded itself in my core, wrapped in fear, loosened some of the old Hazel. Confidence was trickling back in.

I messaged Simon that I'd made the biv and was descending so he'd know my progress: 'Made biv — holy phuck,' I wrote. 'Had snacks, took pics, heading back down now.'

I finally made it up to Sefton Bivouac in Aoraki/Mount Cook National Park after years of thinking about it but not doing it. The view from the tiny hut is surely one of the best in New Zealand — but you wouldn't want to sleepwalk while staying the night.

Phil's caution to me so long ago on Ruapehu rang in my ears as I gingerly downclimbed the steep sections: 'Don't drop your guard on the way down.' A local guide at Aoraki/Mount Cook Village was apparently famous for saying 'It'll be alright . . . if you don't fuck it up', and that also went around in my head as I demanded absolute attention for every step, every foot placement, every handhold. After an hour I was more or less home free, on less deadly terrain, and I dropped my pack to soak my feet in the arctic waters of Stocking Stream.

I'd noticed the old-new Hooker Hut on my ascent, nestled on a terrace below the moraine wall of the Mueller Glacier lake but out of sight of passing tourists on the Hooker Track. Built in 1910, the oldest hut in the Aoraki/Mount Cook National Park, it was removed in 2015 from its perch above the collapsing moraine wall of the dying Hooker Glacier to save it from slipping into the glacier itself. It was the hut's fourth move but access had become almost entirely cut off due to erosion, and as a result it saw only a handful of hardy, determined visitors each year. In spite of the storm around it, it just kept hanging on.

The hut had rumours of being haunted. Peter Graham outlined some experiences of the resident ghost in the book about fellow guide Mick Bowie, *The Hermitage Years*.[5] Graham was known for telling his ghost story around the fire of an evening. Mountain guide Jane Morris told of her encounter with the ghost in 2009.[6] Some say it's the ghost of Darby Thomson, who guided Freda du Faur on her subsequent traverse of Aoraki/Mount Cook along with Peter Graham, and also climbed with Samuel Turner (in 1913, Turner named a peak after himself, north of Ball Pass in Aoraki/Mount Cook).

Anyway, Thomson died in an avalanche on the Linda Glacier in 1914 but his body initially wasn't found. In 1923 the first remnants began to emerge on the surface of the glacier: a skull, a hand, and a knife with a chain attached. Later, a further piece of his body was recovered, and a monument to lost climbers was erected near the Mueller moraine, close to the old Hermitage. Items kept turning up as late as 1939. It's not uncommon for bodies to emerge from glaciers in pieces — they don't always pop out whole.

The ghost could equally be that of Wellington tramper James Butcher, who died at Hooker Hut in 1949 after slipping over a steep rock bluff and rolling into the bed of a creek.[7] He suffered head injuries and lost consciousness after arriving at the hut. Atrocious weather hampered the rescue efforts, as mountain streams turned into torrents. At the inquest, the coroner concluded that Butcher had met his death as a result of his decision to make his own way down the bluff, carrying his pack, rather than waiting for the rest of his party. It was thought that the weight of his pack caused him to overbalance at the edge of the bluff. (Now, everyone carries their own pack, even if you're guided.)

Coming down from Sefton Biv, I was relieved to be off the bluffy terrain. The Hooker Hut came into view as I strode through tussock and pushed past scrub. The intention was to restore it, and that day it boasted a brand-new deck, while the rest of it was to be preserved as much as possible. Old warning signs still hung inside; would climbers please take out all their rubbish, and you might like to consider boiling the water, thank you very much.

Rather than retracing my steps to the Stocking Stream, I decided to continue on the terrace and make a beeline for the Hooker Track, figuring I'd cut some time off. It turned out to be a bad choice. I was in too deep, with scrub taller than me, and couldn't see how to go back or forward. I made small goals: get to that rock, or that clear patch just over there. I came to a massive boulder, at least one and a half times my own height, and the only way forward was to try to belay myself down the side of it using scrub to grab on to as I lowered myself. It sort of worked — towards the end I lost control and fell into a bush that clutched me and didn't want to let go. Spiders were everywhere, their webs stretched between any and every available branch. I could feel them on my neck, tickling my arms, down my gaiters.

I became worried. I'd already fallen several times and what if I whacked my head on something and passed out? Simon had my intentions details and knew I'd gone to Hooker Hut but he didn't know about my ridiculous scrub-bashing mission, and if I didn't turn up he'd have no idea I'd gone off on a tangent. I messaged, just in case, feeling terribly embarrassed: 'Scrub-bashing back from the Hooker Hut, a bad life decision. If you don't hear from me in an hour it's gone very wrong. I'm actually really close to the track but it's all above my head. I'm close though.' It took a lot to admit I'd put myself in a stupid situation. Still, I wanted backup — to know that if I did have an accident, he'd know where to point the LandSAR team to retrieve me, my body half eaten by hungry spiders.

My fears were unfounded. I figured out a technique of throwing myself on the upper parts of the branches on a piece of terrain that sloped rapidly downhill. It seemed to work — I bounced from one bush to the next without falling down towards the roots and getting stuck. Then I hit tussock! Easy, beautiful tussock, a saviour. A few minutes later I looked up and saw a tourist striding past me, tanned legs pumping, appropriately reflective designer sunglasses framing her face, and a perfumed air wafting in her wake. I was sweaty, stinking and scratched all over, and coming out in hives from my allergies reacting to the grasses and scrub.

But I'd made it. Conquered a fear. Got my confidence back.

And confidence is a funny thing.

The so-called confidence gap in the workplace and in learning environments is well documented. Women, overqualified and over-prepared, apparently fail to 'lean in', while men, underqualified and underprepared, simply assume that success is a given and everything is there for the taking. Or so they say. I find that narrative a little too simplistic and it places blame and obligation on women, but it's often true. Transpose that to the world of outdoor adventure and you see much the same paradigm. But women stand to rapidly gain confidence when they engage in challenging outdoor pursuits.[8]

My friend Tessa, who is a bad-ass climber of the highest order, had suffered an accident when a rock fell onto her head while climbing. She was ascending the Ōtira Face in Arthur's Pass and a climber above her pulled some rocks free — most of them bypassed her completely, but one of them came straight for her and smashed her helmet into pieces. She hadn't been on a rope either, as the terrain was suitable for soloing (i.e. climbing unroped without a belay). Fully aware that had one of the bigger rocks hit her or had she not been able to hold on, she would have taken a potentially fatal fall, the incident thoroughly knocked her confidence. So when I mentioned mine had come back, she enquired why — and how.

When I really got to thinking about it, I realised my confidence had become eroded from being treated as less-than. Less than competent, less than capable, less than strong. Not to knock the efforts of a well-meaning

Getting some confidence back on Ball Pass, a trip I thought might be out of my reach. In the background is the Tasman Glacier, where I'd been ski touring the winter before, and Hochstetter Dome (2810 metres), my first Aoraki/Mount Cook National Park summit.

climbing or tramping partner, but men tend to want to help a woman. They see a woman struggling, perhaps not able to carry as heavy a load, or perhaps a little slower going up the hills. Maybe she's smaller, so she struggles a bit going downhill if it involves high steps — always harder on shorter legs. This tendency to help is done out of affection, and it's an admirable thing, and usually quite welcome. But left to its own devices, left unchecked, it can make you feel like you're always *in need* of help, that you couldn't do it on your own. And I'd gotten to that point.

Too much time adventuring with other people — too much time adventuring with your partner — and not enough time battling solo can lead to a gradual erosion of confidence. Before you know it, you feel like you can't do it on your own anymore. (Maybe what you need at that point is a solid hour of bush-bashing through leatherwood while being cloaked in spiders.)

'I guess going on adventures solo makes me feel like I am actually capable and competent under my own steam,' I wrote to Tessa. 'No fault of any of the guys, but when I did stuff with them I would end up feeling slightly less capable. Like, they would carry some of my stuff, or they would be the one to carry the cooker. I can't put my finger on it, but through the mechanism of guys "helping" me, I felt like I wasn't quite able to do it without them. And I think eventually, you begin to take on that attitude towards yourself, too.'

At the head of Lake Tekapo is Godley River, a wide, braided river fed by several glaciers, including the Godley Glacier. It's just over 500 metres' ascent from the lake at the base of the glacier to Sealy Pass, which gives access to the rugged terrain of Westland — down Scone Creek and out Perth River. Sealy Pass provides a stark contrast between bare, rocky riverbeds on the eastern side, and closed-in, steep bushy creeks on the western side.

Godley Hut stands near the outlet of the glacier's lake. Its hut book contains the last entry by Wellington tramper/climber David Cooke, who was on a lengthy alpine traverse in 1989. At that point Cooke was tramping from the Godley over Sealy Pass to Westland. In 2001, two climbers on the Neish Glacier — adjacent to Sealy Pass — found human remains, along with an ice axe. The axe had a set of initials engraved on the handle, which confirmed the remains probably belonged to Cooke. Besides, only one person had ever been known to go missing in the Sealy Pass area. Extensive aerial and ground searching was carried out in February 1989 when he went missing — so it's likely he fell down a crevasse and was carried along, encased in the ice, until the summer of 2001, when the glacier gave him back.[9]

Then, five years later, climbers found further remains on Sealy Pass in the moraine wall on the Godley Glacier — the same general area, but a different glacier entirely. Police at the time said it wasn't uncommon for parts of bodies to come to light years apart — that water often broke up the skeletons of climbers and washed them into different parts of the park.[10]

I'd initially noticed David Cooke's name after seeing his plaque on the memorial at Aoraki/Mount Cook Village, which reads: 'For solitude is sometimes the best society.' At the very least, within solitude there is honesty. There's no risk of betrayal; you can't be disloyal to yourself.

Knocking off Sefton Biv gave me the boost I needed to attack other things I'd been too scared to try. Many were so tame as to not be worth thinking about. Pakituhi Hut was one — a new, small hut on the Te Araroa track just out of Lake Hāwea. I'd read it was steep, exposed, scrambly and demanding. And it was, but I felt in condition for it and equal to its demands. I made the 900-metre climb in three hours and had the hut to myself for the night, chatting to mountain runners and other trampers who breezed through that afternoon. One of them was a young woman drinking elaborate craft beers while she skipped along the track from the hut further along (a 4WD track — much more suited for drunken skipping than the Pakituhi section).

A few things hit me emotionally while sitting in the quiet at the hut, but it helped to know that I could sit tight totally in my solitude and experience the feelings washing over me without the world ending. Eventually the feelings passed, or perhaps I just got bored of them being the same feelings going round and round without ever evolving. It doesn't matter how much you think about a situation, what's done is done and can't be changed.

I got ambitious and went straight from the Pakituhi Hut trip to the Wilkin–Young, a trip I'd wanted to do for more than a decade since hearing that it was even better than the Rees–Dart, while on the Rees–Dart. I was intimidated, sure; the track demands you cross the expansive and swift-flowing Makarora River at least twice, or otherwise get a jet boat, while the Gillespie Pass section is a solid 1000-metre ascent and descent while carrying a full pack. After the ascents of Sefton Biv and Pakituhi Hut, I felt physically up to it. The weather had been baking hot — a teenager had succumbed to heatstroke on the way up to Lake Crucible the day before — so to avoid the worst of the day's blazing sun I departed from Siberia Hut for the pass at quarter to six in the morning.

I made it to Young Hut by 1.30 p.m., and the walk out the next day was equally quick. The only lingering question was if I'd be able to cross the mighty Makarora. Deep, fast and unforgiving, it was known for consuming bodies and I'd been warned against even trying to cross it, particularly solo. But others at Siberia Hut had reported crossing it, and Danielle, the jet-boat driver, on my way in reckoned it was flowing low and well crossable. I thought I'd go have a look, maybe hop in and check the flow, and if it was dodgy I could always back out and walk the extra couple of kilometres to Blue Pools where there was a bridge.

The river level wasn't even enough to get my knickers wet. Before I knew it, I was in the middle of the river at its deepest so I just kept going. The low, slow flow ran cold but not gaspingly so, and it was a warm enough day that I dumped my pack on the other side, stripped down to my merino undies and had a topless dip, cooling off before the blazing road-bash back to my car at Makarora.

I took off to the West Coast for a couple of rest days, then came back and bagged Brewster Hut on the way through — another chicken objective. Three to four hours to the hut, said the DoC sign, but I made the 900-metre ascent in two and a half. After that I ducked into the West Matukituki Valley and finally made it up to overnight at Liverpool Hut then French Ridge Hut, both climbs that require serious '4WD tramping' — using your arms as well as your legs to haul yourself up things and swing down again like a monkey on the way out. I read lots of track info about how steep, slippery and dangerous they were, but tried not to let it get into my head

Happy on the Gillespie Pass circuit, Mount Aspiring National Park, on the tops between Siberia country and the Young River. Carrying a heavy pack, but definitely leaving some baggage behind.

too much and push the new-found confidence out. I reminded myself that such warnings are really meant for those who tramp in sneakers and carry backpacks with wheels that are meant for pushing through airports, not lugging up hills.

I rounded out the trip by climbing Avalanche Peak, where Samuel Edgar Russell had perished in 1933, unnoticed by his companions, likely suffocated under snow while the rest of the party sat in the train carriage on their way home. Avalanche Peak sounded imposing to me but in reality it's little more than a tourist route. I left intentions with a friend, not bothering to get track information from DoC, and elected to ascend Avalanche Peak Track and descend the nearby Scotts Track, which was easier and of a gentler gradient, according to online intel.

Bug-eyed trampers exclaimed over my choice of track as we conversed on the way down; they'd been roundly warned at the visitor centre not to use the Avalanche Peak Track but to ascend and descend via Scotts. They were much the same, I informed groups of hikers. Maybe slightly steeper on the Avalanche Peak Track, but no big deal — just a bit of robust tramping requiring the use of your arms to hold on to things occasionally. Once again, I'd knocked off a tramp that had intimidated me simply because of what I'd been told — just as these walkers had. It was time to make this new-found confidence an everyday thing, not an outlier in my life.

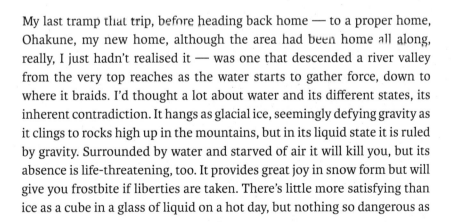

My last tramp that trip, before heading back home — to a proper home, Ohakune, my new home, although the area had been home all along, really, I just hadn't realised it — was one that descended a river valley from the very top reaches as the water starts to gather force, down to where it braids. I'd thought a lot about water and its different states, its inherent contradiction. It hangs as glacial ice, seemingly defying gravity as it clings to rocks high up in the mountains, but in its liquid state it is ruled by gravity. Surrounded by water and starved of air it will kill you, but its absence is life-threatening, too. It provides great joy in snow form but will give you frostbite if liberties are taken. There's little more satisfying than ice as a cube in a glass of liquid on a hot day, but nothing so dangerous as the same substance when slick and with a consequential piece of terrain below it. I felt great affinity with water in all its forms but also fearful respect. This tramp, I felt peace.

When you tramp down a river valley, the river in its steepest reaches crashes incessantly over boulders and around rocks. And as you make your way down the valley, the river changes; it burbles and bubbles and gurgles, making a new and noisy distraction of its own. But gradually the river valley widens into flats and the watercourse braids, splitting itself into smaller sections, and it self-quietens. And as the sound of the water fades, as that fearsome liquid thunder is dispersed into tiny harmless droplets, you realise you are bathed in now-glorious silence. And you can hear the sound of your own two feet, cracking twigs and thudding on rocks. And finally, you know where you're going.

NOTES

Preface

1   I'm not the only one to hold a low opinion of Samuel Turner. The high regard in which he held himself is perhaps best illustrated in climber Jane Thomson's poem 'The Ballad of Sam Turner', held in the Westland National Park archives and published in the *New Zealand Alpine Journal*, vol. 31, 1978, p. 50.

Ruapehu

1   'Climber's death / Fall into crater / Tragedy on Mount Ruapehu', *Otago Daily Times*, 21 May 1936.

2   'Fall into crater lake / Ruapehu tragedy / Fatal slide on frozen cliff', *Evening Star*, 21 May 1936.

3   'Gallant attempts / Rescue unsuccessful', *Stratford Evening Post*, 23 May 1936.

4   'Death of solicitor', *Evening Post*, 21 May 1936, p. 11.

5   'Body recovered from crater lake / Hazardous task accomplished', *Northern Advocate*, 22 May 1936.

6   'Mount Ruapehu tragedy / Death in Crater Lake', *The Press*, 18 June 1936.

7   I recognise that the commonly held belief that Te Heuheu gifted the peak is a narrative that is contested.

8   'Ruapehu victim / Young climber killed / Fall over ice cliff', *New Zealand Herald*, 20 May 1933.

9   'Death on Ruapehu', *Patea Mail*, 22 May 1933, p. 4.

10 Frances Ferguson, 'Auckland man builds snow cave to escape the big smoke', Stuff, 29 August 2016, https:// www.stuff.co.nz/oddstuff/83515176/ auckland-man-builds-snow-cave-to- escape-the-big-smoke (accessed 25 January 2021).

11 Debbie Jamieson, 'Would-be climber alarmed hired crampons fell apart', Stuff, 11 December 2013, http://www. stuff.co.nz/national/9501281/Would- be-climber-alarmed-hired-crampons- fell-apart (accessed 7 February 2021).

12 Originally written up in 'Smashing stereotypes', *Wilderness* magazine, July 2016, https://www. wildernessmag.co.nz/smashing- stereotypes (accessed 7 February 2021).

Aoraki/Mount Cook

1   Freda du Faur, *The Conquest of Mount Cook and Other Climbs: An Account of Four Seasons' Mountaineering on the Southern Alps of New Zealand*, George Allen & Unwin, London, 1915, reprint published by Capper Press, Christchurch, 1977, p. 28.

2   *The Conquest of Mount Cook and Other Climbs*, p. 29.

3   Before the Husky Flat washouts from 2019 onwards, the Ball Hut route was extremely easy and almost entirely flat. Recent erosion has made the trip a much more adventurous affair. The trip described here was undertaken prior to the washouts, when the track went straight across the flat, which has since washed down into the Tasman Glacier lake and disappeared entirely, leaving something of a chasm. The route is now constantly changing.

4   More can be found on the Three Johns Hut tragedy at https://www.wanganuitrampingclub.net/history/ ('Tragedy Strikes: Four Friends Killed').

5   'Tasman Glacier tragedy / New theory advanced / Lightning the cause of death / Mr G. E. Mannering's article', *Otago Daily Times*, 10 July 1930.

6   'Died of exposure', *Auckland Star*, 23 January 1930.

7   Ibid.

8   G. E. Mannering, A.C., 'The Disaster on the Tasman Glacier', *New Zealand Alpine Journal*, June 1930, pp. 119–29.

9   'Blomfield's heroic devotion', *Evening Star*, 22 January 1930.

10 Rob Brown, 'A History of De la Beche Hut', *New Zealand Alpine Journal*, 2011, pp. 102–5.

11 'Blomfield's heroic devotion', *Evening Star*, 22 January 1930.

12 Writer and climber Rob Brown gives an excellent account of the tragedy and the hut's background in the 2011 issue of the New Zealand Alpine Club's journal. Rob Brown, 'A History of De la Beche Hut', *New Zealand Alpine Journal*, 2011, pp. 102–5.

13 Older topographic maps can be accessed via www.mapspast.org.nz. (Users are warned that this pastime can be addictive and affect productivity.)

14 The story of Beverly McClure is told in more detail in Carl Walrond's *Survive! Remarkable Tales from the New Zealand Outdoors*, David Bateman Ltd, Auckland, 2015.

15 When I say 'cute', it's unfortunately very Instagrammable.

16 'Sefton Bivouac to be restored', *Timaru Herald*, 21 May 1998.

17 Emma Bailey, '"Panicky" novice wanted to quit climb', *The Press*, 21 February 2014.

18 'Juvenile alpinists / Climb of 9050 feet', *The Press*, 1 February 1928.

19 Paul Hersey, *High Misadventure: New Zealand Mountaineering Tragedies and Survival Stories*, New Holland, Auckland, 2009.

20 *The Conquest of Mount Cook and Other Climbs*, p. 36.

21 Climbing photos from the time show puttees, also known as gaiters, as long strips of fabric wound around the legs from the boots or shoes upwards to prevent debris and snow from getting in.

22 *The Conquest of Mount Cook and Other Climbs*, p. 37.

23 Janet McCallum, 'Barnicoat, Constance Alice', Dictionary of New Zealand Biography, first published in 1996, Te Ara — the Encyclopedia of New Zealand, https://teara.govt.nz/en/biographies/3b10/barnicoat-constance-alice (accessed 2 February 2019).

24 'Miss Barnicoat's experiences', *Ashburton Guardian*, 26 December 1907.

25 Bee Dawson, *Lady Travellers: The Tourists of Early New Zealand*, Penguin, Auckland, 2001, p. 197.

26 A delicious-sounding word that gives me tingles, 'Schreckhorn' is German for 'peak of terror'.

27 'A lady mountaineer / Notable achievement', *New Zealand Herald*, 14 March 1911.

28 'Evelyn Oxenham's death on Mount Egmont', *The Dominion*, 28 January 1913.

29 *Wairarapa Daily Times*, 3 July 1903.

30 'Lady alpine climbers', *Colonist*, 19 October 1910.

31 Both Haldane sisters were well known on and around Taranaki for their abilities. Their father Andrew Haldane once spent a night at Kahui Hut on Taranaki together with Samuel Turner in 1923 during the search for the Reverend William Murray. As he held forth at great length about his own exploits, Haldane drifted off to sleep. Several times, Turner, noticing Haldane was dozing off, poked him with his feet from the top bunk. The third time it happened, Haldane grabbed Turner's feet and smacked them onto the edge of the bunk to emphasise he had had more than enough. (Described in A. B. Scanlan, *Egmont: The Story of a Mountain*, A. H. & A. W. Reed, Wellington, 1961, pp. 93–94.)

32 *New Zealand Alpine Journal*, vol. 53, 2001, p. 113.

33 G. Langton, 'A History of Mountain Climbing in New Zealand to 1953', unpublished PhD thesis, University of Canterbury, Christchurch, 1996, p. 267. Cited in Karen M. Morin, Robyn Longhurst and Lynda Johnston, '(Troubling) spaces of mountains and men: New Zealand's Mount Cook and Hermitage Lodge', *Social & Cultural Geography*, vol. 2, no. 2, 2001, n. 12, p. 136.

34 Rosamund Harper gives a thorough account of the climb in 'Three girls on a peak', *Otago Daily Times*, 22 December 1934, p. 12.

35 'A guideless climb', *Evening Post*, 14 December 1934, p. 15.

36 *New Zealand Alpine Journal*, vol. 48, 1995, p. 91.

37 Betsy's obituary is provided in the *New Zealand Alpine Journal*, vol. 53, 2001, p. 113.

38 *New Zealand Alpine Journal*, vol. 48, 1995, p. 92. Blunden's climbing partner was almost certainly the same John Pascoe who became a famous photographer and author, as well as chief archivist for the National Archives (now Archives New Zealand Te Rua Mahara o te Kāwanatanga). Pascoe conquered more than 100 peaks, 23 previously unclimbed.

39 The two male climbers are named second in newspaper reports such as 'Mountaineering feat / Ascent of Mount Oates', *New Zealand Herald*, 14 March 1931, p. 12; they are not named at all in a photo caption in *The Press*, 17 February 1931, p. 11.

40 Anna Keeling, 'Women of New Zealand Guiding', *New Zealand Alpine Journal*, 2011, pp. 106–9.

41 John Haynes, 'History & science / Christmas Day 1894: A centennial perspective on the first ascent of Mount Cook', *New Zealand Alpine Journal*, 1994, pp. 87–90.

42 Initial newspaper narrative of the 1913 discovery appears in 'Under the ice: An interesting discovery after eighteen years', *Hastings Standard*, 17 March 1913, p. 3. Guy Mannering's article 'Lost in the ice', *The Press*, 29 July 1939, p. 19, was penned in response to an article by Frank Illingworth, 'Glaciers give up their victims', *The Press*, 1 July 1939, p. 21.

43 *The Conquest of Mount Cook and Other Climbs*, p. 36.

44 *The Conquest of Mount Cook and Other Climbs*, p. 19.

45 https://nzhistory.govt.nz/women-together/women-climbing

46 Lydia Bradey and Laurence Fearnley, *Going Up Is Easy*, Penguin, Auckland, 2016, pp. 49–50.

47 Sam Newton, *Issues faced by alpine clubs in the modern era*, 2015, https://www.communitymatters.govt.nz/assets/WCMT-FRR-PDF/2015-WCMF-Report-Samuel-Newton.pdf (a New Zealand Winston Churchill Memorial Fellowship report, submitted July 2016).

48 Anna Cottrell, 'Climb every mountain', *New Zealand Listener*, vol. 226, no. 3681, 27 November 2010, pp. 31–33.

49 'Her property / Spinster's suicide', *The Sun* (Sydney), 24 September 1935, p. 9.

50 *The Conquest of Mount Cook and Other Climbs*, p. 37.

Kaweka and Kaimanawa ranges

1 https://www.doc.govt.nz/parks-and-recreation/places-to-go/hawkes-bay/places/kaweka-forest-park/things-to-do/tracks/kaweka-road-tramping-tracks/

2 Recommended reading for those interested in the wilding pine problem is Dave Hansford's article 'Wilding Pines', *New Zealand Geographic*, issue 102, 2010, https://www.nzgeo.com/stories/wilding-pines/.

3 'Shelter trees / Dense planting needed', *New Zealand Herald*, 7 April 1934.

4 'Trees to resist salt-storms', *Manawatu Herald*, 5 July 1900.

5 A. Cunningham and Q. Roberts, *A provenance trial of Pinus contorta at 4,800 ft in the Kaweka Range (Assessment after seven years)*, Protection Forestry Branch Report No. 67, Forest & Range Experiment Station, Napier, Forest Research Institute, November 1969.

6 N. J. Ledgard and J. T. Miller, 'Growing trees in the high country', *Tussock Grasslands and Mountain Lands Institute Review*, no. 39, December 1980, pp. 33–40.

7 *Extreme Pine Control*, Bush Telly TV, TVNZ6/Department of Conservation, 2010, https://www.youtube.com/watch?v=cnqrd9CyNOw.

8 Dave Hansford, 'Wilding Pines', *New Zealand Geographic*, issue 102, 2010, https://www.nzgeo.com/stories/wilding-pines/.

9 I recognise that this is feral behaviour.

10 Simon Shepherd, 'Rosemary Ives' mum labels guilty hunters "cowards"', Newshub, 17 May 2011.

11 For the purposes of completeness, I note here that the 'hunters' later protested the claim they did nothing to help, saying they called police and a helicopter, found a nurse at a campsite and sent her to help with a first-aid kit, and went to meet police and direct them to the site. Full details can be found in 'We did everything to get help — hunters', *Nelson Mail*, 21 May 2011.

12 'A lighthearted suicide', *South Canterbury Times*, 22 April 1889.

13 'Answers to correspondents', *Daily Telegraph*, 29 July 1886.

14 'Destructive floods in the North Island', *Clutha Leader*, 8 December 1893.

15 Marty Sharpe, 'Hunter says he "should have died three or four times" in remarkable tale of survival', Stuff, 12 October 2018, https://www.stuff.co.nz/life-style/107797389/hunter-says-he-should-have-died-three-or-four-times-in-remarkable-tale-of-survival.

16 Described in the miscellanea of the *Wellington Independent*, 24 February 1863.

17 'The gold exploring party', *Hawke's Bay Herald*, 18 April 1863.

18 'Discovery of gold in the Kaimanawa Ranges', *Wellington Independent*, 2 October 1869.

19 'Latest from Napier', *New Zealand Herald*, 6 October 1869.

20 'Dr. Hector at Kaimanawa', *Hawke's Bay Herald*, 31 December 1869.

21 'Gold near Hastings / Discovery in river / Grains found in Ngaruroro', *Stratford Evening Post*, 6 August 1932.

22 'Pilots prosecuted for illegal wildlife zone landings', *New Zealand Herald*, 13 December 2012.

23 Gordon Cessford (ed.), *The state of wilderness in New Zealand*, Department of Conservation, Wellington, 2001, https://www.doc.govt.nz/Documents/science-and-technical/Wilderness.pdf.

24 Kaweka Forest Park Management Plan, p. 47; quoted in 'Kaimanawa — Heart of the North Island', 4 September 2017, https://wilderlife.nz/2017/09/kaimanawa-heart-of-the-north-island/.

Taranaki

1 'Dominion telegrams / The record skipper', *Taranaki Herald*, 21 March 1911, p. 7.

2 'A skipping record', *Evening Post*, 15 February 1922, p. 8.

3 In Turner's book *The Conquest of the New Zealand Alps*, T. Fisher Unwin, London, 1922, he gives little credit to Graham and Fyfe for this achievement.

4 'Conquering the impossible in mountaineering', *Sunday Times* (NSW), 28 November 1920, p. 18.

5 'Local and general', *Horowhenua Chronicle*, 26 February 1912, p. 2.

6 *The Conquest of the New Zealand Alps*, T. Fisher Unwin, London, 1922, p. 283.

7 Embarrassingly for Turner, history has proven him wrong on several fronts.

8 *The Conquest of the New Zealand Alps*, p. 7.

9 Letter to the editor, 'Mountain climbing', *Taranaki Daily News*, 12 September 1916, p. 6.

10 If you write a book about yourself, are you by definition an egotist? Asking for a friend.

11 *The Conquest of the New Zealand Alps*, pp. 181–82.

12 The same Mr Cowling who had been a hermit on Ruapehu for 10 years, although he is named as both Alfred and Arthur.

13 *The Conquest of the New Zealand Alps*, p. 182.

14 The word 'conquest' in his book title gives me feelings of rage towards him; it sounds sexual to

me, and the resulting image in my head of the moustachioed, nuggety egotist naked is deeply disgusting.

15   Samuel Turner, *My Climbing Adventures in Four Continents*, T. Fisher Unwin, London, 1911, p. 253.

16   Conrad Kain, 'Long Ago on Mount Cook', *American Alpine Journal*, vol. 1, no. 4, 1932, pp. 490–96.

17   *The Conquest of the New Zealand Alps*, p. 280.

18   *My Climbing Adventures in Four Continents*, p. 256.

19   *The Conquest of the New Zealand Alps*, p. 6.

20   As a small gesture of apology to the abuse Mr Seymour's name endured during this time, I voted on behalf of my father for ACT in the 2020 general election.

21   *The Sun* (Sydney), 18 April 1915, p. 16, https://trove.nla.gov.au/newspaper/article/229313844?searchTerm=freda%20du%20faur&searchLimits=.

22   Royal Geographical Society, The Alpine Club, *Mountaineers: Great Tales of Bravery and Conquest*, Dorling Kindersley, London, 2015, 'The Golden Age of Alpinism – "An Easy Day for a Lady"', p. 158.

23   Nikki Macdonald, 'Too high, too late, two dead', Stuff, October 2017, https://interactives.stuff.co.nz/2017/10/too-high-too-late-two-dead/.

24   Discussed in point 173 in the coroner's report, dated in the report as 13 November 2013 but likely intended to be dated as 13 November 2014, given the hearing dates were 6–9 October 2014, https://www.zoneblue.nz/files/Findings-of-Coroner-Devonport-in-the-matter-an-inquest-into-the-death-of-Nicole-SUTTON-and-Hiroki-OGAWA.pdf.

25   Helen Harvey, 'Climber dies in rescuers' arms', *Taranaki Daily News*, 29 October 2013, http://www.stuff.co.nz/taranaki-daily-news/news/9335455/Climber-dies-in-rescuers-arms.

26   'Mount Egmont mystery cleared up / W. H. Southwood's body found / First fatal accident', *Taranaki Herald*, 8 February 1892, p. 2.

27   'Mount Egmont mystery cleared up / W. H. Southwood's body found / First fatal accident', *Taranaki Herald*, 8 February 1892. p. 2.

28   'Deceased Egmont tourist / The body found', *Patea Mail*, 15 February 1892, p. 2.

29   'Lost on the mountain / No word of the Rev. Mr Murray', *Hawera & Normanby Star*, 2 February 1923, p. 10.

30   'Lost on the mountain / No word of the Rev. Mr Murray', *Hawera & Normanby Star*, 2 February 1923, p. 10.

31   'Lost on the mountain / No word of the Rev. Mr Murray', *Hawera & Normanby Star*, 2 February 1923, p. 10.

32   'Rev. W. Murray / Some notable exploits', *Manawatu Standard*, 24 February 1923, p. 10.

33   'The Rev. W. Murray / Some notable exploits', *Patea Mail*, 14 February 1923, p. 6.

34   'Lost on Mount Egmont / Mr Murray still undiscovered', *Feilding Star*, 3 February 1923, p. 2.

35 'The Rev. W. Murray / Some notable exploits', *Patea Mail*, 14 February 1923, p. 6.

36 'Rev William Murray / Search on the mountain', *Stratford Evening Post*, 6 February 1923, p. 3.

37 Detailed in multiple news articles, including 'Gruesome find / Human bones in river / Mountain tragedy recalled', *Waikato Independent*, 20 May 1924, p. 2. Some dispute that these remains were Murray, but nobody else had been known to go missing in the area, particularly anywhere near the Stony River, and no remains were ever discovered since, so it seems plausible that it was him. There's a full and interesting account in A. B. Scanlan, *Egmont: The Story of a Mountain*, A. H. & A. W. Reed, Wellington, 1961.

38 'Mount Egmont coach service', *Hawera & Normanby Star*, 19 December 1904, p. 2.

39 'Taranaki', *Wellington Independent*, 15 March 1848, p. 3.

40 'Taranaki', *Wellington Independent*, 15 March 1848, p. 3.

41 See 'The Naming of Taranaki', https://taranaki.iwi.nz/our-history/the-naming-of-taranaki/ (accessed 25 June 2020).

42 Another purported name is Pukehaupapa, meaning 'ice hill'. See Deena Coster, 'History reveals Taranaki's peak was once known by a different name', *Taranaki Daily News*, 1 April 2016, https://www.stuff.co.nz/taranaki-daily-news/news/78445421/history-reveals-taranakis-peak-was-once-known-by-a-different-name.

43 I will never do this again.

44 'Three skeletons / A Mount Egmont discovery / No clue to identity', *Evening Post*, 8 February 1923, p. 8.

45 'Mountain skeletons / Who lost the theodolite? on old Egmont in '96', *Stratford Evening Post*, 14 February 1923, p. 5.

46 'Mountain skeletons / Tale of three surveyors', *Hawera & Normanby Star*, 14 February 1923, p. 5.

47 'Skeleton mystery / Bringing the bones in', *Hawera & Normanby Star*, 12 February 1923.

48 'Skeleton mystery / Possible solution', *Hawera & Normanby Star*, 10 February 1923, p. 8.

49 'Mountain skeletons / Remains collected / No clue established', *Stratford Evening Post*, 14 February 1923, p. 5.

50 'Lost on Mount Egmont / The missing missionary / A man of great stamina', *Evening Star*, 8 February 1923.

51 'Mountain climbing', *Taranaki Daily News*, 12 September 1916, p. 6.

52 'Mountain skeletons / Who lost the theodolite? on old Egmont in '96', *Stratford Evening Post*, 14 February 1923, p. 5.

Arthur's Pass

1 Yes, yes, I know, it's a statistically false claim, but you know what I mean, it's more of a feeling. An internet chap, who apparently knows far more than I do about statistics, pulled me up on this after I wrote a column expressing that I'd come to terms with the idea I'd probably die in the wilderness, given how much time I spent there. I liken it to dying in a casino — if you

spent all day there, you'd probably imagine that would be the setting where you'd die, if you were to drop dead from something unrelated to casinos, or the wilderness.

2   'Man spends night at top of steep West Coast ledge before being winched to safety', Newshub, 13 March 2018, https://www.newshub. co.nz/home/new-zealand/2018/03/ man-spends-night-at-top-of-steep-west-coast-ledge-before-being-winched-to-safety.html.

3   R. S. Odell, 'Arthur's Pass / Notes on its place names', *The Press*, 13 October 1934, p. 17.

4   'Search parties' vain quest for missing woman', *NZ Truth*, 7 March 1929, p. 1.

5   'Search parties' vain quest for missing woman', *NZ Truth*, 7 March 1929, p. 1.

6   'The missing nurse / Mystery of disappearance still unsolved', *Hokitika Guardian*, 7 March 1929, p. 5.

7   'Still unsolved / Mystery of missing Nurse McHaffie', *NZ Truth*, 4 April 1929, p. 5.

8   'Search parties' vain quest for missing woman', *NZ Truth*, 7 March 1929, p. 1.

9   Affidavit of Dr Wm. Irving, 26 February 1931, New Zealand Archives Probate Records, 1843–1998, Christchurch Court, https://www.familysearch. org/ark:/61903/3:1:3QS7-L96J-HQJB?i=199&cc=1865481 (accessed 22 December 2020).

10   Affidavit of Jane Trotter, 26 February 1931, New Zealand Archives Probate Records, 1843–1998, Christchurch

Court, https://www.familysearch. org/ark:/61903/3:1:3QS7-996J-HQF5?i=209&cc=1865481 (accessed 22 December 2020).

11   Ice conditions described in 'Wonders of Otira Tunnel', *Shannon News*, 31 August 1928, p. 3.

12   Trolley episode described in 'Casualties', *Otago Witness*, 11 April 1917, p. 43.

13   Meghan Walker, 'A lifetime of summits', *Wilderness* magazine, January 2017, https://www. wildernessmag.co.nz/a-lifetime-of-summits/.

14   Juliet Barker, *The Brontës: A Life in Letters*, Hachette (UK), 2016, p. 302.

15   'Death of climber / The inquiry adjourned', *Waikato Times*, 15 August 1933, p. 4.

16   'Fatal Accident on Avalanche Peak, Arthurs Pass', *New Zealand Alpine Journal*, vol. 5, issue 21, 1934, pp. 444–46.

17   'The late Mr Samuel E. Russell / The coroner's verdict / Advice to mountaineering parties', *Evening Star*, 18 August 1933, p.6.

18   R. S. Odell, 'Arthur's Pass / Notes on its place names', *The Press*, 18 August 1934, p. 17.

19   'Body on peak in alps / Lone deerstalker's fate', *Bay of Plenty Times*, 10 January 1949, p. 3.

20   Rebecca Solnit, *Men Explain Things to Me*, Haymarket Books, 2014, pp. 4–5.

21   https://www.doc.govt.nz/parks-and-recreation/places-to-go/canterbury/ places/arthurs-pass-national-park/ things-to-do/tracks/edwards-otehake-route/

22   Michael Wright, 'Hot pools
      save lost American trampers',
      Southland Times, 11 June 2012,
      http://www.stuff.co.nz/southland-
      times/7076211/Hot-pools-save-lost-
      American-trampers (accessed
      24 October 2020).

23   R. S. Odell, 'Arthur's Pass / Notes
      on its place names', *The Press*,
      6 October 1934. p. 15.

24   Ben Aulakh, 'Tramper recounts
      10-hour crawl to safety, eight day
      wait for rescue', *New Zealand
      Herald*, 21 April 2015, https://
      www.nzherald.co.nz/nz/tramper-
      recounts-10-hour-crawl-to-safety-
      eight-day-wait-for-rescue/QIQOW-
      C34W6OLOGGUYDET4C73EA/
      (accessed 24 October 2020).

25   Matthew Pike, 'A dislocated tale',
      Wilderness magazine, 20 June
      2015, https://www.wildernessmag.
      co.nz/a-dislocated-tale/ (accessed
      24 October 2020).

26   'Julia and Mary Griffin, drowned
      in the Taipo', https://westcoast.
      recollect.co.nz/nodes/view/22988
      (accessed 3 November 2020).
      Originally published in the *Grey
      River Argus*, 17 June 1876 (no title).
      Separately, a book page (title and
      details unknown) on the same
      site names Julia as Ellen, https://
      westcoast.recollect.co.nz/nodes/
      view/22988#idx78048 (accessed
      3 November 2020).

27   'Taipo River (II/III, with optional
      IV/V top section) via Harman
      Pass', posted 8 December 2017,
      https://www.packraftingtrips.nz/
      taipo-river-iiiii-via-harman-pass/
      (accessed 3 November 2020).

28   'Forced landing', *New Zealand
      Herald*, 29 July 1939, p. 12.

29   'Aeroplane leaves Taipo Valley',
      The Press, 1 August 1939, p. 8. See
      also 'Pilot makes a forced landing
      Taipo Valley 1939', https://westcoast.
      recollect.co.nz/nodes/view/17345
      (accessed 3 November 2020).

30   'An accident / Lloyd Parry injured',
      Hokitika Guardian, 24 September
      1937, p. 4.

31   C. Hanson, *By Such Deeds: Honours
      and Awards in the Royal New
      Zealand Air Force, 1923–1999*,
      Volplane Press, Christchurch, 2001,
      p. 384.

32   Photo caption, *Auckland Star*, 8 July
      1943, p. 4.

33   'The Seven Mile Creek, Taipo River',
      Grey River Argus, 11 February 1911,
      p. 1. See also 'Unromantic mining
      narratives', *Greymouth Evening Star*,
      4 December 1907, p. 4.

34   Christine Linnell, 'New hunt
      for "flood" gold a possibility',
      Greymouth Star, 23 August 2012,
      https://www.nzherald.co.nz/
      nz/new-hunt-for-flood-gold-
      a-possibility/BZJHWLOESN
      UBH3SQ2FZQTAW2G4/ (accessed
      3 November 2020).

35   Martin van Beynen, 'Lonely end for
      tramper in mountains', *The Press*,
      2 May 1998, p. 4.

36   Rob Greenaway, 'Old Haunts',
      *New Zealand Adventure Annual &
      Directory*, 1995, pp. 120–22.

37   'The first woman ascent of Mount
      Rolleston', *Evening Post*, 5 April 1927,
      p. 10.

38   Arthur D. Dobson, *Reminiscences
      of Arthur Dudley Dobson, Engineer,
      1841–1930*, W. & T., Auckland, 1930,
      Chapter IV: West Coast Survey, p. 39.

Westland and the deeper south

1   Episode narrated more fully in my piece 'Nightmare at Architect Creek Hut', *Wilderness* magazine, September 2017.

2   Lydia Bradey and Laurence Fearnley, *Going Up Is Easy*, Penguin, Auckland, 2015, p. 197.

3   *Going Up Is Easy*, pp. 194–95.

4   An early account of the hot springs is given by a Tourist Department photographer, T. Pringle, in 1903: 'Westland's hot springs', *Timaru Herald*, 14 February 1903, p. 1.

5   Janet McCallum, 'Barnicoat, Constance Alice', Dictionary of New Zealand Biography, first published in 1996, Te Ara — the Encyclopedia of New Zealand, https://teara.govt.nz/en/biographies/3b10/barnicoat-constance-alice (accessed 5 November 2020).

6   Constance Barnicoat, 'Over the Copland Pass', *The Press*, 25 April 1903, p. 7.

7   'Women will form mountaineer club', *Los Angeles Herald*, 1 September 1907, p. 19.

8   'Conversations Up the Copland', *Wilderness* magazine, 4 September 2011, https://www.wildernessmag.co.nz/conversations-up-the-copland/ (accessed 5 November 2020).

9   Trish McCormack, 'Thomson, Jane', Dictionary of New Zealand Biography, first published in 1996, Te Ara — the Encyclopedia of New Zealand, https://teara.govt.nz/en/biographies/3t34/thomson-jane (accessed 5 November 2020). It seems to be something of a yardstick, i.e. whether or not a woman can do a trip. Climbs that were conquered by women were then labelled by male climbers as 'an easy day for a lady' — in other words, not even worth doing.

10 'Guide tells how three women died in blizzard', *Northern Advocate*, 8 April 1948, p. 6. Also reported in 'Three women perish / Alpine tragedy in blizzard', *Bay of Plenty Times*, 8 April 1948, p. 3.

11 'Guide tells how three women died in blizzard', *Northern Advocate*, 8 April 1948, p. 6.

12 Fox is denied his claim to be the original prospector in his obituary: 'Death of Fox, the prospector', *Otago Witness*, 17 April 1890, p. 12.

13 William Grumitt included Fox's letter in a letter to the editor on the topic of who discovered the local goldfields: 'Discovery of the Wakatipu goldfield', *Otago Witness*, 24 November 1898, p. 19.

14 T. J. Hearn, 'Fox, William', Dictionary of New Zealand Biography, first published in 1990, Te Ara — the Encyclopedia of New Zealand, https://teara.govt.nz/en/biographies/1f16/fox-william (accessed 6 November 2020).

15 Details are related in 'Fall into ice chasm', *The Press*, 18 November 1935, p. 8.

16 'Mountaineering ascents in South Westland', *Hokitika Guardian*, 8 January 1936, p. 6.

17 J. C., 'In the blue ice / Movement of glaciers', *Auckland Star*, 20 November 1935, p. 6.

18 '[T]oday's guides are on the look-out for Tom Christie, a guide who fell

into a crevasse in 1935, and whose body was never recovered. He's expected to make an appearance at the bottom of the ice flow sometime soon.' Liz Light, 'Franz Josef Glacier: White magic', *New Zealand Herald*, 20 December 2010, https://www.nzherald. co.nz/travel/franz-josef-glacier-white-magic/EXR7WIXWQD6 OQKFROJWW7V66TM/ (accessed 6 November 2020).

19 Press release, 'Skyline advances investigations into Franz Josef Gondola project', Skyline Enterprises, 4 October 2017.

20 'Aerial railway / Large ski-ing area / State makes surveys', *Poverty Bay Herald*, 31 March 1938, p. 9.

21 Press release, 'Fox Glacier road closed for indefinite future', Department of Conservation, 24 August 2019, https://www.doc. govt.nz/news/media-releases/2019/ fox-glacier-road-closed-for-indefinite-future/ (accessed 10 January 2021).

22 Sentinel Rock was named for its watchman-like characteristics by early photographer Thomas Pringle of Hokitika. In 'The Glaciers', *Star*, 7 September 1894, p. 4, a reader notes recent (watery) changes at Sentinel Rock, and that it was so-named: 'It was this solitary watch and ward appearance of this dominant rock which caused Mr Pringle to affix the name "Sentinel" to his views of it.'

Fiordland

1 Variously spelled as Quintin, Quinton, MacKinnon, Mackinnon and McKinnon.

2 'The missing guide', *Waikato Times*, 26 January 1893, p. 3.

3 T. M'Kenzie, 'The search for M'Kinnon', *Nelson Evening Mail*, 28 January 1893, p. 4.

4 'Quinton M'Kinnon / Explorer's final journey / A sympathetic tribute', *Evening Post*, 5 April 1923, p. 7.

5 T. M'Kenzie, 'The search for M'Kinnon', *Nelson Evening Mail*, 28 January 1893, p. 4.

6 Captain James Cook, *A Voyage Towards the South Pole and Round the World: Performed in His Majesty's ships the Resolution and Adventure, in the years 1772, 1773, 1774, and 1775*, 2 vols, printed for W. Strahan and T. Cadell, London, 1777.

7 Jock Phillips, 'Sealing — The sealers', Te Ara — the Encyclopedia of New Zealand, http://www.TeAra. govt.nz/en/object/6231/slate-messages (accessed 9 November 2020).

8 Cassell Douglas, 'A mysterious vanishing / The missing tribe of Otago', *Otago Witness*, 23 December 1919, p. 58.

9 Canon Stack, *South Island Maoris: A Sketch of Their History and Legendary Lore*, Whitcombe & Tombs, Christchurch, 1898, p. 89.

10 'Skipper', 'Fiordland mystery', *Auckland Star*, 3 May 1930, p. 11. My own dialogue using details provided.

11 Letter to the editor, 'Makers of Canterbury', *The Press*, 6 May 1930, p. 13.

12 More information on the thigh bone is provided in 'Stalker's discovery / Human thigh bone found /

Interesting theory advanced / Remains of M'Kinnon', *Evening Star*, 14 April 1930, p. 10.

13 'Secret snaps reveal elusive Fiordland moose', *Otago Daily Times*, 21 December 2012, https://www.odt.co.nz/regions/southland/secret-snaps-reveal-elusive-fiordland-moose (accessed 9 November 2020).

14 Mark Price, 'Man's moose tale turns out to be false', *Otago Daily Times*, 8 August 2012, https://www.nzherald.co.nz/nz/mans-moose-tale-turns-out-to-be-false/4GPIVRHSVRT4UGTKQOBPMG75AA/ (accessed 9 November 2020).

15 Elizabeth Binning, 'The question that comes back to haunt Ken Tustin: Is there a moose on the loose in Fiordland?', *New Zealand Herald*, 5 March 2020, https://www.nzherald.co.nz/nz/the-question-that-comes-back-to-haunt-ken-tustin-is-there-a-moose-on-the-loose-in-fiordland/654XFNEHUG76VNPTLSFT2V5F5A/ (accessed 9 November 2020).

16 'The late Miss Reid', *Evening Star*, 26 January 1920, p. 4.

17 'Missing / High school teacher lost', *Otago Daily Times*, 17 January 1920, p. 6.

18 'Missing school teacher', *Otago Daily Times*, 20 January 1920, p. 8.

19 'Milford track mystery', *Western Star*, 10 February 1920, p. 4.

20 'Miss Reid's disappearance and the Milford search', *Evening Star*, 20 Feburary 1920, p. 6.

21 'Milford track mystery', *Western Star*, 10 February 1920, p. 4.

22 'Milford track mystery', *Western Star*, 10 February 1920, p. 4.

23 'Recovery of wedding ring / A Milford romance', *Otago Daily Times*, 28 January 1925, p. 10.

24 'The new river and lake on the West Coast / Captain Alabaster's account', *Otago Witness*, 24 October 1863, p. 4.

25 Public notices, *Grey River Argus*, 13 January 1876, p. 3.

26 'Charge of failing to support a wife', *Evening Post*, 10 May 1881, p. 3.

27 'Wife desertion', *Evening Post*, 17 May 1881, p. 2.

28 *Grey River Argus*, 25 January 1876, p. 2.

29 Jane Elizabeth Fish bore a child, Frederick William Fish, in 1891, who died aged one month.

30 'Magistrate's Court', *Evening Post*, 17 November 1893, p. 2. Bigamy noted in 'Captain DANIEL ALABASTER', https://www.familytreecircles.com/captain-daniel-alabaster-1838-1920-arrived-dunedin-1854-47913.html (accessed 11 November 2020).

31 In 1870 a clearly angry woman named Rosanna Armstrong came from Brunnerton to Captain Alabaster's house and smashed a window and destroyed property without provocation. 'Resident Magistrate's Court', *Grey River Argus*, 13 January 1870, p. 2.

32 Personal, *Marlborough Express*, 12 August 1920, p. 8.

33 His character and actions are detailed thoroughly in Roderick John Bunce's 2013 PhD thesis 'James Macandrew of Otago: Slippery Jim or A Leader Staunch and True?', Victoria University of Wellington, 2013.

34   The area is described by Mr Warden Beetham of Queenstown in 'Martin's Bay', *Evening Star*, 10 January 1873, p. 3.

35   'Steamer Charles Edward', *Nelson Evening Mail*, 16 March 1870, p. 2.

36   'Wreck of the Esther Ann', *Evening Star*, 29 July 1870, p. 2.

37   Railway Commission (Report Of), *Appendix to the Journals of the House of Representatives*, 1880, Session I, E-03.

38   Warden Beetham, 'Martin's Bay', *Evening Star*, 10 January 1873, p. 3.

39   Alice McKenzie, *Pioneers of Martins Bay: The Story of New Zealand's Most Remote Settlement*, Southland Historical Committee, Invercargill, 1947. A self-published revision was released in 1952.

40   'Overland expedition to Martin's Bay', *Grey River Argus*, 7 January 1873, p. 2.

Mount Aspiring

1   J. T. Thomson, 'Reconnaissance Survey of the Northern and Interior Districts of the Province of Otago', Surveyor fieldbook 47, 1858, p. 65, Land Information New Zealand, Christchurch office. Note that there is a question over whether he was actually looking at another mountain altogether; there is a thorough analysis in 'The Naming of Mount Aspiring', https://southernalps. wordpress.com/2011/05/08/the-naming-of-mount-aspiring/#Namin gOfAspiringReferences (accessed 9 December 2020).

2   Siobhan Downes and Marjorie Cook, 'Why are so many people dying in Mount Aspiring National Park?', Stuff, 7 January 2015, https://www.stuff.co.nz/national/64738670/why-are-so-many-people-dying-in-mount-aspiring-national-park (accessed 9 December 2020); Jack Fletcher, 'Climber grabbed at grass tufts before falling 100 metres to her death at Mount Aspiring National Park', Stuff, 3 August 2018, https://www.stuff.co.nz/the-press/news/105990179/climber-grabbed-at-grass-tufts-before-falling-100-metres-to-her-death-at-mt-aspiring-national-park (accessed 9 December 2020).

3   Chelsea Boyle, 'Fatal ordeal on Routeburn Track: The alpine mishap that killed Czech tramper Ondrej Petr', *New Zealand Herald*, 3 September 2019, https://www.nzherald.co.nz/nz/fatal-ordeal-on-routeburn-track-the-alpine-mishap-that-killed-czech-tramper-ondrej-petr/P34MLTDM5IFIJIGXWRZO3JQMNY/ (accessed 9 December 2020).

4   'Latest telegrams', *Christchurch Star*, 15 October 1869, p. 3.

5   'Search for gold', *Waihi Daily Telegraph*, 17 March 1932, p. 2.

6   'Tramper found', *Auckland Star*, 4 January 1944, p. 5.

7   Samuel Turner, *The Conquest of the New Zealand Alps*, T. Fisher Unwin, London, 1922, pp. 54–70.

8   *The Conquest of the New Zealand Alps*, p. 66.

Conquering fears

1   'The Tarndale tragedy', *Marlborough Express*, 26 February 1868, p. 4.

2   'Inquest on the body of Ivanhoe Augarde', *Marlborough Express*, 22 February 1868, p. 5.

3   'Sefton Bivouac', https://www.doc.govt.nz/parks-and-recreation/places-to-go/canterbury/places/aoraki-mount-cook-national-park/things-to-do/huts/sefton-bivvy/ (accessed 1 January 2021).

4   On 14 December 1991, 10 metres fell off Aoraki/Mount Cook (previously 3764 metres) from an earthquake and a massive rock avalanche.

5   Nan Bowie, *Mick Bowie: The Hermitage Years*, A. H. & A. W. Reed, Wellington, 1969, p. 86.

6   Al Williams, 'Pair disturbed by unexplained noises in night', *Timaru Herald*, 8 April 2009, https://www.stuff.co.nz/oddstuff/2295135/Pair-disturbed-by-unexplained-noises-in-night (accessed 10 December 2020).

7   Should James Butcher be haunting the Hooker Hut, he is not the same ghost to have haunted Peter Graham, due to timing, but instead is an additional, auxiliary ghost to the original.

8   '[R]esearch has found that positive outdoor recreational experiences dramatically increase a woman's self-valuation, self-confidence, and belief in her ability to lead.' J. S. Kovach, 'Outdoor Recreation Increases Self-Confidence in Women', *The Journal of Student Leadership*, [Special Issue], vol. 3, no. 1, August 2019, pp. 27–35, abstract, p. 27, https://journals.uvu.edu/index.php/jsl/article/view/342 (accessed 28 December 2020).

9   'Mountain climber's body identified', *New Zealand Herald*, 2 March 2001 (accessed via Newztext).

10 'Match found for bones', *The Press*, 12 January 2006, p. 3 (accessed via Newztext).

SELECT BIBLIOGRAPHY

Bradey, Lydia and Laurence Fearnley. *Going Up Is Easy*. Auckland: Penguin, 2016.

Du Faur, Freda. *The Conquest of Mount Cook and Other Climbs: An Account of Four Seasons' Mountaineering on the Southern Alps of New Zealand*. London: George Allen & Unwin, 1915; Christchurch: Capper Press, 1977.

Fearnley, Laurence and Paul Hersey. *To the Mountains: A Collection of New Zealand Alpine Writing*. Dunedin: Otago University Press, 2018.

FitzGerald, Edward Arthur. *Climbs in the New Zealand Alps: Being an Account of Travel and Discovery*. London: T. Fisher Unwin, 1896.

Graham, Peter. *Peter Graham: Mountain Guide*. Auckland: A. H. & A. W. Reed, 1965.

Grande, Julian. *Constance Grande: War Correspondent, Traveller, Alpinist and Imperialist*. London: Chapman & Hall, 1925.

Hersey, Paul. *Where the Mountains Throw Their Dice*. Auckland: New Holland, 2008.

—— *High Misadventure: New Zealand Mountaineering Tragedies and Survival Stories*. Auckland: New Holland, 2009.

Irwin, Sally. *Between Heaven and Earth: The Life of a Mountaineer, Freda Du Faur*. Hawthorn, Vic.: White Crane Press, 2000.

McKenzie, Alice. *Pioneers of Martins Bay: The Story of New Zealand's Most Remote Settlement*. Dunedin: *Otago Daily Times*, 1963. First published 1947.

Turner, Samuel. *My Climbing Adventures in Four Continents*. London: T. Fisher Unwin, 1911.

—— *The Conquest of the New Zealand Alps*. London T. Fisher Unwin, 1922.

Willoughby, Genevieve. *Life at the Top: Tales from Aoraki-Mount Cook*. Christchurch: Wily Publications Ltd, 2017.

ACKNOWLEDGEMENTS

Thanks to MUP Publisher Nicola Legat, who not only saw merit in the idea of *Solo* but also kindly forgave me for participating in loud, wild parties when I lived next door to her in my twenties. Nicola did a judicious first edit on the text, and I am grateful for her wisdom.

I would also like to acknowledge Mike Wagg, whose edit was thoughtful and insightful and picked up many inconsistencies. Thanks to Associate Publisher Tracey Borgfeldt and Managing Editor Anna Bowbyes, who were lovely to work with. Thanks also to designer Alice Bell, who brought visual life to the text with a beautiful design.

The cover image was shot by photographer Mike Heydon of Jet Productions as part of one of our mad mountain missions, before any words for *Solo* were even on paper. Mike's maxim that the best time to take a photo is when you really don't want to pull the camera out seems to have come to life on so many of our trips. Who would have guessed that our mid-summer outing to find Lake Madness would've ended up on a book cover?

Hat tip to journalist David Fisher, who encouraged me to write the thing in the first place, and fellow writer David Slack, whose enthusiasm as a very early reader also spurred me on.

On a personal note, thanks to my brother Aaron and his lovely other half Victoria for housing me in the Hatfields Beach Burrow from time to time and always making me laugh; and big thanks to Penelope Whitson and Dion and Brian Cruse for being there for me and picking up the pieces when it all hit the fan.

I also want to acknowledge the support and friendship of many people who occasionally housed me while strategically homeless, who came on trips, or otherwise have just been regular garden-variety good bastards: Simon Bainbridge, Jazial Crossley, Laura and Jeremy Chirnside, Vicki and Marty Donoghue, Jane Dudley, David Forsyth and Maria Niva, Preston Hatcher, Kent Hutchins, Ruth Mackenzie, Elliott O'Brien, Tanja Rosendorfsky, Mandy Rothe, Bill Smugs and Nate Wilson.

Finally, a big hug to Papa Smurf and the MTSC Exploding Possums, who are the best partners in crime a lady adventurer could hope for. I love you guys.

ABOUT THE AUTHOR

Hazel Phillips is a writer and communications professional who has worked for a variety of media, from the *National Business Review* (where she learned how to read a balance sheet) to *CLEO* magazine (where she learned how to use a hair straightener to iron a skirt).

She has written two previous books: *Sell! Tall tales from the legends of New Zealand advertising*, a popular history of the advertising industry; and *Wild Westie*, a biography of Sir Bob Harvey. She is always working on a new book, even if it's just inside her own head.

Hazel holds a BA(Hons) in French and an MA in Media Studies.

In her spare time she enjoys multi-day tramping, skiing, ski touring, mountaineering, scuba diving, motorbiking, and sitting on the couch with a good book when it all gets too much.

MASSEY
UNIVERSITY
PRESS

First published in 2022 by Massey University Press
Private Bag 102904, North Shore Mail Centre
Auckland 0745, New Zealand
www.masseypress.ac.nz

Design by Alice Bell
Cover photographs and photograph page 237 by Mike Heydon, Jet Productions
(Mount Ruapehu)

A catalogue record for this book is available from the National Library of New Zealand

Printed and bound in Singapore by Markono Print Media Pte Ltd

ISBN: 978-0-9951354-5-1
eISBN: 978-1-9910160-8-9